Complete Garden Guide
to the
Native Perennials of
California

Complete Garden Guide
to the
Native Perennials of
California

Glenn Keator

CHRONICLE BOOKS
SAN FRANCISCO

The illustrations in this book are from the classic
The Wildflowers of California
by Mary Elizabeth Parsons
illustrated by Margaret Warriner Buck.
Additional illustrations are by Brenda Rae Eno.

Printed in the United States of America

Library of Congress Cataloging in Publication Data

Keator, Glenn.
    Complete garden guide to the native perennials of California /
Glenn Keator.
       p.   cm.
    Includes bibliographical references.
    1. Perennials—California.   2. Landscape gardening—California.
I. Title. ISBN: 0-87701-699-2
SB434.K43   1990
716'.09794--dc20   89-71258
                                                          CIP

Editing: Carey Charlesworth
Book and cover design: Brenda Rae Eno
Typography: TBH/Typecast, Inc.

10 9 8 7 6 5 4 3

Chronicle Books
275 Fifth Street
San Francisco, California 94103

YERBA BUENA—*Satureja.*

Contents

Part II. Encyclopedia of Families, Genera, and Species . . . 51

Preface

This book was inspired by a desire to extend the available knowledge on gardening with native plants. At present, my garden bulges with over three hundred species of natives. Even so, I have only scratched the surface of what is possible to try. In my present location—Sebastopol—I am limited to certain plant categories; our winters are somewhat colder and wetter than in many parts of the immediate San Francisco Bay Area and, to make matters worse, my garden lies on an east-facing slope so that gardening is difficult in winter, though also tempered by later afternoon coolness during hot periods of the summer. The soil is also difficult, being a powdery sand, not easily wetted when dry and poor at retaining moisture at the height of the summer drought. I think all of this reinforces what is so special about gardening in California; the numerous microclimates and habitats which make it so difficult to generalize about such important matters as hardiness and watering.

Obviously, there are many plants in the present book which I have not had the opportunity to grow, or simply cannot grow. Many of the coastal southern California, Channel Islands, and desert plants fare poorly here. At the other extreme, the alpine and subalpine mountain flowers are often uncomfortable with the wet winters. Still, I am always willing to try something at least once.

The book was undertaken because I felt frustrated with what is now available; most books either ignore the perennials altogether—there are books on woody plants—or they're treated in a rather piecemeal fashion. The present volume does not correct this situation entirely but attempts to present to the reader a fair sampling of the numerous genera and species with which I am acquainted and that I feel deserve garden trial. Some I have grown for years. Others I have only recently introduced to my garden, and still others I have never grown; nonetheless, I have tried to give an idea of how I think they would fit into a landscape and the conditions they would do best under. Please bear this in mind, as you peruse the entries here.

Finally, I'd like to note that gardening is an avocation for me; by training, I am a botanist and teacher who specializes in California natives. The reader is asked to forgive the strong emphasis on things botanical which has crept in. I do believe botany and horticulture should be brought together more often.

The book is divided into three clearly organized parts:

1. A compilation of whys and wherefores of obtaining, growing, and designing landscapes with native perennials.

2. An encyclopedia detailing attributes, cultivation, and propagation of hundreds of families, genera, and species of perennials. Turn to p. 51 for a convenient alphabetical listing of these entries and their equivalent common or scientific names.

3. A reference and resources section complete with detailed glossary to terms and index.

Well, there it is. I hope that this will pave the way to more complete works on a fascinating and worthwhile subject.

TOOTHWORT—*Dentaria.*

part one

Collecting, Growing, and Designing Landscapes with Native Perennials

Perennials are plants which live more than two years. On the one hand, they differ from annuals, which complete their life cycles in less than a year and have a single flowering, and on the other, they are unlike shrubs and trees in being nonwoody, or herbaceous. Technically, of course, all shrubs and trees are also perennial, but horticulturally the herbaceous perennials are put into a class by themselves.

Most perennials have a rest period or dormancy during part of the year, or at least they slow their growth at certain specific times. Those in the latter category remain evergreen, never dying back to their roots; thus, they often form broadly spreading clumps and new growth appears along the forefront of the clumps. Such perennials are easily divided into new plants.

Other perennials lose their leaves either during the dry part of the year or during the cold season. Since dry and cold periods occur at different times in the California calendar, dry-dormant perennials differ from cold-dormant kinds in cultural needs: dry (summer) dormant kinds need to be kept dry, so that neither growth nor rot is encouraged; cold (winter) dormant kinds are difficult in lowland gardens because they require a thorough chilling for best results. Both kinds have underground structures to which water and food are sent for storage during dormancy: these include rootstocks, rhizomes, tubers, corms, and bulbs. Each kind differs in some technical detail and in shape and depth; for example, bulbs are often deeply seated, as much as a foot below the soil surface. All seasonally dormant perennials are propagated by offsets from the parent storage organ and sometimes by divisions or cuttings of the storage organs themselves.

This book is devoted to native perennials for the very reason that this group usually is neglected, while much has been written on California's beautiful shrubs or its great variety of trees. Also, woody plants are the mainstay of nurseries specializing in natives. Even so, among perennials there are far more

1

species with far greater variety than amongst the woody plants. Perennials also are easier to propagate, and grow to full size more quickly. I am including all the bulbous plants and ferns in the perennial category.

There are a variety of applications for perennials in the garden, and these uses will be noted throughout the book. Typically perennials are incorporated into some kind of "border" intended to go in front of shrubbery or hedging, or as liners for lawns and pools, yet there are several other worthwhile applications. Because they create a "natural" setting they are fine subjects for woodland gardens, rock gardens, and ground covers between stepping stones and beds. Two other uses for a natural or wild garden: a pond surrounded by moisture-loving plants, and clumps of bunchgrasses which form a matrix in which colorful perennials fill the spaces. Finally perennials can be displayed as specimen plants for pots, boxes, and tubs.

At times, my concept of perennial is stretched a bit, if a particularly intriguing group of subshrubs is worthy of the garden: the line between perennial and shrub is rather tenuous.

Climates and Physical Geography of California

Gardeners really cannot determine how to make best use of a plant unless they are conversant with the habitats and climates the plant grows in. It is a paradox that not every aspect of the original environment need be recreated to adapt a plant to its new home, and some aspects of behavior cannot be predicted from the environment alone. For example, plants which grow on soils derived from serpentine or lava seldom require those in cultivation; in fact, many grow better in an ordinary garden soil. The key to the proper soil is closely related to drainage (and it is always better to err on the side of good drainage) and to its pH value. Plants from acid soils in the wild should be given acid soils in the garden.

Aspects to be learned about the natural environment include:

1. growth cycles, 2. moisture cycles, 3. temperature cycles, 4. shading

For the most part, growth cycles can be determined by the interaction of moisture and temperature, which is generally what we call climate. The degree of shading or exposure to sun can be learned from direct observation, bearing in mind these important considerations:

- the direction of the slope—north, south, east, or west
- in full sun, what the average high temperatures are
- the degree of shading (determined by density of foliage and branching pattern)—mottled shade, shade in morning, high shade, dense shade, or other

For example, plants of the immediate coastal fog belt or of the high mountains which grow in full sun are not subjected to the high temperatures that foothill plants are. Consequently, in most gardens, coastal plants need light shade to keep them cooler and to lower transpiration (evaporation) from leaves.

Climate is better regarded as a set of complex interactions between seasonal and daily temperature changes together with the seasonal nature and form of precipitation. Understanding these interactions is the key to success with a plant in the garden.

To understand California's climates, it helps to know a bit about its physical geography. The most imposing physical features are the mountain ranges and rivers. The coast, from Santa Maria in the south to Eureka in the north, is bordered by a series of ridges and hills called the Coast Ranges. Between ridges lie major river valleys, and there are almost everywhere four or more major ridges between the ocean and the great Central Valley inland. The various ridges are referred to as outer Coast Ranges (immediately back from the ocean), middle Coast Ranges, and inner Coast Ranges (hills nearest the Central Valley). The outer Coast Ranges receive the lion's share of summer fogs, with the results of extra moisture and cooling; the middle Coast Ranges receive intermittent fogs; and the inner Coast Ranges receive none. Also strong summer winds prevail along the outer Coast Range and are absent from the inner. In winter, most storms move from the ocean across the Coast Ranges, so one would expect each part to differ as to the amount of water received: generally, the outer ranges receive the greatest brunt from the storms and the inner the least, but because ridges interjoin in complex patterns, this is an oversimplification.

Along the coast south of Santa Maria, the mountains and ridges run east and west rather than north and south: these are referred to as the Transverse Ranges. They include several named groups, such as the Santa Ynez, Topa Topa, Tehachapi, and San Bernardino mountains. Since the coastline also runs west to east here, the relationship to shore is not much different from that in the Coast Ranges.

As the coast turns southward again new south-north ridges are referred to as the Peninsular Ranges, in Orange, Riverside, and San Diego counties.

North of Eureka the mountains form complex patterns where some of the main ridges run at various angles and appear to be of much greater age: taken together they form the Klamath Ranges, which include such distinctive local groups as the Marbles, Siskiyous, Trinities, and Scott-Salmon Mountains.

All of this is by way of saying that different families of mountains are to be found behind the coast at different latitudes. They all have effects similar to those discussed for the predominant Coast Ranges. But not all mountains are equal, because of different maximum elevations: the higher the mountains, the more precipitation they are likely to receive because the inland-moving storms are coaxed to dump their moisture as they rise and cool. The Coast Ranges immediately around San Francisco Bay are relatively low, and it is important to note the effect of the gap created by the Golden Gate and the Bay, which allows fog to flow further inland and keep summer temperatures lower in that region. There, mountains seldom exceed 3,000 to 4,000 feet. Further south they become progressively lower except for the immediate coast, where the Santa Lucia range, just south of Monterey, has peaks to almost 6,000 feet. The Transverse Ranges are of comparable elevations near the coast, but inland they reach to nearly 11,000 feet. The Peninsular Ranges are only modestly high, up to about 6,000 feet. To the north of the Bay, mountains climb ever higher, and the inner north Coast Ranges may exceed 7,000 feet. The Klamaths are generally higher yet, with some peaks topping 8,000 feet.

Inland to the Coast Ranges lies the great Central Valley, arbitrarily composed of the San Joaquin Valley in its southern half and the Sacramento Valley in its northern part. This valley may extend more than 50 miles at its widest, stretches 450 miles in length, and is uninterrupted by mountains except for the singular volcanic ranges in the north: the Marysville (Sutter) Buttes.

The valley is further characterized by the major river systems of California, which drain the full extent of the Sierra Nevada and, in the north, parts of the Klamath and Cascade mountains. The climate here is hot to very hot in the summer—only near the Bay gap does it get cooler, so that the two ends of the valley, typified by Bakersfield and Redding, are the hottest. Winter rainfall is relatively scant because so much moisture has been wrung from the clouds on their journey across the Coast Ranges; it is minimal in the southwestern portions, where relatively high mountains and generally fewer major fronts create so little rain that the area is technically desert.

The Central Valley is completely bordered by mountains. We have seen how the north Coast Ranges and Klamaths surround it to the northwest; to the northeast, the great volcanic cones of the Cascade Ranges appear. The two most striking mountains of this range are Mt. Lassen at 10,500 feet and Mt. Shasta at more than 14,000 feet. These ranges receive the remainder of winter storms moving in from the north coast across the Klamath Mountains, and the highest peaks show a respectable precipitation, but the lower parts of these mountains are relatively dry. Beyond the Cascade chain, which runs roughly north to south, lie extensive volcanic tablelands at elevations of 3,000 to 6,000 feet. This is a high desert region, cut off from moisture by the intervening Klamaths and Cascades, yet high enough to experience very cold winters.

Just where the Cascades end near Mt. Lassen, the mountain building processes south have continued the mountains as the Sierra Nevada. This mountain block has had several separate episodes of uplift, and contains sediments as well as the nearly ubiquitous granites so typical of the higher elevations. The block is tilted toward the east with the result that the western slopes and foothills pass gradually to higher and higher mountains. From the crest, the plunge east to the high desert country is quite abrupt. Thus, the Sierra shows itself as forbidding and rugged from the east side, and as a gentle undulating range from the Central Valley side. The Sierra extends the remaining length of the valley and is the longest and most impressive of California's mountain ranges. The crest rises to little more than 8,000 feet in the extreme north but grows ever higher and more rugged to the south, culminating in Mt. Whitney at 14,495 feet. From there the mountains decline again for a short ways to their end.

Obviously, a massif as impressive as the Sierra has startling effects on climate:

nearly all moisture which passes across the Central Valley gets wrung from the clouds before they pass over the crest, which is subalpine. The greatest amount is dumped at the middle elevations typified by the great yellow pine belt. The country along virtually all of the eastern Sierra scarp is desert, the only sources of water the eastward-trending streams which once watered the Mono and Owens valleys.

At the southern extremity of the Central Valley lie the east-west Transverse Ranges. To the extreme southeast, abutting the Sierra, are the Tehachapi Mountains, and to the southwest, the Topa Topas. These mountains show varying degrees of desert climate according to how far inland they lie and how high they ascend. The Tehachapis, in particular, receive scant moisture. They mark this mountain chain as the northwestern edge of the Mojave Desert. The bulk of the Mojave Desert is almost exclusively Californian (a bit in Nevada and Arizona) and lies east of the Transverse Ranges; in the extreme north it gradually merges with the high desert country along the east side of the Sierra.

The Mojave, far from being a monotonous plain, consists of a complicated series of plains, valleys, and plateaus between a number of separate mountains. Most of these mountains are less impressive than those to the west, but a few, especially around Death Valley, reach elevations exceeding 10,000 feet, and those higher mountains receive considerably more moisture than the adjacent slopes and flats. Overall, the Mojave is a moderately low desert with an average elevation of less than 4,000 feet and consequent hot summers and mild to cool winters.

The Mojave is bordered along much of its southern edge by Transverse Ranges such as the San Bernardino and Little San Bernardino mountains. These are high enough to form a barrier to plant migration, and the lower basins to the south belong to a second desert known as the Colorado. Technically the Colorado desert extends from the eastern boundary of California, the Colorado River, to the western mountains—the Peninsular Ranges. The largest basin is centered on the Salton Sea and has elevations averaging lower than those of the Mojave, even below sea level, with the result that the Colorado is a very hot, dry desert with mild winters.

Now let's turn to the consideration of climate patterns. We have at least three major kinds of climate:

1. Mediterranean, 2. montane, 3. desert

We'll examine each in turn.

Mediterranean climates are noteworthy because they're only found in five places in the world: lowland California, central Chile, the Mediterranean basin, the Cape Province of South Africa, and southwestern Australia. Since most of California's population, and hence gardens, occur in this climate, the greatest stress will be laid here. Mediterranean climate has its major precipitation during the short days of the year—winter and spring, when temperatures are also at their lowest. This means that when water is available two factors negate its use for growth: relatively low temperatures and short days, the opposite of what is optimal for plant growth. However, toward the end of the rainy season—mid to late spring—days are long and temperatures rapidly climb, so that there is a period which coincides with moisture and favorable day length. But this period is limited by the other part of a Mediterranean climate—hot, dry summers and falls. Thus, at least half of the long days are lost to drought, with many plants requiring a dormancy then to survive.

In the garden, of course, the natural drought can be modified by extra water in summer and fall, but it is important to consider the origin of natives from this climate, and the need for many to rest.

Mediterranean climate holds sway over the foothills of the Coast, Transverse, and Peninsular ranges as well as the Sierra foothills and Central Valley. Only the higher mountains in these areas have a rather different climate. From our discussion of California's geography it should also be obvious that, within the large Mediterranean province, there is great variation in certain details of the climate:

- Overall precipitation varies from near desert to 40 inches annually (more in some modified climates).
- Winter coldness varies from nearly frost free along the south coast to several nights of below freezing in the inland valleys.
- Summer heat varies from mild, even cool on the coast to scorching hot in the interior valleys.

Plants growing or originating in various parts of this province should be reckoned with accordingly; coastal plants need partial shade and cool situations inland in summer and protection from frost in winter. Perhaps the most dramatic subclimate is the immediate central and northern coast. Here not only do winter lows seldom go below freezing, but summer fogs blanket the land to keep temperatures low and add important fog drip during the driest months. Consequently, plants adapted to this belt, especially those from the coastal forests where fog condenses to add extra rain, need summer moisture and protection from overheating and drying out.

Montane climates predominate through most of the higher mountains, especially where they form a continuous chain, as in the Sierra. There, precipitation from late fall through early spring comes as snow, and snow melt coincides with the longest days and warmest temperatures. Some mountain areas experience a later drought—from late summer through early fall—after snow melt has been absorbed and used up, but in some years the high country has sporadic thunderstorms to supplement summer water. Thus, the montane climate has much colder winters, a dormancy during the short, cold days, and a nearly optimal usage of long days, warmer temperatures, and available water. Plants from such climates must be handled to allow dormancy in winter and, if at all possible, with winter chill, and with abundant moisture in summer during flowering and seeding. The higher the elevation and the further north the latitude, the more strictly this climate is felt.

Desert climates are characterized by their paucity of water—generally less than 10 inches annually—and their hot summers. Beyond these parameters, there is considerable variation. The Mojave Desert receives most of its rain in late fall, winter, and early spring, with occasional snows. It is usually waterless through the remaining months, when temperatures are elevated. The Colorado desert, in contrast, may experience occasional abrupt and violent summer showers, so that some annuals there germinate when temperatures are warm while others germinate only in winter, when it's cool. Finally, the high desert country north of the Mojave and east of the Sierra and Cascades is characterized by severely cold winters with snow, and warm to hot, mostly dry summers. Occasional thundershowers here sometimes relieve summer drought. Although I will mention few strictly desert plants in this book, it may be useful to experiment with them where hot sunny days and dry climate are the rule.

One last item must be stressed about the natural growing conditions for native plants: several species come from permanently wet situations regardless of climate, because they live on flood plains of permanent streams or in marshy or boggy areas. Such plants (regardless of general climate) must have moisture at their roots at least in summer in order to survive; some may require soggy soil at all times. Such plants come from the plant communities referred to as freshwater marsh, sphagnum bog, and riparian woodland.

Microclimates

In addition to understanding broad climatic requirements, one needs a strong familiarity with the concept of the microclimate, and with the characteristics of microclimates in one's own garden. Most gardens of ordinary size will contain these pockets, which differ in temperature, moisture, and sunniness as compared to other parts of the garden. Some of the most dramatic changes relate to temperature, at both ends of the spectrum: freezing and searing hot.

Here are some factors in microclimates by which to recognize them or mitigate their effects:

- South and west sides of buildings retain heat best in winter; they also receive the greatest heat in summer.
- Conversely, north and east sides of buildings are coldest in winter; they remain cooler in summer.
- Overhangs, patios, and other extensions from buildings help protect from frost damage and summer heat.
- Low valleys, gulches, and ravines collect cold air in winter; cold air drains from high places into low, where it settles.
- Deciduous trees and shrubs allow sun to come through in winter, whereas evergreen trees and shrubs create shade all year.
- The denser the foliage and branch pattern of trees and shrubs, the heavier the shade they create.

- Tall trees with high limbs (the lower limbs missing) create high shade, allowing the sun to reach what's underneath when its angle is near the horizon.

- Plants that are under trees gain some protection from frost, as compared to those fully exposed.

- Ponds create cooling local microclimates in summer and may help mediate winter chill.

- Shade can shift patterns according to season and time of day to greatly varying effects.

- The color of the soil or of mulch or other dressing may determine the temperature of the soil surface; dark soils absorb heat and can become unbearably hot in full sun.

- Likewise, dark containers on decks get much hotter than white or light-colored ones.

- Roots that need cool soil in summer can find protection in crannies under rocks.

- Soils in shade dry out much less rapidly than those in full sun. Allow for the fact that the trees which create the shade do have thirsty roots.

- Shallowly rooted trees create much drier conditions for perennials than deeply rooted trees.

- Mulched surfaces lose moisture much less rapidly than fully exposed soils.

- Plants in hanging pots are less likely to freeze than plants at ground level.

Sources of Natives

One of the most important questions for the gardener is where to obtain a particular species. The answer must be qualified and expanded when it comes to natives because of the rather narrow range available from nurseries, even those dealing exclusively in natives. This would seem contradictory were it not for the economic realities of business: most native nurseries are small and depend upon moving enough of each item to make it worthwhile; only those natives already well known are those that sell. It's a sort of Catch-22 in which new material has no place; so it is seldom introduced. There are, however, quite a number of native nurseries; see the list in Appendix 3.

There is one other commercial outlet that does offer the more unusual natives, and this outlet also helps support a number of nonprofit organizations whose specialty is plants: the sales of various botanical gardens, arboreta, and plant societies. Most such sales occur only annually, so it is important to find out the dates. An especially fine source of material is the local chapter sales of the California Native Plant Society. The society is instrumental in helping preserve and teach the value of natives, and membership is quite reasonable. See Appendix 2 for a list of the society and other organizations.

There are several advantages to obtaining material from propagators:

- Material is usually accurately named.
- The more decorative cultivars of species are offered.
- Material is grown under garden conditions; root systems may be more vigorous than otherwise is possible.
- Reputable firms propagate their material from already established garden stock rather than depleting wild populations.

One of the biggest problems with nursery material is that the time at which it looks best may be the worst time to plant it. If yours is a garden with little summer water, natives should not be planted in the late spring or summer. Instead, wait until late fall or even winter before planting. Such a plan follows nature's cycles better, allowing the natural rains to do the watering and inducing the least amount of shock in the plant at transplanting time because of its semidormancy.

A third commercial source for natives is seed houses (also listed in Appendix 3), although there are several disadvantages:

- Plants from seed take considerably longer to reach maturity, and they do so with less uniformity (cultivars do not come true from seed). Bulbs are especially slow, requiring three, four, or even five years before flowers appear.
- Some seed outlets do not have accurate identification of their material.
- Some seed outlets do not check the fertility of their seed, with the result that some batches may have low viability (this is partly because some seed is gathered directly from the wild).
- Germination of native seeds is occasionally trickier than propagation by cuttings or division.

Aside from these drawbacks, seeds give a considerably broader range of available material than do other means of propagation, and they are interesting because of the variation found in the offspring. This is the way a new and desirable form may appear.

If you cannot find the species you desire from these sources, there is only one other way to go: natives from their own homes in the wilds. Before embarking on this route, however, the reader should be acquainted with the reasons for *not* using this source. Problems include:

- accurate identification of the plant
- finding the plant at the right stage (especially for mature seeds)
- doing the removal legally (there are fines and laws covering such removal)
- establishing a vigorous plant in the garden
- serious depletion of plants in the wild—disturbing the population and its breeding potential

- risking the high probability of killing a plant which is unable to adapt to garden conditions

If you feel you can deal with these problems reasonably, then read on—there are ways of obtaining natives from the wild with minimal impact and high chances for success. Let's look at each problem.

Accurate identification. The means of identifying your plant may be available at a local university. However, don't rely on experts to identify large numbers of plants; they don't have the time. A better way is to have access to a library of books covering various parts of the state—unless you're already an expert and can use the technical manuals, such as Munz's *A California Flora.* You're apt to need many books for cross-referencing and for the sake of completeness; no one book covers everything unless it's a technical book, written at the level of advanced students. The use of line drawings, photographs, and flower color guides is helpful but is only a beginning. One of the best bets is to take plant identification courses from your local university extension or community college so you know the important traits to look for and how to use an identification key. Appendix 4 lists some identification guides.

Finding the plant at the right stage for propagation. The right stage depends on the kind of propagation used. If, for example, you take sections or rooted portions of a plant, they'll move better when the plant is *not* in flower or fruit, at a time when it's harder to recognize the plant. And, if seeds are your goal, they are usually ripe after the flowers have passed. Many plants out of flower are not showy and may be almost impossible to find in the field. The solution? Learn the plants in a given area, and when they flower tag them so that you can identify them later. The tag may be visible when the plant itself fades into the background vegetation.

Removing parts of a plant legally. For legal removal you need a state collecting permit or permission from owners of private land. Many ranchers are glad to learn about plants on their land and, once they understand what you intend, are generous. Finally, *if* there is a new housing development or new road in an area formerly covered with mature vegetation, rescue work is not only legitimate, it's a way of saving some of the gene pool which would otherwise be lost.

Establishing a vigorous plant in the garden. This is a problem we'll devote considerable attention to in the next chapter. Remember that timing is all important and that to expect a rooted plant to adapt to a new home, it must be removed when growth has slowed or halted during the rainy season. Another rule is that the greater the difference in climate between the plant's home and yours, the less likely rooted portions will move successfully. When the difference is considerable, plants should be started from cuttings or from seed.

Now let's turn our attention to a few of the rationales behind *not* taking natives from their environment—after all, many species and varieties are threatened in various ways: they are already rare, they are in a sensitive habitat that is being threatened, they have been sought by too many other collectors, or they have been wiped out by agricultural or other development. A list of rare and endangered plants is available from the California Native Plant Society; any plant on the list should be left alone in the wild and obtained only from already existing sources. What is the impact of taking natives, if they are not threatened or endangered in any way? Well, it depends upon the method used. Let's examine each:

Collecting seeds. This is one of the most appropriate ways of taking perennials. Consider that perennials live several years and so have many chances to make new seeds before they die; annuals are by definition more sensitive this way. Seeds are needed in quantity in the wild to maintain genetic diversity and supply enough seeds to overcome the pitfalls that await them—pests and diseases, consumption by animals and birds, and landing in the wrong place or at the wrong time. For this reason, don't collect large quantities of seeds at any one spot. You have better chances for more interesting variation, too, if you collect seeds from several different plants in different locales.

Taking cuttings. This is the single least harmful way of removing material as long as you don't deplete any single plant of too many branches. Cuttings may actually stimulate the original plant to grow more vigorously, just as though you were pruning it. Be sure to observe the methods discussed further on to minimize any injury to the plant.

Taking divisions. Many perennials grow into ever-larger clones which can be divided into rooted sections. This is seldom harmful to the plant because removal of one section stimulates it to produce new sections. Again, discretion is necessary as to the number of sections to be removed from any one clone.

Digging the entire plant. This method is the one which does the real damage to native populations. It leaves a hole in the population which may or may not be filled by a new seedling. Therefore, this should never be resorted to unless you are doing salvage work, where the whole population is threatened by development. Here are some general rules to keep in mind for collecting wild material:

1. Know the plant's identity.
2. Have a spot ready for it in the garden.
3. Collect it in the right season—for example, when the seeds are fully ripe or the plant divisions are dormant.
4. Obtain permission.
5. Prepare to transport the plant properly.
6. Take prompt care of it when it's home.

Here are suggestions for each method of propagation.

Seeds. Use paper bags, envelopes, or seed packets, not plastic bags. Label each envelope separately. Check for fully ripe seeds; nearly ripe seeds may continue to ripen if the stalk is kept in a low concentration of sugar water, but this is risky. Seeds are ripe when they have turned dark brown, black, or purple, *not* green or white. Some plants produce seeds inside hard ovaries (achenes) or fleshy berries; in this case, they're ripe when the achene turns brown and falls easily from the parent, or when the berry is brightly colored. Practice makes perfect in recognizing the signals. Seed pods are ready to open when they've turned brown and started to split. The big problem is arriving just when the pods open, so seed hasn't spilled all over, but late enough that the seed is fully ripe. It's often best to tie a small cheesecloth bag or paper bag around the immature pod and return later—the seeds fall into the bag. Seeds should be stored away from light, in a cool, dry place, until planting time. Refrigeration is a good idea.

Cuttings. Each species has a best time for taking cuttings. For perennials, softwood or semihardwood cuttings are best, and the timing depends on when new growth first starts. Softwood cuttings can be taken on many foothill species in spring, and on mountain plants in early summer; semihardwood cuttings become possible later in the season. Cutting length should seldom exceed three to four inches. In order to make the cuts clean and even, they should be made with a sharp knife or pruning shears. Otherwise, torn tissues could result in the introduction of pathogens and the eventual demise of the plant. Put cuttings in Ziploc plastic bags with a few drops of water, small bunches of the same kinds together, then label and seal them. Put the bags into an ice chest. Keep them *out* of the sun. Plant material will cook if the bags are left exposed. If you're out in the field for several days, it's a good idea to rinse the cuttings periodically, to remove fungus spores and to keep the plants as cool as possible.

Divisions. Since most divisions are already rooted, the method here is much like transplanting the whole plant. Dividing should be done in late fall or winter to minimize disturbing growth and introduce the new plant into the garden when moisture is plentiful. Winter-dormant plants should be divided just before they lose their leaves, usually sometime during autumn. Sever the section with a sharp knife and put it immediately into a plastic bag with a few drops of water. Then handle the plants as with cuttings, in an ice chest and out of direct light. An alternative method is to set up a temporary planting bed in old milk cartons or wooden flats and immediately put the rooted sections into these. Cover them with a large plastic bag and keep them away from light. Cuttings or rooted sections may even be held in their plastic bags for a day or two in the refrigerator.

Propagation of Natives

Natives are propagated by:

- seeds
- divisions
- cuttings
- layering

Assume that you have already obtained the plants, or you simply want to increase what you already have in the garden. What is involved with each kind of propagation?

Seeds

The handling of seeds can be broken into component parts:
seed storage, cleaning, pretreatment, planting, seedling establishment
We'll look at each in turn.

Seed storage. Seeds should be stored in airtight containers, away from heat and humidity. Glass jars are good containers, although cardboard boxes and paper bags may suffice. Not only do seeds need careful storage, they must be planted within a minimum time in order to realize maximum viability (fertility). If you have collected seeds in late spring and summer, don't plant them until the fall rains begin, from October through January or February, so that the normal rain/short-day cool temperature cycle stimulates germination. Of course some seeds will germinate nearly immediately after collection (for example, lupine), but then the life cycle is out of synch, and extra care is needed to bring the seedlings along. A major portion of seeds lose their viability after one year, although some native shrubs and annuals are surprisingly long lived, being adapted to sprout after fires. Generally, the smaller the seed the less food reserve is available to carry the embryo through long dormant periods.

Seed cleaning. It is not always necessary to clean pods or other chaff from seeds meticulously, but the more chaff is present, the greater the chance of contamination by fungal spores. This in turn leads to fungal infection and the demise of seedlings. Some seeds separate readily from their containers, and it is merely a matter of dumping them out to separate the chaff. Other pods become brittle, flaking off as seeds are prodded from them; in still other cases, the seeds are firmly enveloped by their containers, which must be broken open to release them. Where there is lots of chaff, gentle blowing may suffice to remove the lighter chaff, leaving the heavier seeds behind. Sometimes a little mechanical help eases the task. Various sizes of screens are available that will retain the seeds while allowing the chaff to pass through.

For seeds contained inside a tough ovary wall, methods are used according to size: the larger nuts (oak acorns, for example) are best handled by being individually cracked to remove the seed inside, or by being planted intact. Smaller hard fruits, such as the achenes of composites and buttercups, are handled by crushing the achenes inside a paper bag, then winnowing away the chaff. In many cases, the achenes are so tiny (in the wild buckwheats, for example) that the whole achene is planted as though it were the seed.

Finally, a number of seeds are embedded in fleshy fruits. Often, a useful method here is to soak the seeds thoroughly, then force the pulp through a sieve which holds back the seeds. Fruits may also be left to ferment or rot, to make the removal of the flesh easier. This rotting process promotes softening of the seed coat, a necessary step for many since the fruits normally pass through the digestive tracts of animals before germination.

If seeds are contaminated with extraneous material or you suspect that fungal spores are present, rinse the seeds in a weak solution of bleach, which oxidizes and kills foreign matter. Be sure the solution does not penetrate the seed, and that it is not strong enough to remove the seed coat. Gauge this by starting with a 10 percent solution of bleach to water as a trial on a few seeds; if the seed coat is removed by so doing, then bleach is penetrating the seed.

Seed pretreatment. Native seeds are quite unpredictable in their readiness to germinate. Usually, the right combination of moisture (wet soils), day length (short days), and temperature (cool to cold nights) is necessary for germination, but even then many seeds steadfastly refuse to germinate, or do so only after months or years. Such seeds need pretreatment to break dormancy. Here are general guidelines (to which there are always exceptions) to determine whether seeds need pretreatment.

- *High-mountain plants* most often require stratification (described below). Stratification can be tried for one month, six weeks, two months or even more, to determine the optimal time for each species.
- *High-desert plants* also require stratification.
- *Fleshy-fruited plants* frequently produce seeds with hard coats which need softening or partial removal. Removal may be accomplished by filing the coat or by passing the seeds across sandpaper; softening is done by placing them in a weak acid solution for a few minutes, then rinsing. Sometimes the act of soaking the seeds is sufficient; you can tell by noting whether the seeds swell, an indication that water has been taken in through the coat.
- *Chaparral plants* often are sensitive to fire. Such seeds may require the fire pretreatment (also described below) in order to germinate. Stratification may be substituted with more even results for some species.
- *Beach plants* frequently have very heavy coats. Treat them as for fleshy-fruited plants above.
- *Any seed with a very tough or hard coat* should be treated as for fleshy-fruited plants above.
- *If germination is poor without pretreatment,* try stratification. It is always best to retain some seeds for future trials.

Stratification is a cold treatment often needed by plants that are subjected to freezing winters, in order to trigger germination. To stratify, put seeds into damp perlite or sphagnum moss in a plastic bag, and put the bag into the refrigerator. Usually the regular cold compartment is sufficient, but certain seeds do better in the freezer. Some seeds even germinate while in the refrigerator; hence the advantage of using plastic bags to check progress. Plant immediately if you see signs of roots or leaves.

The special fire (also called burn) pretreatment is to plant seeds in the soil, then place pine needles or excelsior paper on top and set them on fire.

Experimentation will determine how deep to plant seeds and how thick to make the fuel. The idea is to let the heat of the fire crack the seed coats but not destroy the embryo inside.

Planting seeds. This is a surprisingly simple task, given a little common sense. Seeds may be started in shallow flats, in separate plastic pots, or in peat pots. Each has its advantage: flats hold greater numbers of seeds; plastic pots are cheap and each may hold only one kind of seed; peat pots are directly plantable in the garden without disturbing the seedlings, though they tend to dry out quickly. The only soil to use is well-known commercial potting mixes. This cannot be overstated; potting soil has the advantages of good aeration and lack of disease pathogens and pests. An additional precaution is to water with a pan-drench-type fungicide. Damping-off and other fungal diseases are the worst foes of newly germinated seeds.

Two other points to consider are planting depth and thickness of sowing. Planting depth should be roughly once to twice the diameter of the seed; very fine seed may be sprinkled on top of the soil and secured with a sprinkling of fine sand or fine sphagnum. How thickly you sow the seeds is determined by whether you intend to thin seedlings soon or leave them in place for some time. Sow thickly if you feel mortality of seedlings is likely to be high, or if you intend to thin quickly. To broadcast seeds more sparsely, mix them with fine sand beforehand.

Seeds need frequent watering; soil should remain damp but *not* soggy. It is especially important to have a soil mix which drains quickly; extra coarse sand may be added for plants which live in habitats with soils of grit or gravel. Seed beds should never dry out and should not be in direct sun. Special attention is needed with peat pots, because they dry so quickly—a saucer of water might be put under the pots or the pots plunged into a tray of moist soil, but capillary action may form a salt crust on the soil surface this way. The best general way to water seeds is with a fine misting attachment so that soil is not disturbed in the process. Otherwise, seeds may be washed from their secure hole or clumped together.

Seed beds also need extra protection from snails, slugs, and birds. Snail bait takes care of the first two; mesh or netting above the seed bed should keep birds out. Otherwise, birds peck out seeds before they sprout, and later cut off tender seedlings.

Seedling establishment. Much failure occurs at this critical step. At some point, the new seedlings need to be transplanted into their permanent environment, unless that environment is to remain a pot. Certain seedlings move poorly (for example, many bulbous plants) and should be started in deep pots and left there for several seasons, until adult plants are ready for moving.

Most plants, however, can be moved into the garden in two or three stages. When seedlings have their first or second set of *true* leaves (as opposed to cotyledons), they are ready for thinning and transplanting. If there is an excess of plants at this stage, the weaker seedlings may be discarded. Seedlings generally need to be moved into deeper flats or small pots as an intermediate stage. These can then be gradually placed in ever stronger light to toughen the seedlings, and to allow maximum growth until they have reached gallon-can size. It is difficult to generalize about this size. Seedlings should be vigorous and have several sets of leaves before they are ready for the cans. When they have finally developed a vigorous root system throughout the can, they are ready for the garden.

When seedlings are moved into their permanent position in the garden, they should be watched for at least two months. If seedlings have not reached a transplantable size by early spring, they should be carried over in the cans until the next rainy season for easiest establishment. Seedlings transplanted in late spring would otherwise have to be watched diligently and watered often. Even if seedlings are transplanted by early spring, they need to be checked for signs of wilting and may require watering between rains. Some seedlings—even drought-tolerant species—do not establish deep roots fast enough to carry them through their first summer. Attention is needed to assure survival for that first critical dry period. By the second dry season, plants should be on their own.

Divisions

Divisions comprise two categories: rooted pieces and offsets. Rooted pieces are made by dividing clump-forming clones; offsets come from bulblets, cormlets, and bulb scales.

Establishment of rooted sections is much the same as transplanting mature plants. If sections are made in summer, it is better to hold them in flats or pots in a potting mix before moving them to the garden. There they will develop vigorous roots and can be separately monitored for water. Full transplanting should be done *only* during the rainy season, and new plants should receive some supplemental summer water their first year. To assure minimal loss in the transplanting process, follow these rules:

Maintain moisture at the roots at all times. Mortality and setback are caused by fine root hairs drying out.

Remove any flowering or fruiting parts of the plant. It is better to move material that is in its vegetative stage. Otherwise, the plant puts any extra energy into developing flowers and seeds.

Remove vulnerable tender new growth, and pinch back young leaves to reduce transpiration. Roots have been damaged in the process and cannot provide the water the leaves require until new roots have developed.

Keep the root ball as much intact as possible to minimize root damage. However, if roots are wound into a ball, they need to be unwound and opened up; and if too much taproot is present it can be pruned to encourage side roots.

Dig a hole bigger than the root ball before attempting to move the plant, and be sure soil is thoroughly wetted.

Gently firm the soil all around the root ball to eliminate air pockets, so long as soil texture allows good drainage.

Provide extra shading to help the newly moved plants until the roots have recovered. This slows down water loss and consequent wilting.

Provide special protection from snails, slugs, and other pests. Newly moved plants are weakened and are most vulnerable to attack.

Offsets may be handled in a variety of ways. These are sometimes stored in cool, dry places until they are ready for planting in the rainy season. Be sure, however, that they don't shrink too much—it is better to leave offsets in sand or peat moss and sprinkle them occasionally than to leave them in hot, dry air. When they are ready for planting, place them in containers such as pots filled with potting mix. This way they have time to grow healthy roots and mature into flowering-size plants before they go into the garden. Too often, small offsets planted directly in the garden are lost to predators or competition with bigger, more vigorous plants. Offsets usually mature faster than seeds but still require time before a flowering size plant is reached.

Many bulbous plants never should go directly into the garden—for example, if the garden is summer watered so that they require a summer rest (otherwise, summer-dormant bulbs will rot), or if the garden has gopher problems. Gophers are particularly fond of plants with fleshy roots, although a few of these are poisonous to them (as, for example, the irises). The gopher problem may also be handled by placing bulbs in wire baskets or raised beds covered with wire mesh, but often it is simply easier to grow bulbs in large tubs, boxes, or pots.

Cuttings

Many perennials cannot be started from cuttings, since their stems are simply too soft to strike root before rotting. Fortunately, most of these can be readily propagated by division, and this is an easier way to go. Cuttings are most successful in perennials with semiwoody to woody tissue in their stems. There are three categories of perennial cuttings:

1. Herbaceous cuttings. These are useful for a few species, such as certain succulents (for example, *Sedum*) which never produce woody tissue.

2. Half-woody cuttings. These are taken from perennials which develop woody tissue toward the base of the plant. Half-woody tissues occur when growth has halfway hardened, and this, in turn, depends upon the growth cycle. For example, perennials which begin to grow in spring won't develop half-woody tissue until early summer, while those which commence growth in summer won't develop it until the summer's end. Half-woody cuttings are often the easiest way to increase perennials such as various salvias, diplacuses, and penstemons.

3. Ripe-wood (or fully woody) cuttings. These are taken after a full year's growth has occurred, because in many plants the secondary growth which produces bark and wood doesn't get into full swing until a year has passed.

While many shrubs may be propagated this way, few perennials strike root as well from ripe wood as they do from half-ripe wood. In case half-woody cuttings fail, it doesn't hurt to try ripe-wood cuttings.

Obviously, then, to make successful cuttings some experimentation is necessary. Most important is the timing of taking the cuttings, and this can only be determined after getting acquainted with a particular species' growth cycle.

Some definite rules need to be laid down for taking cuttings. These are summarized below:

1. Never take so many cuttings from a plant that no primary branches are left. The bigger the original plant, the more cuttings it will yield.

2. Cuttings should always be made with a clean, sharp knife or pruning shears. To be meticulously clean, dip the shears in bleach before using.

3. Cuttings should be no longer than three or four inches.

4. Remove the lowest leaves of a cutting from the nodes, and rub or scratch the nodes to stimulate root growth (new roots develop from them). Incidentally, there's some controversy over whether rubbing the node is beneficial or not.

5. Remove flowers or fruits from the cutting (otherwise all the reserve food will go toward completing their development).

6. Nip back the upper leaves so that only part of each is left for photosynthesis; this way you reduce the surface area exposed to air and consequent wilting.

7. Rinse the cuttings, or if you suspect fungal contamination, dip them in a fungicide or in bleach.

8. Dip the tips of cuttings in a rooting hormone (this speeds up the rooting process, but will not cause roots to form if they would not otherwise) and shake off the excess.

Cuttings normally shouldn't go into ordinary garden soil, although there are always those plants that seem to root easily no matter what you do. For best results, set up a special cutting bed with the following considerations in mind:

• The bed should be in a shallow tray so that cuttings can be moved around to different sites as needed.

• Drainage holes in the tray are of utmost importance. Equally important is the medium used in the tray; ordinary garden soil should never be used. The ideal medium allows rapid drainage (to prevent rot) and good aeration. Most propagators use perlite, vermiculite, or sand, or a combination thereof. Some like to add chopped sphagnum moss or peat for better water retention.

• Cuttings should be inserted into the medium up to the intact leaves.

• Cuttings should be watered frequently, since they have no roots by which to absorb water.

• The rooting process can often be speeded by a special cable placed under the propagation bed to provide bottom heat. Cables for this purpose are available at many nurseries. The ideal temperature is around 70 degrees Farenheit. You could alternately rig a number of incandescent lights below the starting bed, but be sure to eliminate any risk of electrical shock from water. Check the soil temperature with a soil thermometer; elevated temperatures will cook cuttings.

- The cutting bed should be placed out of bright or direct light, since this only increases wilting and water loss. Commercial growers use glasshouses whose windows are heavily glazed or whitewashed.

- Covering the cutting bed with plastic or frequent misting helps reduce wilting, but care is needed to provide ventilation or the cuttings will certainly rot. Automatic misters are available for those with the money and inclination.

Cuttings vary greatly in the speed with which they form roots; most take one to two or three months, so don't give up if roots don't form right away. You may gently loosen the cutting from the medium to check progress; if the lower stem feels mushy, the cutting has rotted; if the lower stem ends in a swelling (callus), root formation may soon begin. Be careful not to overdo your probing; too much disturbance is bound to retard root formation. Sometimes you can trim off the rotted portion of a cutting before it's gone too far and try again.

Cuttings should have several roots each, the roots an inch or more long, before they are ready to be moved. As with seedlings, you don't move a rooted cutting directly into the garden but into a small pot, which is carefully watched. Pots with rooted cuttings should be gradually exposed to more sun until the new plants are hardened off. If cuttings have been started in a glasshouse, the cuttings also need to be gradually habituated to fluctuating temperatures. As with seedlings, it pays to move your new plant from a small pot to a gallon can before making the final move into the garden. You will know when plants are ready to be moved by checking to see if the roots protrude through the bottom drainage hole. Care should be exercised to prevent the plant from becoming root bound in its pot; this condition is obvious when you tamp the plant from its pot and see a series of roots wound tightly around the edge of the exposed root ball.

Layering

Layering is a variation on making cuttings; it involves a newly rooted section which is still attached to its parent plant. Layering is most often used on shrubs, where a branch may be bent to the ground and held there by a pin or simply the weight of soil placed over it. The part which is buried is irritated by partially breaking the stem at that point, and by removing leaves from the nodes in that area and rubbing the nodes. Layering may take several months, but it has the advantage that the newly rooted plantlet is nourished and watered by the parent plant. When vigorous roots have formed, the new plant may be severed from the parent by a sharp knife.

Another kind of layering is to select an upright branch, remove leaves from and irritate a node at which you wish to have roots form, then wrap it in moistened sphagnum moss in a plastic cover. Many house plants are layered in this manner.

Both of these layering techniques have limited use with our perennials, but there are occasions when a half-woody perennial with decumbent or prostrate stems may be encouraged to strike root in this fashion.

Management of Soil and Water

No other factors are so important to successful culture of plants than soil and water. Probably more plants have been killed by improper management of these two factors than from all other factors combined. Yet despite these failures, the basics of soil and watering are straightforward: soils should be loose, friable, well-draining, and amended with organic materials; water should be given so that soils are temporarily saturated to their full depth, then allowed to dry thoroughly on the upper surface before being watered again. If those rules are adhered to, few problems should result for the majority of plants. Of course, there are always those exceptions where plant roots need to be in constantly soggy soil, but even then, some movement of water is necessary to maintain health. Soils that never drain and are finely textured with few pores are to be avoided. If you have soil such as heavy clay with an underlying hardpan, you must either improve the soil in some way or water with extreme caution. It is always better to change the soil condition to a more favorable one than to try to compensate by not watering much. Let's look at these two factors in more detail.

Soils

The ideal garden soil is one whose texture (due to the pores between soil particles) is loose and crumbly, but not so coarse or porous that water moves right through. Sandy soils are too coarse and have major problems with proper water retention; clay or adobe soils are too fine and have little pore space for the needed oxygen exchange between roots and air. They also drain too slowly. The ideal soil is therefore a loam with intermediate properties. Another consideration is that the upper topsoil layer have some organic material in it—this allows better pore structure while helping retain water, and adds minor amounts of needed minerals.

Let's see what to do in the likely case that you have either a sand- or clay-type soil. In some ways, sandy soils are the most difficult: although they drain well, they dry out rapidly and are hard to rewet after drying. And, most sandy soils are low in organic matter. Consequently, the only effective way to deal with these soils is to add lots of vegetable matter—a compost pile is a handy source, as are various sources of peat moss, leaf mold, and shredded bark. One caution should be observed with regard to adding organic matter: some types of leaves and twigs break down to create an uncommonly high acidity (especially pine and other conifer needles)—these are best used for plants whose habitats match those conditions (for example, rhododendrons and ferns from redwood forests).

Homemade compost, if properly heated, should be relatively safe in this respect. There are books available which detail the ways to make a workable compost pile.

Strangely enough, the way to improve a clay soil is also to add lots of organic matter. You can also add sand or various other amendments such as perlite or vermiculite, but the quantities needed and the general loss of them through the soil makes this costly and wasteful. Adding organic matter year after year finally results in an airy, crumbly soil.

For both sandy and clay soils, there is another solution which is swift and effective: build your garden with good soil on top of the original soil. This has two advantages: it raises the overall level of soil to give improved drainage, since the beds are now raised, and it introduces soil whose structure is better suited to plant growth right from the start. Two words of caution:

1. Mix the new and old soils together at their interface so there is a gradual transition from old to new (otherwise water accumulates or runs off at the interface).

2. Allow plenty of root room by creating the proper depth of the new soil layer—a minimum is around a foot.

The ideal way to utilize this concept is to create raised beds bordered by wood planks or rocks so that the bed is totally independent of the original soil cover.

One final alternative to the poor-soil syndrome is to garden in containers—if you have a deck or lawn around which to place planters, this may be the ideal solution. You can fill containers with the best possible soil—a potting mix which has already been sterilized.

Questions frequently raised about soil for native plants are:

• Do natives require special soils when they have grown on unusual soils in nature (for example, serpentine)?

• How often do you fertilize?

The answer to the first question is a resounding "no." Natives grow naturally on special soils—dolomite, limestone, serpentine, lava—not because they need those soils but because they avoid competition there, since these soils provide unfavorable growing conditions for the majority of plants. Experiments have shown that many serpentine plants actually perform better when planted in ordinary garden soil so long as they don't have to compete with other plants.

Two exceptions to this rule are drainage and soil pH. Plants from rocky soils need sharp drainage; plants from acid soils seldom grow well in neutral or alkaline soils. Litmus paper can be used to get a rough idea of pH conditions. Remember that soils from conifer forests and, in general, from damp cool climates are acid, and soils from hot desert areas range toward alkalinity. Lime (calcium carbonate) will sweeten an acid soil; pine duff and leaching help to correct alkalinity. The process of leaching involves passing water through the soil to remove excessive salts; it would be successful only where drainage is excellent.

With respect to fertilizer, the general rule is—don't worry about it. Few natives are used to highly rich soils. Thus, for most natives, a light fertilizing is all that is needed for ordinary growth, and that is sometimes unnecessary. In general, soils low in organic matter and sandy soils need nutrient supplements more than other soils. Also in general, woodland plants may need extra fertilizing because of hungry tree roots. Excess fertilizer is likely to be harmful to most natives, particularly fertilizers rich in nitrogen, since this makes growth unnaturally prolific. When natives grow faster than they would in nature, their growth may become spindly or they may burn themselves out, thus shortening their usual life span. The best fertilizers are those with slow release of nutrients: for containerized plants, Osmacote; for bedded plants, an organic source such as manure which has been well rotted beforehand. In general, garden conditions may shorten natives' life cycles through their nutrient richness; one does not need to compound this by adding rich fertilizers. However, when seedlings or new divisions are just starting out, it is beneficial to boost vigorous new growth with a dressing of Osmacote pellets.

Mulches for Soils

One final word about soils is a word much in favor today: mulch. Mulches are top dressings of soil other than the soil itself; they vary almost as widely as do soils. The several sound reasons for mulching are as follows:

1. Mulches may gradually release trace nutrients to the top soil.

2. Mulches gradually break down into smaller bits of organic matter, which help improve upper soil texture and maintain crumbliness.

3. Mulches often improve the appearance of beds, giving them a tidier look.

4. Mulches smother and suppress growth of weed seedlings.

5. Mulches help retain soil moisture so that much less water is lost.

The last two reasons are perhaps the most important and persuasive for using mulches. Mulches are applied everywhere but on the desired plants, thus keeping weed pulling chores low. And because a mulch helps cover vulnerable top soil, loose particles are not carried away by winds, nor are they dried rapidly by heat and winds as they normally would be. In gardens where water is minimized to begin with, mulches make extra summer water even less necessary.

What materials can be used for mulching? The list is a long one, and even inorganic materials are used (but are less desirable). Here are some possibilities:

- black plastic (strictly for keeping weeds down; does not amend soils)

- ordinary leaf duff or mold (pine and other conifer needles help create acid soils)

- compost (please—well rotted only)
- grass trimmings
- cocoa hulls
- pressings from grapes
- coarsely ground bark (again, conifer bark helps maintain acidity)
- gravel

The thicker the mulch, the more effective it is for reducing evaporation and weeds, but remember that the mulch must be coarse enough to allow plenty of air channels to keep that oxygen flowing into the soil for healthy roots!

Watering

If your soil is loose and friable, and your drainage good, it is much easier to gauge watering. Remember that the advantage of many natives is that they seldom need to be watered. Their cycles are geared to the climate you live in—namely late-fall/winter/spring rains and a dry period in summer and early fall. But note that there are many important exceptions to this rule. Here are the outstanding ones:

1. All native seedlings and cuttings need constant moisture.
2. Most natives, even if planted during the rainy season, need some summer water their first year to establish deep roots.
3. Most natives look better if they receive occasional, thorough summer water.
4. Natives from bogs, marshes, and wet meadows must have summer water.
5. Natives from the higher mountains need summer water.
6. Natives from redwood forests and other coastal forests need some summer water.
7. Natives planted in sandy soils may require some summer water.
8. Natives from coastal situations when planted inland need summer water.

The biggest worry about watering natives in summer (other than the extra time needed to do so) is that some are actually killed this way. Water molds and other soil fungi (such as oak root fungus) grow rapidly when conditions are both wet and warm, in summer. They grow so slowly or poorly in winter that wetness is seldom a problem. The only way to learn about which natives are sensitive to these fungi is through trial. In general, many chaparral shrubs are sensitive, as are native oaks. If you have a native oak in your garden, it may be weakly infected with this fungus pathogen, which may then pass from oak roots to adjacent roots of other natives, so extreme caution is needed.

There are a few rules about how water is applied that will help assure success:

- Water in the early morning, if possible. Evening watering may encourage mildew; watering during the warm hours of the day promotes leaf burn and wastes water through evaporation.

- Water thoroughly. Each situation differs with respect to how long it takes for a thorough soaking, but remember it is always better to water thoroughly a few times than to water skimpily many times. Water needs to penetrate to the bottom layers of soil in order to encourage roots to reach deep. Deeply penetrating roots carry the plant over dry periods much better than shallow roots. In general, sandy soils need to be watered longer than loams; clay soils require the shortest time. You can determine how thoroughly the soil is wetted by digging down.

- The frequency of watering should depend upon soil type, the original environment of the plant (as outlined above), the amount of organic material in the soil, the angle of slope, and the season. Remember that organic matter helps retain water, making frequent watering less necessary. The steeper the slope, the more poorly it retains water. And, of course, on hot summer days soils dry much faster than they do on cool winter days. Another condition to watch for is wind: wind can evaporate water from leaf surfaces just as rapidly as hot sun.

- It is best to apply water through a fine sprinkler or mister, or from the slow seepage of a drip system. However, drip systems are best used where large, discrete plants are located such as shrubs and trees. In general, a sprinkler system does a better job for a garden of perennials than any other method, and is also one of the easiest ways of getting the job done. There are sophisticated computerized timer systems which simplify this task for a large garden.

Designing Native Landscapes

You might find the title to this section contradictory; natives are wild natural plants without seeming design. Therein lies the essence of successful native plant design—to create a landscape without contrived design. One way to achieve this is simply to plant in a hodgepodge fashion, but this usually produces worse results than a deliberately carried out design. If you have country property, another option is to leave the landscape in its original condition, assuming it is still in a natural state. With such an option, careful additions and removal of weedy plants enhance an already pleasing setting. The majority of gardens, however, need some deliberate plan.

Rather than belabor design parameters, this section attempts to provide plans for using natives in natural and pleasing ways, and to suggest groupings of species which result in attractive contrasts, similar cultural requirements, and pleasing color schemes. (See also Appendix 1, "Species Pairs and Triplets for the Garden.")

The scale of the native garden requires careful attention—a small garden space can attempt only part of certain designs, while an exceptionally large garden can incorporate all suggested species. Important considerations are:

- the slope of the land
- the amount and timing of sun
- the presence of natural rocks
- the presence of water features, such as streams and ponds
- the presence, number, nature, and location of trees

All determine the direction to go in creating a natural garden.

Unless you want to create a collector's garden, another design parameter is to use certain key plants for tying together and unifying the theme of each kind of garden. Such plants may be repeated several times, but remember to make repetitions look random rather than evenly spaced; plant in drifts or odd groups rather than even. Nothing is worse than to space all plants in geometric designs.

The next pages deal with each situation item by item, and suggest several possible groupings of natives for that situation. The groupings are the mixed border, the woodland garden, the water garden, deck planters, the meadow garden, and the rock garden. Each category is followed by a list of appropriate plants arranged according to height and listed alphabetically. Sometimes a genus name (for example, lupines) will be qualified by the words "some forms," meaning that only those species with the appropriate height and cultural requirements are to be used. Also note that for species not detailed in Part II scientific names are given in parentheses after the common names.

The Mixed Border

Rather than the usual perennial border I am using the mixed border, because it allows greater latitude in design. For example, annuals can be added at times when perennials are not flowering. Also, many bulbs help to fill out and add variety to a mixed border, as do background subshrubs.

Mixed borders are useful in many landscaping situations: to border a path or walk, in front of foundation shrubs and hedges, to line a lawn, or to edge a long drive. They are designed so that the lowest plants go in the foreground, the medium-sized plants behind those, and the tall plants (four, five, six feet) behind those. Rigid adherence to this pattern results in a formal, stiff effect, but since few plants are the same height, a pleasing mixture of low, medium, and tall plants results from planting a wide variety of species in the border.

Other considerations for choosing plants in a border should include:

- pleasant foliage contrasts in color and texture
- flower color combinations which blend well
- extension of flowering times over a long period and with early bloomers mixed with later blossoms
- dormancy requirements—interplanting summer- and winter-dormant plants to cover for each other
- water requirements—are all plants summer water tolerant or drought resistant?

• shade/sun requirements

Because these factors call for separate border designs, I have categorized them as dry border (full sun), watered border (full sun), and shaded border (some summer water).

The Dry Border. This is the best border in terms of maintenance, since it requires little summer water. Unfortunately, however, it takes special design to achieve a pleasing look when so many natives are summer dormant. It is important to include plants which continue to hold their leaves and even flower during this critical dry period. Considerable time is needed to remove the dead and browned parts of summer-dormant plants to prevent shabby appearance; such plants must grow in proximity to "evergreen" types which help hide the dead growth. This border is ideal for a sunny garden where watering is not practical—it can hold its own for the most part with only the water from natural rains and fogs.

Into this come the complicating factors of summer heat and soil texture. If the dry border is built on sandy soils, some supplemental summer water will probably be necessary, since sand retains water so poorly. Even the most drought tolerant native may succumb to the lack of water in such situations. Here it would help to amend the soil with lots of organic matter and mulch heavily.

In gardens where the mercury frequently soars to 90 or 100 degrees even the most drought tolerant natives may have trouble or look poorly without summer water—some may even lose their leaves (although they are "normally" evergreen) without summer water. And coastal plants which are drought tolerant in their homes cannot cope with the tremendous increase in transpiration they experience in hot situations—they must have some summer water, and even a bit of shade. The design of a dry border must take all of these factors into account.

Low Plants	Medium Plants	Tall Plants (for the Background)
Alpine penstemon	Adobe lily	Beargrass (*in flower*)
Blue-eyed grass	Antioch dunes—	Blazing star
Bluff goldfields	evening primrose	California sunflower
Brewer's lupine	Apricot mallow	Chaparral lily
Brodiaeas	Balsamroots	Climbing penstemon
California milkweed	Beach bursage	Creamy eardrops
California phacelia	Blochman senecio	Golden eardrops
California poppy	Blue flax	Hooker's evening primrose
(*coastal forms*)	Blue nightshades	Matilija poppy
Checkerbloom	Buckwheats	Prickly poppy
Coast goldenrod	California goldenrod	St. Catherine's lace
Coast goldfields	California poppy	Santa Cruz Island
Coast paintbrush	Coyote mints	buckwheat
Coast strawberry	Deerbroom	Tree coreopsis
Douglas's violet	Douglas's senecio	Tree lupine (*Lupinus*
Dune aster	Foothill wallflower	*arboreus*, a shrub)

Low Plants

Dune knotweed
Four o'clocks
Golden aster
Gumweed
Horkelias
Hummingbird fuchsia
Ivesia
Johnny-jump-up
Low-growing morning glories
Lyall lupine
Mountain pride penstemon
Mountain nightshade
  (*Parish's nightshade*)
Perennial linanthus
Phloxes
Pussy toes
Sand verbena
Sapphire flower
Sea thrift
Shooting stars
Sierra lotus
Siskiyou daisy
Skullcaps
Small-leafed buckwheat
Sonoma sage
Suncups (*golden eggs*)
Sunrose
Tansies
Wallflowers
Western larkspur
Wooly sunflower
Yarrow (*some forms*)

Medium Plants

Golden stars
Golden yarrow
Hummingbird fuchsias
Indian paintbrushes
Larkspurs
Little California sunflower
Lizardtail sunflower
Lupines
Mariposa tulips
Mountain phacelias
Mule's ears
Pearly everlasting
Penstemons
Rayless aster
Sea dahlia (*Coreopsis*)
Seaside daisy
Shaggy bee plant
Showy milkweed
Sky rocket
Triteleias
Wandflower
Western thoroughwort
White fritillary
Wild hyacinths
Yarrow
Zygadenes

Tall Plants (for the Background)

Washington lily
Wild morning glories
  (vines)

The Watered Border. The watered border offers more possibilities than does the dry, as long as soil drainage is good. Under these circumstances, many natives—even those classified as drought tolerant—will grow and bloom longer and look better than with no summer water. Certainly some species are so sensitive to summer water that their roots succumb to root-rotting fungi; many others burn themselves out by rapid growth and prolific blooming under these circumstances. Still, if good looks are desired, this is a better way to go. The main question is how much summer water is needed, and the answer varies according to soil texture, summer high temperatures, and the actual plant material selected. Some material for the watered border needs frequent irrigation—on the order of one thorough watering a week or every other week. This is best determined by careful study of the plant's original home. For example, most mountain meadow species fall here.

Low Plants

Acaena
Alumroots
Arnicas
Bicolor lotus
Blue-eyed grass
Bluff goldfields
California phacelia
Checkerbloom
Coast rockcress
Dune aster
Gentians
Geraniums
Geums
Gold-eyed grass
Grass-of-Parnassus
Gumweeds
Horkelias
Ivesias
Meadow lotus
Mouse-eared chickweed
Musk monkeyflower
Native clovers
Northern hummingbird
    fuchsia
Penstemons
Perennial linanthus
Phloxes
Pussytoes
Sea thrift
Siskiyou daisy
Skullcaps
Small-leafed buckwheat
Star tulips
Stonecrops (sedums)
Suncups (golden eggs)
Tinker's penny
Violets
Wallflowers
Woodmints
Wooly sunflower
Yarrow (some forms)
Yerba mansa

Medium Plants

Arnicas
Asters
Balsamroots
Blue dicks (*brodiaea*)
Blue flax
Buckwheats (*some*)
Burnt orange senecio
Buttercups
California poppy
Cardinal monkeyflower
Columbines (*some shade*)
Common daisy
Coyote mints
Davis's knotweed
False lupine
Foothill wallflower
Fountain star lily
Golden monkeyflower
Golden yarrow
Goldenrods
Horsemint
Hummingbird fuchsias
Indian paintbrushes
Irises (some shade)
Island snapdragon
Jacob's ladders
Jeffrey's shooting stars
Large-leafed geum
Larkspurs
Leopard lily
Long-rayed brodiaea
Meadow daisies
Meadow lupine
Milk lily
Pink monkeyflower
    (mountain monkeyflower)
Mule's ears
Nightshades
Pearly everlasting
Potentillas
Rayless aster
Sea dahlia (coreopsis)
Showy milkweed
Single-leaf onion
Sky rocket
Sneezeweeds
Swamp onion
Wooly sunflower
Wooly woodmint
Yarrow

Tall Plants

Annual paintbrush
California coneflower
California sunflower
Canyon sunflower
Cardinal lobelia
Coast woodmint
Common butterwort
Fireweed
Giant larkspur
Goatsbeard
Hooker's evening primrose
Humboldt lily
Monkshood
Red columbine
Tower larkspur

The Shaded Border. Although shaded areas lose water more slowly, this is partly mitigated against by the enormous thirst of tree roots. Some plants will tolerate dry shade, but a far greater number thrive in moist shade; again, remember that good drainage is the key to success. The shaded border can replace the woodland garden where a more formal design is desired, or can interface with the more natural feel of a true woodland garden. Some coastal and high mountain plants which receive full sun in their natural homes would succeed best in the shaded border of hot, inland gardens.

Low Plants

Blue-eyed grass
Brook saxifrage
California saxifrage
California strawberry
Candy-stripe
Coast goldenrod
Common stonecrop
    (sedum)
Dog violet
Enchanter's nightshade
False lily-of-the-valley
Fawn lilies
Globe tulips
Golden brodiaea
Grouse flower
Indian pink
King's gentian
Milkmaids
Mist maidens
Modesty
Mountain strawberry
Oregon gentian
Piggyback plant
Pussy ears
Redwood sorrel
Redwood violet
Shooting stars
Single-leaf onion
Moss spring beauty
    (small-leaf montia)
Star flower
Sugar scoops
Tinker's penny
Twinflower
Vanilla leaf
Waterleaf
Western bleedingheart
Wild gingers
Wild savory

Medium Plants

Alumroots
Andrew's beadlily
Arnicas
Baneberry
Broadleaf lupine
Brook orchid
Buttercups
Cardinal monkeyflower
Checker lily
Columbines
Common daisy
Fairy bells
Firecracker brodiaea
Fringe cups
Globe tulips
Golden brodiaea
Golden monkeyflower
Grass-of-Parnassus
Heartleaf milkweed
Horsemint
Hound's tongue
Hummingbird sage
Inside-out flowers
Irises
Island snapdragon
Ithuriel's spear
Jacob's ladders
Jeffrey's shooting star
Large-leaf geum
Larkspurs
Louseworts
Meadow saxifrage
Meadowrues
Pink monkeyflower
Potentillas
Rein orchid
St. Johnswort
Scarlet fritillary
Smooth yellow violet

Tall Plants

Annual paintbrush
Beargrass
California aralia
California coneflower
Canyon sunflower
Chain fern
Columbia lily
Common butterwort
Corn lilies
Fireweed
Giant larkspur
Humboldt lily
Indian rhubarb
Leopard lily
Meadow knotweed
    (meadow polygonum)
Meadow lupine
Monkshood
Ranger's buttons
    (whiteheads)
Tower larkspur

Short Plants	Medium Plants
Woodland anemone	Solomon's plumes
Woodland phlox	Swamp onion
Woodmint	Trilliums
Wormskjold's clover	Western coltsfoot
Yerba buena	Western heartsease
	Wooly woodmint

The Woodland Garden

Many of the perennials suggested for the shaded mixed border actually do and look better as part of a natural woodland garden where design is not formalized. In fact, it is the mark of a well-designed woodland garden that it has a natural feel without looking planned. The four major factors dictating planting themes in such a setting are:

1. the size of the area
2. the density of shade (remember, deciduous trees give different shade according to season)
3. the side of the tree(s) plantings are done on—north sides stay shady longer than south sides, for example
4. whether the trees are water tolerant or not—most oaks need summer dryness while redwoods require water

Other factors include:

- slope
- natural objects in place, such as rocks or a stream channel
- depth and breadth of tree roots

It is difficult to plant around shallow-rooted trees because there is little root room for other plants and much competition for water and nutrients.

Only experience can alert the gardener to all of these factors, but direct observation in nature helps. For example, the larger plants—giant herbs, ferns, and shrubs—generally occur where there is plenty of moisture, as along stream banks, or at an opening in the tree canopy that allows light to pass through. The low ground covers, spring bulbs, and ferns most often grow in the deeper, poorly lighted situations.

These basic facts help in arriving at some kind of general design for your woodland garden: the larger, taller plants go not only behind others but near the edge of the tree line for better light. The ground cover plants can weave an interesting pattern in dense shade near tree trunks, and be interrupted by islands of taller plants where light passes through longer—islands of ferns, spring bulbs, and small shrubs. Finally, if there is room for a stream course, dry or not, it greatly enhances the design and creates a site for the moisture-loving stream followers—large ferns, lilies, orchids, and saxifrages. These aspects—dim forest floor, islands, background edge plantings, and streamside plants—suggest a loose design which may be filled in with varied detail. One final aspect of your woodland garden might be a steep slope with moss-covered rocks which make a home for other specialized plants found nowhere else. The plants in the following lists are given according to these categories.

Plants for the Forest Floor (ground covers)

Bride's bonnet
California strawberry
Coast waterleaf
False lily-of-the-valley
Mitreworts
Modesty
Piggyback plant
Redwood sorrel

Redwood violet
Star flower
Sugar scoops
Twinflower
Vanilla leaf
Western bleedingheart
Wild gingers
Woodland anemones

Plants for Islands

Alumroots
Andrew's beadlily
Bolander phacelia
Broadleaf lupine
California sword fern
Checker lily
Common sword fern
Dudley's sword fern
Fairy bells
Fringe cups
Hound's tongue
Hummingbird sage
Inside-out flowers

Irises
Lady fern
Lilies
Lobed violet
Lowland meadowrue
Milkmaids
Polypody ferns
Red columbine
Smooth yellow violet
Solomon's plumes
Trilliums
Western heartsease
Wood ferns

Background Plants (forest edge)

Beargrass
California aralia
Canyon sunflower
Cardinal lobelia
Chain fern
Coast lily
Common sword fern
Fireweed

Fringed corn lily
Giant larkspur
Goatsbeard
Indian rhubarb
Lady fern
Lilies
Meadow lupine
Monkshood

Background Shrubs

California rosebay (*Rhododendron macrophyllum*)
Cascara sagrada (*Rhamnus purshiana*)
Columbia manzanita (*Arctostaphylos columbiana*)
Creek dogwood (*Cornus stolonifera* and others)
Evergreen huckleberry (*Vaccinium ovatum*)
Mock orange (philadelphus) (*Philadelphus lewisii*)

Red huckleberry (*Vaccinium parvifolium*)
Salal (*Gaultheria shallon*)
Salmonberry (*Rubus spectabilis*)
Snowbell bush (*Styrax officinalis*)
Snowberries (*Symphoricarpos* spp.)
Thimbleberry (*Rubus parviflorus*)
Twinberry honeysuckle (*Lonicera involucrata*)
Vine maple (*Acer circinatum*)
Western azalea (*Rhododendron occidentale*)
Western burning bush (*Euonymus occidentalis*)
Western spice bush (*Calycanthus occidentalis*)
Wood rose (*Rosa gymnocarpa*)

Streamside Plants

Brook orchid
Brook saxifrage
California aralia
California coneflower
Canyon sunflower
Cardinal lobelia
Columbia lily
Deer fern
Fireweed
Five-finger fern
Giant larkspur
Goatsbeard
Grass-of-Parnassus

Horsemint
Humboldt lily
Indian rhubarb
Lady fern
Leopard lily
Meadow lupine
Meadowrues
Monkshood
Red columbine
Skunk cabbage
Spiny wood fern
Sticky columbine
Water ferns
Western coltsfoot

Plants for Rocky Banks

Alumroots
Broadleaf lewisia
Brook saxifrages
California lace fern
California maidenhair
California saxifrage
Coffee fern
Common stonecrop (sedum)
Common wood fern
Fawn lilies
Globe tulips
Goldback fern
Ground iris
Grouse flower
Hound's tongue

Inside-out flowers
Lowland meadowrue
Merten's saxifrage
Milkmaids
Mist maidens
Modesty
Montias
Northern hummingbird fuchsia
Polypody fern
Red larkspur
Shooting stars
Skullcaps
Twinflower
Western heartsease
Yerba buena

The Water Garden

The term water garden can mean many things, but I'm using it here to indicate a garden designed strictly around a body of still water such as a pond or small pool. Much of the success of the design rests on the careful, artful creation of the pool and its partners: rocks. Well-placed rocks, an attractively shaped pool, and the lining of the pool all go far to make this a convincingly natural and restful setting. Strict symmetry should be assiduously avoided, as should even placement of like-size rocks; asymmetry and variation in rock shape and size are the cornerstones to pleasing design. On the other hand, too many kinds of rock leads to confusion and chaos—similar rock material ties the whole together.

Pools can vary tremendously in size and depth, but even the smallest should measure no less than 12 to 18 inches deep from surface to bottom. The lining of the pool can vary from a simple heavy-duty urethane black plastic liner to heavy-duty concrete. Each choice has its advantages and drawbacks. The greatest liability with plastic is that it punctures; properly poured concrete should last a long time, but when leaks develop, they're difficult to find. In order to minimize the visual impact of a liner under water, the liner color should be as dark and neutral as possible, and the bottom should be covered with coarse pebbles or gravel, or by a several-inch-thick layer of soil, if bottom planting is wanted. Another possibility for submerged aquatics is to place them in sturdy boxes or pots and plunge them into the bottom soil layer. This prevents roots from wandering, as many aquatics are wont to do. Finally, the theme of poolside rocks may be continued into the water itself, the rocks helping to hide side views of pond liners.

Pool design is enhanced by varying the rate at which the edge drops off toward the bottom; shallow shelves or gradual slopes allow marsh edge plants to be incorporated which soften pond design. In fact, to vary the pond margin, shallow bays might be created for the several clump-forming marsh plants which naturally grow in such situations. Another way to help create asymmetry is to install a small island in one part of the pond.

Finally, the consideration of site for your pond must be done before starting construction. Be sure the following criteria have been taken into account:

- as level a site as possible
- easy access to a water source (or a pipe that you bury)—water must be aerated from time to time
- easy access for wading into the pond for periodic cleaning
- location of the pond to make a visual statement
- positioning the pond where the front receives sun and the back filtered shade

One efficient placement is to install a pond at the end of an open lawn or meadow and in front of a backdrop of tall shrubbery or trees. Such a setting gives several different habitats for the natives you place around the pond.

Two factors need careful consideration in your decisions on which plants to use:

1. Plant height—tall plants naturally go behind the pond and in front of shrubs and trees while short plants are grouped in front of the pond.

2. Tolerance to water—some want constantly moist soil but no standing water; others are best with water over their roots; still others grow only submerged.

Low Plants—Pond Periphery

Arnicas (shade)
Bicolor lotus
Blue-eyed grass
Bluff goldenrod
Brook saxifrages (shade)
California maidenhair (shade)
Candy-stripe (shade)
Deer fern (shade)
Dog violet
Enchanter's nightshade (some shade)
Gentians
Gold-eyed grasses
Grass-of-Parnassus
Moss spring beauty (little-leaf montia; shade)

Native clovers
Pt. Reyes checkerbloom
Primrose monkeyflower
Purple star tulip
Single-leaf onion
Suncups (golden eggs)
Tinker's penny
Venus-hair fern (shade)
Waterfall buttercup
Waterleafs (shade)
White mountain violet
Wild savory
Woodmints
Yerba mansa

Medium Plants—Pond Periphery

Asters
Bistort
Brook orchid (shade)
Buttercups
Camasses
Cardinal monkeyflower
Coast lily
Common daisy
Dotted saxifrage
False lupine
Five-finger fern (shade)
Fountain zygadene
Golden monkeyflower
Horsemint
Jacob's ladders
Jeffrey's shooting stars
Lady fern (shade)
Large-leafed geum
Long-petaled iris

Long-rayed brodiaea
Meadow paintbrush
Meadow saxifrage
Meadowrues
Milk lily
Mountain hollyhocks
Mountain iris
Pink monkeyflower
   (mountain monkeyflower)
Potentillas
Rein orchids
Red columbine (shade)
St. Johnswort
Siskiyou dentaria
Sneezeweeds
Swamp onion
Water ferns (shade)
Western coltsfoot (shade)
Wooly woodmint

Tall Plants—Pond Periphery

California aralia (shade)
California coneflower
Canyon sunflower (shade)
Cardinal lobelia
Chain fern (shade)
Coast woodmint
Common butterwort
Fireweed
Giant larkspur

Goatsbeard
Hooker's evening primrose
Humboldt lily
Indian rhubarb
Lemon lily
Leopard lily
Meadow knotweed (meadow polygonum)
Meadow lupine
Monkshood
Tower larkspur

Shallow Water Plants

Ball rushes
Buckbean (bogbean)
Cattails (allow room to spread)
Jussiaea
Marsh potentilla
Pennywort (invasive)

Sedges
Silverweed (invasive)
Skunk cabbage (shade)
Speedwell (invasive)
Tules (allow room to spread)
Yerba mansa

Deeper Water—Submerged Plants

Bladderworts (*Utricularia* spp.), (insectivorous)
Elodea
Hornwort (*Ceratophyllum demersum*)
Pondweeds (*Potamogeton* spp.)
Water buttercups
Water shield (*Brasenia schreberi*)
Yellow pond-lily

Shrubs and Small Trees for Behind the Pond

Creek dogwoods (*Cornus stolonifera* and others)
Hazelnut (*Corylus cornuta californica*)
Labrador tea (*Ledum glandulosum*)
Mock orange (philadelphus; *Philadelphus lewisii*)
Mountain dogwood (*Cornus nuttallii*)
Mountain maple (*Acer glabrum*)
Native crabapple (*Malus fusca*)
Sierra laurel (*Leucothoe davisae*)
Snowbell bush (*Styrax officinalis*)
Stink currant (*Ribes bracteosum*)
Twin honeysuckle (*Lonicera conjugialis*)
Twinberry honeysuckle (*Lonicera involucrata*)
Vine maple (*Acer circinatum*)
Western azalea (*Rhododendron occidentale*)
Western burning bush (*Euonymus occidentalis*)
Western spice bush (*Calycanthus occidentalis*)
Willows (*Salix* spp.; allow room to spread)

Deck Planters

Tubs, large pots, and planter boxes are containers for plants to be displayed as specimens, where space is limited to a deck, or for easy protection and removal of plants such as bulbs and tubers. Plants may be containerized where protection from gophers is needed, or where especially fine drainage is desired. Thus, plants suitable for deck planters belong to several categories. Regardless, the basic treatment of these plants is similar, and is described below.

All containers need to have generous holes at the bottom for good drainage. This is seldom a problem with commercially available pots, but planter boxes and tubs need to have holes drilled in them; the larger the container, the more holes needed per square area. The bottom of any of the larger containers should be covered with coarse gravel to aid drainage. Although it is advised to put broken crockery at the bottom of ordinary flower pots, studies have shown that these may actually impede proper drainage. It is always a good idea to use potting soil since it has the advantage of being easy to handle, is sterile (without fungus spores), and drains quickly. For most natives, fertilizer does not need to be added right away, but a light dressing of Osmacote can be added later after the plants are well established.

Although containers are easily moved from spot to spot to take advantage of shade or sun and later to store when bulbs go dormant, the largest need castors or wheels, and these should be added *before* filling the container with soil. Containers also need to be checked fairly often for water—even drought-tolerant natives *require* some water when containerized! A good rule is to leave an inch to several inches (according to container size) between the soil and the rim of the container, and to fill this with water each time you water. Small containers, and clay pots in particular, may dry quite rapidly on hot, sunny, or windy summer days—you may actually need to water every few days.

Although virtually all native perennials can be containerized, the following lists suggest some of the most appropriate bulbous plants, specimen plants, and rock garden plants. Criteria for these choices are:

- plants that thrive with protection to their roots and require excellent drainage

- plants that may be shy of competition in the garden, or are displayed to better advantage by themselves

- plants that make bold statements in containers

- plants that may have a complete dormancy and can be moved out of sight by being in containers

Bulbs, Corms, and Tubers for Containers

Andrew's beadlily (shade)
Brodiaeas
Brook orchid (shade)

Douglas's violet
Fawn lilies (some shade)
Fritillaries

Bulbs, Corms, and Tubers for Containers

Globe tulips (light shade)
Golden stars
Jepsonia
Johnny-jump-up
Larkspurs
Lewisias
Lilies
Lobed violet (some shade)
Mariposa tulips
Milkmaids (shade)

Rein orchids
Shelton's violet (shade)
Shooting stars
Skullcaps
Star flower (shade)
Star tulips
Trilliums (shade)
Triteleias
Wild hyacinths
Zygadenes

Specimen Plants for Containers

Apricot mallow
Beargrass
Blazing star
Blue flax
Bush penstemons
California sunflower
Chain fern (shade)
Creamy eardrops
Dudleyas
Golden eardrops
Humboldt lily
Island snapdragon

Lewisias
Matilija poppy (large container needed)
Nightshades
Penstemons
Prickly poppy
Sand verbenas
Scarlet locoweed
Sea dahlia
Sky rocket
Tree coreopsis
Wandflower
Washington lily

Rock Garden Plants for Containers with Extra Fine Drainage

Alpine alumroot
Alpine buckwheats
Alpine buttercup
Alpine columbine
Alpine geum (nodding avens)
Alpine penstemons
Alpine rattlepod
Bead ferns (*Cheilanthes* spp.)
Bladderpods
Brake ferns
California lace fern
Daisies (small varieties)
Dudleyas
Goldback fern
Indian pinks
Indian's dream fern
Ivesias
Larkspurs
Lewisias
Mist maidens

Mountain mariposa
Mountain pride penstemon
Phloxes
Purdy's fritillary
Pursh's rattlepod
Pussytoes
Rockfringes
Scarlet locoweed
Serpentine fritillary
Showy penstemon
Sibbaldia
Sickle-leaf onion
Skullcaps
Sky pilot
Steer's head
Stonecrops (sedums)
Sulfur flowers
Tiny-flowered zygadene
Werner's senecio

The Meadow Garden

Relatively few gardens are designed this way, yet this is one of the best natural concepts. While lawns can be converted to a sort of meadow garden they can never wholly fulfill the requirements for successful design, since lawn grasses are sod formers whereas many meadow grasses are bunched or clumped. The problem with a solid sod is that it allows few openings for other plants, such as flowering perennials and bulbs. By having the grass cover with many openings (through the use of bunchgrasses and sedges), you can achieve the requisite pattern for a true meadow.

A visit to a Sierran meadow will reveal how closely integrated all of the parts of the system are: it is nearly impossible to extricate flowering plants from grasses and sedges because of their close proximity and intertwined roots. A more practical aim in the garden is to allow a greater spacing between grass and sedge clumps, in order to give room for perennials to expand and for ease of maintenance.

Other differences between a true meadow garden and a lawn planted to flowers are these.

- Lawns are regularly mowed; meadows are not (the latter do need periodic trimming of dead flowering stalks and old leaves).

- Lawns are heavily fertilized; meadows need little or no feeding.

- Lawns are used for recreation; meadows are for beauty only, with paths meandering through for easy access.

Of course, both lawn and meadow need regular summer watering because the plants in both grow actively then, although it is also possible to create a foothill prairie, which is summer dormant.

Other factors of importance for the meadow are its design and the source of plants. Meadow gardens can be small or expansive, but they always look best when used with a backdrop of shrubbery or woods, and a small pond can be included at one end to establish a definite focal point for the whole. Plantings of perennials should be made so that they have a random look, but the best plantings should include large masses of few species, which gracefully interweave with one another. Plants of stature comparable to the grasses and sedges are best, but taller flowers are effective toward the back or sides of the meadow, to grow next to shrubbery or trees beyond.

The source of plants is important and will determine in large part the kind of care and maintenance the meadow garden requires. For example, you can design a foothill meadow garden in which most of the plants are summer dormant and require little summer water. Such a garden would include foothill bunchgrasses which are part of the coastal prairie and valley grassland communities; the flowers used would be bulbs which flower in spring and are summer dormant.

The true mountain meadow is one which is summer active and, of course, reflects the plants' source as the mountains. The particular elevation they are from should be determined by the elevation of the garden. For lowland gardens, middle-elevation mountain plants work best, since they are most likely to adapt to the lack of a prolonged winter cold period. For mountain gardens, plants from higher elevations can be included.

For suggestions on appropriate grasses to use for the matrix of your meadow garden, turn to the section on grasses and grasslike plants (beginning page 42). Genera and species are listed there with their habitats—some do best at the end of a woodland, others in lowland, open meadows which are summer dormant, still others in mountain meadows which are winter dormant. Summer-dormant plants which nonetheless need water have this noted.

Foothill Flowers (for use with foothill grasses—summer dormant)

Adobe lily
Asters
Beargrass
Bicolor lotus (water)
Blue-eyed grasses
Brodiaeas
California buttercup
California poppy
Cardinal monkeyflower (water)
Checkerbloom
Coast lily (water)
Coast paintbrushes
Common daisy
Douglas's violet
False lupine
Fireweed (water)
Golden aster
Golden monkeyflower (water)
Golden stars
Goldenrods
Gold-eyed grasses (some water)
Irises (most species)
Ithuriel's spear
Johnny-jump-up
Larkspurs (most species)
Lowland gentians (water)
Lupines (certain varieties)
Mariposa tulips
Milk lily
Mouse-eared chickweed
Mule's ears (most varieties)
Pink monkeyflower (mountain monkeyflower; water)
Rayless aster
Seaside daisy
Shooting stars
Showy milkweed
Sneezeweeds (water)
Star tulips
Sticky potentilla
Suncups (golden eggs)
Wallflowers
Western buttercup
White fritillary
Wild onions
Woodmints
Wormskjold's clover (water)
Yarrow
Yerba mansa (water)
Zygadenes

Mountain Flowers (for use with a summer-wet meadow)

Alpine goldenrod
Alpine shooting stars
Arnicas
Asters
Balsamroots
Beargrass
California coneflower
Canada goldenrod
Common butterwort
Common corn lily
Elephant snouts
Fairy lily
Fireweed
Giant larkspur
Glacier lilies
Golden monkeyflower
Grass-of-Parnassus
Green gentian

Mountain Flowers (for use with a summer-wet meadow)

Hooker's evening primrose
Horsemint
Jacob's ladders
Jeffrey's shooting stars
Large-leafed geum
Leopard lily
Long-rayed brodiaea
Meadow daisies
Meadow knotweed (meadow polygonum)
Meadow lotus
Meadow lupines
Meadow paintbrushes
Milk lily
Monkshood
Mountain blue-eyed grass
Mountain buttercups
Mountain clover
Mountain gentian
Mountain gold-eyed grass
Mountain hollyhocks

Mountain iris
Mountain meadowrue
Mountain mule's ears
Pearly everlasting
Pink monkeyflower
   (mountain monkeyflower)
Potentillas (most varieties)
Pussytoes
Ranger's buttons
Rayless aster
Red columbine
St. Johnswort
Showy milkweed
Smooth yellow violet
Sneezeweeds
Swamp onion
Tower larkspur
White mountain violet
White rein orchid
Whorled penstemons
Yarrow

The Rock Garden

Rock gardens are a real challenge for successful design and take the most careful planning. Rock gardens provide an opportunity to display various small plants individually and at the same time achieve excellent drainage. They should always be constructed on a slope or bank if possible; otherwise it is necessary to create a raised bed for the purpose. Before ever attempting to obtain and plant such a garden, the site should be ready to go.

There are many books on the subject of how to build a successful rock garden; the reader is referred to these for explicit detail. Here are some useful hints:

Choose rocks which blend well with one another—the idea is not to design a garden of rocks but to use rocks to assure drainage and complement the plants. It is best to use only one or two kinds of rocks rather than a hodgepodge.

In constructing a wall of rock, be sure to leave some chinks or openings for planting. Plants on rock walls help to soften them, and the walls provide plants with superb drainage.

When placing rocks along the surface of soil, be sure to bury enough of each rock to make it look realistic. Rocks seldom sit around loose on the ground in nature.

If you choose rocks with rounded contours stick with that pattern. It is jarring to see sharply angular and rounded rocks together.

If there is a hardpan at the base of your raised rock garden, you may need to install a drain through it, or fill in the bottom of the rock garden with gravel for extra drainage.

For extra protection with plants that need superb drainage, you may dress the soil surface with small pebbles around the plants' crowns—this helps to prevent rot.

Although the typical rock garden often includes high-mountain or alpine plants, there is no reason a rock garden cannot consist entirely of lowland plants from coastal bluffs and cliff faces. This is the kind of rock garden recommended for the average lowland gardener. The following lists also give typical high-mountain plants for a mountain rock garden.

Foothill Rock Garden Plants

Bead fern (*Cheilanthes* spp.)
Blue bedder penstemon
Blue-eyed grass
Bluff goldenrod
Bluff goldfields
Bluff lupine
California phacelia
California saxifrage
Cliffbrakes
Coast buckwheat
Coast rockcress
Coastal wallflowers
Common stonecrop (sedum)
Coyote mints
Douglas's violet
Dudleya
Dune aster
Dune knotweed
Eriophyllums
Fawn lilies
Four o'clocks
Golden aster
Golden vancouveria

Goldwire
Gumweeds
Indian pinks
Indian's dream fern
Johnny-jump-up
Leather fern (shade)
Little California sunflower
Little-leaf buckwheat
Low-growing brodiaeas
Low-growing onions
Lowland lewisias
Merten's saxifrage
Mouse-eared chickweed
Pearly everlasting
Pinnacles buckwheat
Sapphire flower
Sea thrift
Seaside daisy
Siskiyou daisy
Siskiyou rockfringe
Skullcaps
Sonoma sage
Star tulips
Sulfur flowers

Mountain Rock Garden Plants

Alpine alumroot
Alpine aster
Alpine buttercup
Alpine columbine
Alpine daisy
Alpine geum (nodding avens)
Alpine goldenrod
Alpine Jacob's ladder
Alpine lady fern (shade)
Alpine larkspur
Alpine locoweed
Bead ferns (*Cheilanthes* spp.)

Bladderpods
Blue flax
Brewer's lupine
Flat-stemmed onion
Golden brodiaea
Holly fern
Indian's dream fern
Ivesias
Lewisias
Lyall's lupine
Mountain buckwheats
Mountain cliffbrakes

Mountain Rock Garden Plants

Mountain coyote mint	Sierra lotus
Mountain fritillary	Sierra mariposa
Mountain hummingbird fuchsia	Sierra onion
Mountain paintbrushes	Sky pilot
Mountain penstemons	Sky rocket
Mountain phacelias	Steer's head
Mountain wallflower	Stonecrops (sedums)
Perennial linanthus	Werner's senecio
Phloxes	Western anemone
Pine violet (shade)	Western pink
Pussytoes	Western thoroughwort
Rockfringe	Wooly rattlepod
Shasta fern	Wooly sunflower
Sickle-leaf onion	Wooly violet
	Yarrow (mountain forms)

All about Grasses and Their Kin

Grasses can play a vital role in the native garden. We are so used to thinking of grasses in restricted terms—for a lawn, or the larger kinds (bamboo and pampas grass) for background and foundation purposes—that we forget that smaller grasses and their relatives also have ornamental uses. First, let's turn to the natural environment and see what native grasses are all about.

The foothills and lower valleys, including much of the Central Valley, were once home to bunchgrass lands, where clumped perennial grasses dominated. Between these grasses there were colorful spring annuals and bulbs by the thousands. Along coastal bluffs and open hills, a comparable equivalent existed: the coastal prairie. We know that many such areas were maintained as grasslands, or even enlarged, by fire management used by the Indians (to increase certain food plants and the availability of grazing animals). All has been drastically changed in the last two hundred years: today grasslands are mainly dominated by European annual weedy grasses—various fescues, bromes, foxtails, ryegrasses, wild oats. There are still a number of areas which have escaped this fate: to see pristine grasslands, visit the serpentine areas north of San Francisco Bay—the alien grasses cannot compete with the natives on this special soil. The majority of native grasses form perennial bunches, whereas the alien kinds are mostly annuals with single to few stems from a limited root system.

The other major grass areas are the meadows of the middle to high mountains, particularly in the Sierra Nevada. The grasses in these meadows vary with altitude and moisture so that there is great variety. Many fewer alien grasses have gained a foothold here. Most alien grasses are adapted to lowland conditions with mild climate; montane conditions, where winters are freezing cold, discourage many of the intruders. In general, meadows consist of bunch-forming as well as some sod-forming grasses, with a prominent component of sedges and rushes in the permanently wet spots by bogs, ponds, permanent streams, and seeps.

Thus, when we look at grasses for the native garden we have two basic sources: undisturbed foothill grasslands and open woodlands, and mountain meadows. In discussing the meadow garden, it was noted that both sources give possible candidates for its framework—foothill grasses where drought-tolerant perennials are used, and mountain grasses where summer-moisture-requiring perennials are chosen. But the meadow garden is by no means the only place for these plants. Low, sod-forming kinds could be used between stepping stones as a basic ground cover (the majority, however, require summer water). Bunch-grasses, sedges, and rushes are also useful as accents of different texture and color between flowering perennials, and as a way of softening the edge of a pond or stream. Leaf colors range from yellow-green through emerald and dark green, blue-green, and even silvery. These colors fade in summer if the plants receive no water—and in that case they should be trimmed back severely. But if you judiciously remove old leaves and give summer water, many of these plants retain an attractive appearance most of the year. The flowering stalks (culms) usually rise a few inches to a few feet above the leaf tufts, and may or may not add a graceful note in season—you may prefer to remove them, but in any case, they need to be cut off as the flower heads turn brown and go to seed.

Propagation of grasslike plants could not be easier: slicing through the clump with a sharp knife divides it into new rooted sections, or there may be "baby" clumps beside the parent. Be sure to dig deeply to get a full root ball—these grasses have deeply penetrating, fibrous roots, and may die if the roots are unduly damaged, or too much root mass has been damaged. Raising large numbers of grasses from seed is easy, too: simply sow the seeds in the usual potting soil, and separate while still quite young—otherwise the roots of adjacent seedlings become inextricably entangled. Care is needed during this process to keep the soil free from weeds, especially weed grasses which are difficult to distinguish at first from the native kinds. Usually, careful study of weedy grasses in the garden beforehand will acquaint you with what to look for. *Poa annua* is one of the most likely villains, especially in winter and spring.

Here is a summary of grass groups and the species with possible garden merit:

True Grasses

These usually have rounded, hollow stems with two rows of leaves; the leaves consist of a blade, a sheath which partly surrounds the stem below the blade, and a ligule or tiny flap of whitish tissue just above the junction of blade and sheath. True grasses bear flowers in clusters called spikelets; each spikelet consists of a pair of bracts (the glumes) above which are one to several tiny flowers (florets). Each floret consists of two more bracts (the lemma and palea), which surround the three stamens and single pistil with an ovary topped by two feathery stigmas. Normally, the spikelet and other spikelets will be in their male or female stage at different times—in the male stage, the stamens dangle beyond the bracts; in the female stage, the feathery stigmas protrude. The flower clusters or spikelets are themselves arranged in larger groupings—racemes, panicles, or spikes. The shape of these clusters and the details of their arrangement may be helpful in learning to recognize many species. Unfortunately, no simple key exists to make identification easy for the amateur, and accurate recognition depends on learning a complex vocabulary, using a dissecting microscope, and having plenty of time. Some grasses are so distinctive that their identity is without question as you peruse the illustrated manuals on grasses. But most often, learning the identity of grasses is the most difficult obstacle to using them in the garden. Here are some of the best bets for ornamental native grasses.

Agrostis scabra. **Ticklegrass.** Moderate bunchgrass with very fine leaves and rough flowering culms to about two feet. Spikelets small in open panicles. Good for mountain meadows. Some summer water.

Aira caryophyllea. **Hairgrass.** This introduced annual is so charming, even though it isn't native, that I've included it here. It self-sows readily. Small leafy culms of dull green, fuzzy leaves with spikelets borne in airy, wiry-stemmed panicles. Demure in groups in a rock garden. Grows and flowers in spring.

Briza maxima **and** *minor.* **Rattlesnake or Quaking Grass.** Other pretty, annual European grasses. Small leafy culms with bright green blades, and nodding panicles of broad spikelets resembling rattlesnake tails. Self-sows. Late spring. The first species has spikelets an inch long; the latter spikelets one-fourth the size. Both make fine dried arrangements if cut *before* the spikelets turn brown and shatter.

Bromus carinatus. **Keeled Brome.** A substantial short-lived perennial bunchgrass with smooth to hairy leaves and flowering culms to three and a half or four feet. Flattened, long-awned spikelets are borne in open panicles and often nod. One of the few native bromes; this one can be used in a large-scale meadow.

Calamagrostis nutkaensis. **Nutka Reed Grass.** A large bunchgrass with moderately wide blades of bright green, and flowering culms to four feet or more. Typical of windswept coastal bluffs and edges of coniferous forests. Good for background or accent in a woodland garden or partially shaded meadow. Summer moisture.

Calamagrostis purpurascens **var.** *ophitidis.* **Serpentine Reed Grass.** A large bunchgrass with narrow blades a dull, sometimes gray-green; flowering culms to three feet. Grows on hot serpentine slopes where it forms graceful tufts over rocks. Good in the mixed border or lowland meadow.

Danthonia californica. **California Oatgrass.** Not to be confused with the invasive, alien wild oats. Low perennial bunchgrass with fuzzy, dull green leaves and half-decumbent flowering culms with nodding spikelets. In flower, rather inconspicuous, but a good basic grass for a lowland meadow or rock garden.

Deschampsia caespiotsa **(and** *holciformis***). Hairgrasses.** Robust bunchgrasses with green, firm leaves and flowering culms to three and a half or four feet.

Spikelets in loose open to rather compressed panicles, the flowers with hair-like awns, hence the common name. Pretty and reliable grasses for a mountain meadow or pond. Summer water.

Distichlis spicata. **Salt Grass.** Like its relative, Bermuda grass, this kind has a limited use since it is rather invasive by its creeping stolons. It forms large patches of leafy stems, the leaves two-ranked, dark green, and stiff. In flower, the culms rise a few inches with an umbrella-like arrangement of several one-sided spikes of small spikelets. Saltgrass is recommended near the coast for helping hold sand or in brackish to salty places where few other ground covers can grow.

Elymus cinereus. **Desert Ryegrass.** Much like common ryegrass. The leaves are mostly green, and the culms up to five feet or more. Good for dry gardens for binding sandy, loose soils.

Elymus condensatus. **Giant Ryegrass.** Rhizomatous with closely spaced, very tall leafy culms to five or six or more feet. Stout and invasive. Good on a large scale for stabilizing soils along the edge of woodland and coastal gardens.

Elymus glaucus. **Common Ryegrass.** Much like coastal ryegrass, but leaves vary from green to blue-green, and the leafy culms are often spaced closer together. May be quite invasive, but excellent for binding soil on steep woodland slopes.

Elymus mollis. **Coastal Ryegrass.** A rhizomatous species which does an excellent job of binding loose sand and tolerates some salt and wind. The wandering rhizomes produce upright leafy culms at some distance from one another so that they don't exclude other vegetation between them as does the introduced European dunegrass (*Ammophila*). Leafy culms grow to three feet with graceful blue-green leaves and tight flattened spikes of spikelets. Excellent in coastal gardens and nice contrast with green leaves.

Festuca californica. **California Fescue.** A large bunchgrass with gracefully drooping, narrow, dull green leaves. Flower culms may stand up to three or four feet. Fine for dappled shade, especially on terraced or moderately steep slopes.

Festuca idahoensis. **Idaho Fescue.** A modest-sized bunchgrass with very narrow leaves, often of a striking blue- to gray-green color. Flowering culms to 12 or 18 inches, and rather insignificant. Good for texture/color contrasts in dry borders.

Festuca occidentalis. **Western Fescue.** A medium-sized bunchgrass with narrow green leaves and flowering culms to three feet tall; spikelets on wiry side branches. Good for dappled shade, especially in mountain gardens.

Festuca rubra. **Red Fescue.** A modest-sized bunchgrass (may travel by rhizomes) with narrow leaves. Flowering culms to two and a half feet, sometimes tinged purple to reddish, in paniclese. Nice for a mountain meadow or watered rock garden.

Glyceria spp. **Manna Grass.** Large, somewhat tufted grasses, but also with creeping rhizomes. Bright green leaves and flowering culms to three and a half or more feet. Spikelets borne in graceful, drooping panicles and red to purplish in color. A very attractive grass for mountain meadows or behind ponds. Summer water.

Hierchloe occidentalis. **Vanilla Grass**. An unusual grass with bright green, rather broad, sweet-scented leaves. Grows as small clumps with some rather close spreading by rhizome; flowering culms to eighteen inches with tight panicles of spikelets. Excellent for the woodland garden, and compatible with many redwood forest plants. Summer moisture.

Hystrix californica. **Bottlebrush Grass**. This is a rare grass related to the foxtail and squirreltail grasses. It is a short-lived perennial forming small clumps with the culms bearing both fuzzy leaves and above, often several feet high, the narrow spikes of two ranked spikelets with long awns, the whole resembling a bottlebrush. An interesting, bold grass for the woodland garden.

Koeleria cristata. **June Grass**. A modest bunchgrass with gray-green to green and fuzzy leaves and flowering culms to two feet. Spikelets densely arrayed in a spike-like cluster, purplish or silvery in the best forms. This widespread species grows from coastal woodlands and prairies to high mountains. It is well adapted to the meadow garden or in rock gardens and is relatively drought tolerant.

Melica imperfecta **and** *californica.* **Coast Range and California Melics**. Both are dense to loose bunchgrasses with bright green leaves and flowering culms to one and a half to two feet tall. Spikelets are mosty borne in narrow (sometimes open) panicles and are purplish in the former and whitish in the latter. Both grasses can be included in the dry margins of woodlands or lightly shaded meadows, although the former tolerates more sun and drought.

Melica stricta. **Flag Melic**. This is a small, distinctive subalpine bunchgrass with narrow, fuzzy gray leaves and flowering culms to perhaps one foot. The charm of this grass is the one-sided, flaglike attachment of the spikelets to the flowering culm. Nice for the alpine rock garden.

Muhlenbergia rigens. **Meadow Muhly**. A large, robust bunchgrass with rather stiff, narrow light green blades and tall stiff flowering culms to four feet. Spikelets borne in a narrow spike. This is a good grass for large scale, in wet meadows, or in a watered mixed border.

Oryzopsis hymenoides. **Indian Ricegrass**. A modest bunchgrass with narrow, bright green curled leaves and flowering culms to one or two feet. Spikelets in open panicles with curved wiry branches, the individual grains relatively large and edible. Distributed through the deserts and dry mountains; excellent for hot, interior gardens and good with plantings of desert species.

Panicum pacificum. **Panic Grass**. This is an utterly distinctive grass with prostrate to decumbent, widely spreading leafy stems (rather than underground rhizomes). The leaves are a broad lance shape, bright green and softly hairy to the touch. The tiny spikelets are borne in upright, much-branched airy panicles on threadlike stems. Good for a ground cover with no foot traffic, or wandering about a lowland rock garden.

Phleum alpinum. **Alpine Timothy.** Here is another distinctive subalpine or alpine grass; this one has bright green bunched leaves, and flowering culms to a foot tall with tight clusters of numerous spikelets into a rounded to ovoid spike—the whole a pleasing dark purple color. For rock gardens.

Poa nevadensis. **Mountain Blue Grass.** A medium-sized bunchgrass with stiff, roughened leaves and flowering culms to about two and a half feet; spikelets greenish. At middle elevations and above in meadows; good for the meadow garden. Needs some summer water, but does not go dormant so readily as the former.

Poa scabrella. **Pine Blue Grass.** A medium-sized bunchgrass with soft pale green leaves and flowering culms to three feet tall; spikelets may be purplish on good forms. Wide ranging, with tendencies to go dormant at low elevations and for the leaves to wither at flowering time. Given supplemental water, this should be avoided. Versatile.

Poa unilateralis. **Coast Blue Grass.** A small bunchgrass with narrow dull green leaves and flowering culms to about one foot high. It is highly tolerant of winds and salt spray; use it in a lowland meadow or for a coastal rock garden.

Polypogon monspeliensis. **Rabbitsfoot Grass.** One more pretty annual European grass. Modest leafy culms are terminated by a dense rabbitsfoot-like spike of spikelets—the whole soft and furry. Summer. Self-sows. Good for dried arrangements.

Sitanion jubatum **and** *hystrix.* **Squirreltail.** These are low, short-lived bunch-grasses, sometimes best treated as annuals. Leaves are gray-green, soft; flowering culms grow to two feet with dense, brush-like spikes of spikelets; the brush is narrow and reddish in flower, but then opens into a bushy "squirreltail" in fruit, the many parts separating and blown about by wind because of their long awns. Unlike the related foxtail, these awns are not dangerous to animals or a nuisance to socks. Squirreltail is a good, general grass for foothill meadows, and readily self-sows.

Sporobolus airoides. **Alkali Sacaton.** A large bunchgrass with flat to rolled blades and flowering culms to three and a half feet. The tiny reddish spikelets are numerous in graceful open panicles and are quite attractive. This is an excellent grass for dry meadow gardens, especially where the soil is alkaline.

Stipa **spp. Needle Grass or Needle-and-Thread.** Medium-sized, modest bunch-grasses, and some species have an extensive range in the former valley grasslands. Leaves dull to gray-green with flowering culms to two or three feet depending upon species. Spikelets are borne in open, airy panicles with narrow outline and distinctive bent or twisted awns extending far beyond the grain (these later help plant the grain by twisting and turning with changes in moisture). Good basic grasses for the dry meadow; choose species according to locality.

The Sedges

The sedge family is large and it takes an expert to identify the individual species in the genus *Carex*. (There are 140 species in California alone.) But the family is easy to recognize, and the kinds used in the garden might be best appreciated by seeing them in their native habitats first. Generally, sedges form clumps which may remain as mounds, or may travel by underground rhizomes (avoid these unless you have plenty of space). The leaves are arranged in three rows, and are tough, with an upper channel running down the middle and a keel running down the middle bottomside. The stems are normally three-sided (hence the jingle "sedges have edges") and bear spikes of flowers (sometimes very small). In some sedges, the flowers are unisexual, the male spikes borne above the female. The flowers are very simple, usually with a brown, purple, or green bract at the base and three stamens and a pistil (sometimes the pistil is inside a green sac called the perigynium). Sedges are most often found along swamps, bogs, and marshes or stream sides, or in the wettest parts of meadows, but there are exceptions. A few live in forests on rocky banks or in full sun amongst rocks. Size ranges from a few inches high in the alpine (where some form the equivalent of an alpine lawn) to several feet tall for the tules. The following are some of the genera:

Carex. **True Sedges.** This is the genus most often thought of when the word sedge is used—there are more than 140 species in California, and most are difficult to key even with the aid of a microscope. The gardener should choose the carexes according to their habitat and size and not worry about identifying species. This is the only genus with unisexual flowers, and usually both are found on the same plant, male above female. The leaves are always three-ranked and the flowering stalks three-angled (triangular in cross-section). Some carexes are good for banks in the woodland garden, others are ideal for rock gardens, still others are excellent in boggy spots. Beware the species with underground rhizomes; these are quite invasive. Leaf color ranges from dark to bright green, and occasionally a lovely glaucous or silvery green. Spikes may be decorative in flower; yellow to cream color for the male, and white to pinkish for the female, and in some, the seed stage has pretty brown or purple bracts, but sooner or later the stalks lean over and look ragged, so must be removed.

Cyperus. **Grassnut.** Although some are native, the commonly met-with ones are invasive weeds. Cyperuses resemble carexes in the basal leaves and triangular flowering culms, but the spikes are arranged in umbels or heads and the flowers are bisexual. There is usually a row of leafy bracts surrounding the flower umbrellas. Two species likely to be found in the garden are *C. esculentus* (the common grassnut), which is extremely invasive (especially on wet soils), and *C. alternifolius* (umbrella sedge), which is often grown for the umbrella-like flower clusters but reseeds itself abundantly in wet places. Neither is native.

Eleocharis. **Spike "Rushes."** Contrary to the common name, these are really sedges. Most are low growing (sometimes only inches high), tufted, grass-like plants with very narrow green leaves and short flowering culms (often only inches high) with tiny green to brown spikes of bisexual flowers. It is the tiny scale—like grasses designed for a bonsai landscape—that lends them great charm. Although short lived, they reseed easily.

Eriophorum. **Cotton-Grass.** Our single species, *E. gracile,* is a most unusual sedge and has a circumboreal distribution. You find it in acid bogs of mountain meadows, where whole fields are white with it in midsummer. Unlike most sedges, the three- to four-foot flowering culms bear dense heads of bisexual flowers, each flower with several long, cottony white strands that give the appearance of balls of cotton from a distance. Excellent for an unusual accent around a pond or in a wet mountain meadow.

Scirpus. **Tule.** Actually this is a varied genus with moderate sized to giant grass-like species. The smaller kinds look more like sedges with leafy, often three-sided stems and open clusters of tiny, bisexual flowers. Some might grow by a pond or such, but they tend to spread by rhizomes and/or seeds, and so are of questionable garden value. The true tules are giant plants with green stems to six or eight or more feet which dominate wide tracts of freshwater marsh. The leaves are reduced to scales, and the bisexual flowers are borne in brown spikes at the tops of the stalks. Most tules are simply too large for the scale of the everyday garden.

The Rushes

The rushes are straightforward as a family, and are limited to a mere 50 or so Californian species. Although the familiar jingle states that "rushes are round," there are many exceptions. Rushes are best identified by their flowers, which are borne in umbels, heads, or small clusters. The typical rush flower has a true perianth—petals and sepals—albeit reduced to scale size and not brightly colored—mostly green, white, or brown. The six perianth parts are arranged in two circles, inside of which are three or six stamens and a pistil with two or three stigmas. Close up, many rush flowers are works of art—bronzy perianth like a six-pointed star, yellow stamens, and stigmas of strawberry pink. Leaves vary greatly—the typical "round" rushes have long, narrow, pointed leaves which are dark green and round in cross-section. In some, the leaves are clumped into large bunches and are easily visible and identifiable as rushes from far away because of the dark green color and stiff, upright bunching. In others, however, the leaves are attached to wandering rhizomes so that they are strung out over several feet; in still others the leaves are flattened and lance shaped or even sickle shaped, or flattened and folded together in overlapping groups just like iris leaves.

It is impossible to attempt to list rushes for garden purposes—again, experience in the field is the best guide. Large, stiff-clumped kinds make bold statements around ponds; tiny clumped rushes fit into an alpine garden. A few annual rushes are common weeds in foothill gardens which are moist in spring, and are not attractive for the garden. The iris-leaved rushes make an interesting statement in boggy spots.

All of the rushes described above belong to the single genus *Juncus*. But a second, smaller genus *Luzula* (woodrushes) also occurs. The most common species, *L. subsessilis*, is frequent in woods and is told by its rosettes of light green, grass-like leaves edged by curious curly white hairs. Flowers on this are rather inconspicuous, but it is a pleasant plant for the natural woodland garden. A second species, *L. subspicatus*, comes from the high mountains and is charming in a rock garden. Its leaf rosettes are similar but without the hairs, and the airy panicles of orange-brown flowers create the effect of bronze smoke from a distance.

The Ball Rushes

A fourth group, scarcely known, is the distinctive family of ball rushes, all in the genus *Sparganium*. The foliage is grass-like and spongy inside—ball rushes live in soggy soils in wet meadows and marshes—but the distinctive ball-like configurations of the flowers make them readily identifiable. All flowers are unisexual, and the male yellow balls are at the top of a spike-like stem above the whitish female "balls." These plants, especially the high-elevation species, make pleasing additions to ponds or stream sides.

part two

Encyclopedia of
Families, Genera, and Species

The following entries represent the bulk of information in this book; genera are arranged alphabetically within each family according to the *scientific* genus name. Family names, in turn, also have been listed alphabetically, but this time according to their *common* name. A typical example is the birthwort family with its two genera: *Aristolochia* and *Asarum*.

Each genus entry is given accompanied by common names and the common name of its family; this is followed by a highlighted abbreviated section to give the reader basic information at a glance. Entries in this section run like this: height of the plant (abbreviated HT), flower color (abbreviated FLW CL), flowering time (abbreviated FLW TM), means of propagation (abbreviated PRPG), exposure to sun or shade (abbreviated EXP), and watering regime (abbreviated WT). Where the genus is large and varied, specific recommendations for watering regime or other attributes may not be given. Lack of entries on flowers denotes a nonflowering plant, such as the ferns.

Below the highlighted section the genus is discussed in more detail with a summary of the visual attributes, habits and habitats, distribution, and finally, use in the garden and any pertinent cultural information. If the genus has several distinctive and worthwhile species, these are listed last, with particulars on each. Some notable similar species pairs or complexes are instead discussed together.

Here is a list of family and genus names for easy reference: the column entitled "Names used in book" denotes common names for family and scientific names for genera; the column entitled "Equivalent names" gives the equivalent scientific name for family and the equivalent common names for genera.

Agave Family

(Agavaceae)

A small family of desert plants in California, closely related to the lily family. All have exceptionally large rosettes of fleshy and toughly fibrous leaves; most are suitable for desert gardens. Most of the yuccas and the genus *Nolina* are excluded here because they are woody.

Agave. Agave, Century Plant, Maguey. Agave family.

HT: in flower 5 to 15 feet, but leaf rosettes much lower   FLW CL: cream to yellow   FLW TM: April to June   PRPG: "pups" from edge of mother rosette or seeds (many years to large size)   EXP: full sun   WT: occasional summer water in sandy soils

Here are some of the boldest leaf succulents of any desert. Agaves are typical of rocky warm deserts from our Southwest through Mexico; California only has a few species. Deep, fibrous roots anchor the very broad leaf rosettes, each leaf sharply pointed with a spiny tip and gradually broadening to a wide base. Leaves are lined with recurved spines, tough and fibrous, gray to pale green, and with the impression of other leaves left from when the leaves were together in bud. Agaves are often referred to as century plants because it takes so long for the leaf rosette to grow large enough and store sufficient food to make the flowering stalk, but actually the process is more like 10 to 20 years than a century! Just before it flowers, a slender, plump asparagus-like bud appears in the middle of the leaf rosette. Over several months this elongates, growing ever higher into the air until at last a massive panicle of flowers develops. Flowers are long and tubular, bright yellow, laden with nectar (hummingbirds love these), and produced by the hundreds. In fact, so much energy is expended in producing the flowers that the parent rosette dies by the time seeds have ripened. Before that happens, however, the parent has made a circle of smaller rosettes around its periphery; these are referred to as pups.

In the garden, agaves are surprisingly tolerant of cool, coastal conditions as long as they have a well-drained soil and full light, but they really shine in the hot interior or desert gardens. Their bold design demands space, and they are best used as specimens or far in back of a sun-drenched rock garden, or widely spaced with other desert plants such as cacti and mesquite. The only truly common species in California is *A. deserti*, which is typical of the mountains bordering the Colorado desert, such as in Anza Borrego State Park.

Yucca whipplei. Our Lord's Candle, Yucca. Agave family.

HT: in flower to 6 or more feet   FLW CL: creamy white   FLW TM: varies   PRPG: pups or seeds (several years from seed)   EXP: full sun   WT: little summer water

The yuccas are a typical desert group, with much the same range as for the agaves. Most form woody-looking trunks which carry the leaves ever higher

SPANISH DAGGER—*Yucca baccata.*

with age, and so are not included here. But one species, *Y. whipplei*, stands out—its leaf rosettes are right at ground level, and it lives on the hottest chaparral-covered slopes of central and southern California. There, its rosettes are protected by their dagger-sharp tips and tough fibers. The leaves themselves are narrowly lance shaped, and a pretty gray-green to silver color. By themselves these leaf rosettes are very decorative. But after several years, enough food is laid down to produce stalks which soar several feet into the air with panicles of hundreds of large, pendant, bell-shaped, creamy white flowers, a true spectacle. A hillside with many flowering yuccas looks from afar like so many giant candles.

Our lord's candle does well in most well-drained soils from near the coast to hot inland and desert gardens. Its boldness demands forethought for placement: in large tubs, the back of a large-scale rock garden, or in a desert garden with agaves and cacti.

Amaryllis Family
(*Amaryllidaceae*)

All are bulb- or corm-bearing plants and most are summer dormant. Most all adapt to garden culture, although some of the rarer members of the brodiaeas and their relatives have been omitted. The genus *Muilla* has been left out because of its unshowy flowers, and the genus *Androstephium* because it is so uncommon.

Allium. Wild Onion. Amaryllis family.

HT: 2 inches to 3 1/2 feet   FLW CL: white, pink, rose, purple   FLW TM: varies   PRPG: offsets or seeds (a few years to flower)   EXP: mostly full sun   WT: varies

The onions are widely distributed across the northern hemisphere; our usual ones come from the Mediterranean basin and Europe, including the sometimes naturalized "wild" onion of shady coastal gardens. The genus is not often grown for ornament, although even our edible vegetables—leeks, chives, onions, shallots, and garlic—have attractive umbrellas of flowers. In California alone, there are well over three dozen species, most poorly known even amongst native bulb enthusiasts. Most are diminutive plants with charming small flowers, but make up in form what they lack in size. A few are robust enough to include with other meadow plants. Habitats are most always open—rocky scree, coastal prairie, foothill grasslands, and meadows—but range in elevation from sea level to timberline. All come from edible onion- to garlic-flavored bulbs which send up one to several leaves as spring nears—leaves may be tubular, flattened, grass-like, or even sickle shaped. Flowers are borne in rounded umbrellas protected in bud by papery bracts—the developmental process of the flowers opening makes onions worthy of garden space. The six tepals are arranged in two rows forming various designs from open stars to vase shapes with colors ranging through the purples and pinks, or on occasion, pure white. Most are easy to grow and once established multiply readily. The foothill kinds need summer drought, but the mountain kinds go dormant only at the end of summer or beginning of fall.

The majority of alliums are best used in rock gardens, planted in groups where they can accompany some of the short brodiaeas and calochortuses. Only a sampling of species is given here:

A. amplectens. Lava onion. Foothills around the Sacramento Valley, usually confined to rock outcroppings. Leaves dry by flowering; stalks a few inches high carry ball-shaped umbels of open white flowers. Easy culture.

A. burlewii. From granite outcroppings in the southern Sierra and higher mountains of southern California. Single flat leaf with a scape only inches high with pink-purple flowers. Mountain rock gardens.

A. campanulatum. Sierra onion. Common on gravel and scree in the mid to high mountains. Leaves dry by flowering; stalks are a few inches tall with open umbels of starry pink and purple flowers. Rock gardens.

A. crispum. Wavy onion. Inner Coast Range foothills in grasslands. Leaves dry by flowering; stalks to about a foot with dark purple flowers, the inner tepals prettily crisped or wavy.

A. dichlamydeum. Bluff onion; coast onion. On wind-swept coastal bluffs of central California. A few flat leaves which dry; scapes to six inches high with cheerful clusters of narrow dark purple flowers. Ideal for coastal rock gardens with *Calochortus tolmiei* and *Brodiaea terrestris.*

A. falcifolium. Sickle-leaf onion. Open rocky slopes and scree in north Coast Ranges. Very low with small umbels of pink to nearly white flowers. Choice and easy for rock gardens.

A. fimbriatum. Widely varied with races from rocky foothills of the Coast Ranges, middle elevations in the Sierra, and on deserts. Single tubular leaf which is longer than the inches-high scape. Pale to deep pink-purple flowers.

A. haematochiton. A rather rhizomatous species with flowering stalks to a foot high; flowers white to rose; leaves flat. Southern coastal mountains.

A. hyalinum. Grasslands moist in spring in the central and southern Sierra foothills. Two folded leaves and flower stalks to around a foot with open white flowers. Lowland meadows.

A. lacunosum. Serpentine onion. Mostly on serpentine rocks from the Bay Area to the south Coast Ranges. One or two tubular leaves dry by flowering; inches-high scapes with many open starry white or light pink flowers. Coastal rock gardens.

A. peninsulare/serratum. A pair of species from interior foothills around the Central Valley. A few leaves, which dry by flowering; stalks to about a foot with pink to rose-purple, narrow flowers.

A. platycaule. Flat-stem onion. Similar habitats to *A. campanulatum,* but leaves sickle shaped and stem conspicuously flattened. Tight clusters of narrow purple flowers. Rock gardens.

A. unifolium. Single-leaf onion. Grasslands moist in spring, or forest edges. Actually two or more flat leaves with flowering stalks to over a foot with open, starry flowers of pink-purple to white. Spreads quickly in the garden.

A. validum. Swamp onion. This is the onion which gives the name to Onion Valley and other place names in the Sierra. The vigorous rhizomes form large patches with flat, upright leaves, and flowering stalks to three or more feet with tight clusters of pink-purple flowers. Excellent for moist meadows.

Bloomeria crocea. Golden Stars. Amaryllis family.

HT: 8 to 18 inches   FLW CLR: yellow   FLW TM: May to July   PRPG: offsets or seed (3 to 4 years to flower)   EXP: full sun   WT: summer dry

The bloomerias are a small group with only one readily available species, which lives in dry foothills of southern California in grasslands, open woodlands, or the edge of chaparral. It must have summer dormancy and tolerates soils ranging from adobe to light loam.

Golden stars grows to a foot or more with open umbels of many golden yellow flowers from May on. The overall appearance is similar to some triteleias, alongside which they may be planted in full sun. Like other family members, they are most effective when massed, and the flower color blends nicely with other yellows, or contrasts vividly with the blues and purples of brodiaeas, dichelostemmas, or triteleias.

Brodiaea. Harvest Brodiaea, Harvest Lily. Amaryllis family.

HT: 2 to 18 inches   FLW CLR: blues and purples   FLW TM: April to July   PRPG: from offsets or seeds (3 to 4 years to flower)   EXP: full sun   WT: summer dry

Brodiaeas grow from true corms, making low mounds of narrow leaves in late winter to early spring. Leaves brown when flower buds have swollen. Most have umbels of glossy blue or purple flowers which last well. Plants die back by midsummer. All brodiaeas are dwellers of open grassland situations, the majority in the foothills, but a few wandering up into mountain meadows. Several species are restricted to unusual soils, often of the heavy adobe variety. In the garden, brodiaeas need full sun, and a definite summer rest.

The true brodiaeas fall into two horticultural groups: those with low flower scapes—fine for rock gardens or the fronts of borders—and those with tall stalks which mass together behind or with other bulbs, such as mariposa tulips, wild hyacinths, or zygadenes. Most will flower reliably from year to year with minimal care. Here are some good species:

Low-Growers

B. jolonensis. Jolon brodiaea. Similar to *B. terrestris*, but flowers mostly darker blue.

B. nana. Dwarf brodiaea. Also low growing; flowers with narrow petals, pale blue-purple flowers pinched in at the top of the flower tube. Tolerates adobe soil.

GOLDEN STARS—*Bloomeria crocea.*

B. stellaris. Star brodiaea. Fine, clear blue, star-like flowers with white centers.

B. terrestris. Ground brodiaea. Scapes seem to emerge directly from the ground; flowers are light blue, mass well.

Tall-Growers

B. californica. California brodiaea. The tallest kind, and vigorous. Blooms latest. Flower color ranges from pale to deep purple. Stately appearance. Sometimes multiple flowering stalks from single bulb.

B. coronaria var. *rosea.* Rose brodiaea. Rare and choice. Waxy flowers of pink-purple.

B. elegans. Common harvest lily, common harvest brodiaea. Intensity of color and number of flowers varies. Very handsome.

Dichelostemma. Blue Dicks, Wild Hyacinth, and Others. Amaryllis family.

HT: 8 to 36 inches   FLW CLR: blue, purple, pink, red   FLW TM: March to June   PRPG: offsets or seeds (3 to 4 years to flower)   EXP: sun to light shade   WT: summer dry

The dichelostemmas are closely related to and confused with the brodiaeas. They generally have longer, twisted or curved scapes, up to two feet long, and grow in habitats including open grasslands, foothill woodland, openings in the yellow pine belt, and the edge of coastal forests. Each kind has its own charm and distinctive flowering period. Soils are well drained except for those of the foothill grasslands which tolerate heavy adobe and grow with the true brodiaeas. They should be treated like the latter in terms of a summer rest.

Dichelostemmas are seldom eye-catching unless massed together since the individual flowers are quite small. A possible exception is the unique firecracker flower, whose flowers are considerably larger and of such striking colors—red and green—that they immediately arrest the eye. Most grow well with other native bulbs in the middle of a mixed border. Some do best along the edge of a woodland.

The easiest one, which increases rapidly by offsets, is the common blue dicks—*D. capitatum.* It is variable, generally with handsome metallic purple bracts around the tight heads of blue-purple flowers; flower color ranges from white through blues and purples to almost pink. Vigorous corms produce three or more scapes under good conditions. Since different races flower at different times, from early March through May, experimenting with them may result in a long flowering time in the garden. This is one bulb that flowers from seed in as few as three years, and so may be started and increased readily by seeds.

Two other species are frequently confused with blue dicks, but flower later: *D. congestum* (ookow) and *D. multiflorum* (wild hyacinth). Both produce large clusters of pale blue-purple to red-purple flowers from late April to early June. Ookow grows best in light shade.

The remaining two are grown for their distinctiveness. *D. volubile* (the snake lily) has a scape which winds its way around supports: it may be trained through the branches of open shrubs, for example. The scapes reach three or more feet, and by late April to May produce tight balls of pink flowers. *D. ida-maia* is the striking firecracker flower, whose umbels of flowers hang. Each flower is a work of art—a bright red tube tipped by recurved green petals, a crown of white staminodia and pale yellow stamens. These establish themselves slowly and should be grown in light shade with woodland plants such as fairy fans clarkia, California fawn lily, and coast wood fern. It often grows in company with other hummingbird flowers, such as Indian pink and scarlet larkspur.

Triteleia. Ithuriel's Spear, Milk Lily, and Others. Amaryllis family.

HT: 8 to 24 inches   FLW CL: white, yellow, blue-purple   FLW TM: April to July   PRPG: offsets and seed (3 to 4 years to flower)   EXP: sun to light shade   WT: summer dry

This genus is yet another brodiaea relative, whose corms may be treated in much the same manner. Triteleias vary in habitat, so that each kind has its own special environment: some prefer full sun, but many thrive in light shade and cool temperatures; some even need wet soils through flowering.

Triteleias are of average height for bulbs. The open umbels of star-like to trumpet-shaped flowers vary from the blues and purples of the true brodiaeas to white, red-purple, and yellow. A few are suitable only for the rock garden, but these are rare and not readily available. Here are some decorative species:

T. bridgesii. Looks similar to *T. laxa*, but is a shorter plant of rocky situations with very handsome flowers of varied shades of red-purple. Late spring.

T. hyacinthina. Milk lily. This kind prefers open grasslands where the soil is temporarily wet before flowering, but dries later. Milk lily should naturalize well even in a garden with some summer water. Massed, the white to pale purple flowers are effective. Some have large, snowball-like umbels of flowers and are handsome by themselves.

T. ixoides. Golden brodiaea. These grow from medium to low according to variety. Taller plants grow in open forests of the Coast Ranges; short plants from Sierran meadows. Flower color varies from pale straw color to golden yellow. Blooming varies according to elevation but does not start until May.

T. laxa. Ithuriel's spear. Easiest to grow and most common. Flowers borne on stiff scapes through middle spring. Many color forms from small dark blue to large, pale blue-purple.

T. peduncularis. Long-rayed brodiaea. This is a late bloomer, flowering even into July. It is always associated with permanently wet areas such as stream edges, swales, and small marshes, where it may grow with rushes. It mixes nicely with wet-growing lilies such as leopard lily, and will tolerate summer water. The short, trumpet-shaped flowers are usually white, but flushed purple on the outside.

Arum Family
(Araceae)

The arums are basically tropical, and our only reasonably common native is the attractive skunk cabbage discussed below.

Lysichiton americanum. Skunk Cabbage. Arum family.
HT: up to 3 or more feet   FLW CL: yellow   FLW TM: March to April   PRPG: divisions or from seeds (3 to 4 years to flower)   EXP: shade   WT: wet all year

Skunk cabbage should not be confused with the eastern species of the U.S. nor the Sierran meadow plant sometimes called by that name. Western skunk cabbage lives in cool swamps and bogs near the coast from central California north to British Columbia. It must have saturated soil on the acid side and shade. Hot summers are not to its liking. Skunk cabbage demands ample space, with its monstrous tropical-looking leaves; it could be planted with other large vigorous plants such as other arums (for example, calla lily) or California spikenard and chain fern.

Skunk cabbage grows where many plants would die: with poor drainage and low aeration. It is not for the small garden; but in a natural shaded garden, it is handsome around the back of a pond or stream. The leaves lend a decided tropical effect, and the bright yellow flowers are showy on large clones. Plan for the gap that the plants leave in winter; they go dormant to creeping rhizomes.

Barberry Family
(Berberidaceae)

Most of the native barberries belong to the genus *Berberis* (*Mahonia* to some), and are woody shrubs not discussed here. Two small genera, however, are followers of moist forests and belong to the perennial category.

Achlys triphylla. Vanilla Leaf, Sweet-After-Death. Barberry family.
HT: with flowers to 18 inches   FLW CL: white   FLW TM: April to June   PRPG: root divisions   EXP: shade   WT: some summer water

Vanilla leaf creates a loose ground cover in damp spots of coastal forests, and is common in northern redwood forests. It may exclude other plants, spreading by underground runners much as other members of the barberry family do. The three large leaflets are of intriguing shape and long lasting, but finally die back in winter. Although they are said to smell of vanilla, the odor is scant. Stalks, less than eight inches high, produce numerous tiny petalless whitish flowers in late summer.

SKUNK CABBAGE—*Lysichiton americanum.*

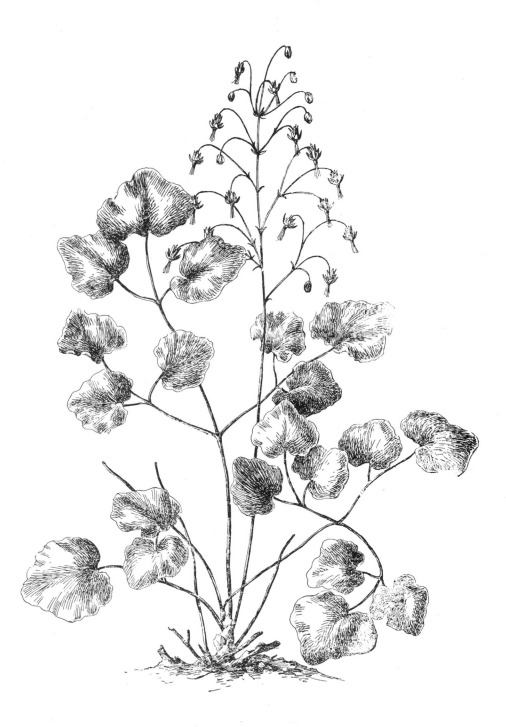

REDWOOD IVY— *Vancouveria.*

Vanilla leaf is a fine ground cover for the woodland garden, and needs summer water for best performance. Although it spreads readily once established, vanilla leaf may require a year or more for the roots to accommodate to their new home, and it does not compete well with other more vigorous ground covers which travel by similar underground runners. It needs a place of its own and contrasts well beside spring-flowering trilliums and woodland ferns.

Vancouveria. Inside-Out Flower, Redwood Ivy. Barberry family.

HT: in flower to 18 inches   FLW CL: yellow or white   FLW TM: April to June   PRPG: divisions   EXP: light to moderate shade   WT: some summer water

This second herbaceous genus is more widely distributed and less fussy. Two species come from steep, rocky banks in coastal forests, along the edge of redwoods or mixed-evergreen forests. In nature, they often cling precariously to the very edge of a cut-away bank by creeping rootstocks. Like vanilla leaf, they are slow to establish, but once settled quickly expand their leafy clumps. They favor well-drained woodland soils.

Inside-out flowers should be planted where their fine and unusual foliage shows to advantage. The unfurling of the coarse, maidenhair-fern-like leaves signals the stirrings of other spring events, although *Vancouveria planipetala* retains some of its old leaves through mild winters. This species has polished deep green leaves when mature, whereas *V. hexandra* is fully winter deciduous and has delicate, apple-green foliage. Both display airy stalks of white flowers, more interesting for their curiously turned back petals than showy. A third species, *V. chrysantha* (golden inside-out flower), has yellow flowers of slightly larger size and grows on brushy, rocky slopes in open forests in the Siskiyou Mountains near the Oregon border. The latter is not readily available and is difficult to transplant, but should be a fine addition to a lightly shaded rock garden or woodland border. Vancouverias serve much the same function in the garden as the Asiatic epimediums.

Bellflower Family
(*Campanulaceae*)

In California, the bellflowers and their close relatives the lobelias consist mostly of annuals living in the special niches of our grasslands called hog wallows or vernal pools. What perennial species there are have limited attractiveness for the garden; consequently, *Lobelia* is the only genus discussed here.

Lobelia. Lobelia, Cardinal Flower. Bellflower family.

HT: 6 inches to 5 feet   FLW CL: blue or red   FLW TM: May to September   PRPG: root divisions   EXP: light shade   WT: moist all year

This is the only native perennial genus of horticultural merit, although a quick mention might be made for the Scottish bluebell, *Campanula rotundifolia*, which enters our borders but is not common here. The other campanulas are shy, drab plants with little to recommend them. One could grow C. *prenanthoides* in a forest garden, but there are many showier plants.

The lobelias differ from the campanulas by their irregular, two-lipped flowers. Our two species are distinctive: both come from permanently wet areas: *Lobelia dunnii* (blue lobelia) forms low clumps and has pale blue flowers and is found on mossy seeps and rocky stream banks in southern California. There it grows with saxifrages (for example, *Boykinia*), brook orchids, and Venus-hair ferns. It could be planted in much the same company in the garden along a stream or the edge of a lightly shaded pond. It is winter dormant.

The second, *Lobelia cardinalis* (cardinal lobelia), is occasional by springs in the mountains of southern California. It is also winter dormant, but makes dark green clumps of leaves in spring (selected forms have red-purple leaves), and tall flower spikes of cardinal-red flowers in summer. It is a favorite with hummingbirds, and makes a handsome backdrop for a pond or in the background of a mixed border which receives summer water. It is short-lived under favorable conditions such as in rich soils, but the roots are easily divided and seeds quickly establish new plants.

Birthwort Family

(*Aristolochiaceae*)

We have but two genera in this curious, nearly exclusively herbaceous perennial family. One is an odd but attractive vine; the other has three species of shade-loving ground covers.

Aristolochia californica. California Pipe-Vine, Dutchman's Pipe.
Birthwort family.

HT: climbs several feet in a season   FLW CL: brown, green, and purple   FLW TM: early spring/late winter   PRPG: stem cuttings   EXP: light shade   WT: some summer water

Here is perhaps our most curious native vine. Roots penetrate deeply between rocks on brushy or wooded hillsides; stems wind their way around surrounding vegetation to reach light. Stems are covered with attractive, fuzzy narrowly heart-shaped leaves; flowers are often borne before new leaves appear at the end of winter. These are always sure to catch attention—they are distinctly pipe-shaped, the sepals with three maroon-purple lobes at the opening to the "pipe." The rest of the floral envelope consists of brown and white stripes which surround and hide the stamens and pistil. Insects are fooled into entering the pipe, lose their orientation, and remain trapped until pollination is completed. Pipe-vine is capable of extending stems several feet in a season, but the new growth and leaves are normally lost in winter, to be replaced the following season. Cuttings and rooted sections are quite easy ways of propagating pipe-vine.

WILD GINGER—*Asarum.*

Since pipe-vine is more odd than beautiful, it might be displayed on its own up a trellis, rock wall, unsightly shrub, or simply up a small tree in the woodland garden. Since the pipe-vine swallowtail butterfly depends upon the leaves as food for its larvae, planting this species will attract these beautiful butterflies.

Asarum. Wild Ginger. Birthwort family.
HT: up to 6 inches or so   FLW CL: maroon   FLW TM: April to July   PRPG: rooted sections or divisions   EXP: shade   WT: moist all year

The three species of asarum live on moist, dark forest floors from redwood forests into the yellow pine belt of the mountains. There, they form handsome ground covers, evergreen in one species, with broad, dark green and attractively veined heart-shaped leaves. The flowers are strange maroon-purple affairs, some with spidery "tails" and some without, and hide under the leaves next to the ground. They add to the strangeness of the plant, but are not easily seen.

Asarums have such attractive, ginger-scented leaves that they are one of the best ground covers for shade. They multiply vegetatively with summer water, and will survive but not look good with minimal supplemental summer water. Inland, they would perish with none. They form mats low enough to fill in between taller woodland plants such as ferns, trilliums, and vancouverias. They complement another forest ground cover: redwood sorrel.

Of the three species, *A. caudatum* is most amenable to lowland gardens and most readily available; *A. lemmonii* is closely similar, from higher elevations, but adjusts to gardens. *A. hartweggii* forms discrete clumps rather than wandering about, and some forms have very handsome, white-veined leaves, but this species is much more difficult to establish and slower to spread.

Blazing Star Family
(*Loasaceae*)

Most of the blazing stars and relatives are desert plants, often rather inconspicuously flowered annuals, although there are a couple of desert perennials not mentioned here because of dubious ability to adjust to gardens or of uncertain horticultural merit: *Eucnide* (desert nettle) and *Petalonyx*.

Mentzelia laevicaulis. Blazing Star. Blazing star family.
HT: 4 to 5 feet   FLW CL: yellow   FLW TM: June to September   PRPG: seeds (soak)   EXP: full sun   WT: occasional deep summer water

This is the only native *Mentzelia* which is nearly perennial; it really is biennial. The first year a taproot carries a low broad mound of rough, gray-green coarsely toothed leaves, and the second year a tall flowering stalk branches out candelabra fashion with dozens of large yellow starry flowers. Each flower is filled with long bunches of yellow stamens and opens from late afternoon until early

BLAZING STAR—*Mentzelia laevicaulis.*

morning, closing when the sun is directly overhead. Blazing star is a summer bloomer on sandy, gravelly, or talus-covered slopes of mountain canyons from the chaparral of southern California to the east side of the Sierra. It flourishes where there is little competition and lots of summer heat. Natural companions include showy milkweed, certain native thistles, and prickly poppy.

Because of the showy flowers produced during the peak of the hot summer months, blazing star is valuable in the back of the mixed border for a long show of color. It would do best in inland gardens where it receives the heat it needs, and must have excellent drainage.

Borage Family

(*Boraginaceae*)

The borages are among our commonest natives, but the majority are rather small, sometimes unshowy, annuals. Thus, the fiddlenecks (*Amsinckia*) and pop-corn flowers (*Cryptantha* and *Plagiobothrys*) are not included here, nor are several even more obscure genera.

Cynoglossum grande. Hound's Tongue. Borage family.

HT: to 2 feet with flowers   FLW CL: blue   FLW TM: March to April   PRPG: seeds (2 to 3 years to flower)   EXP: light shade   WT: summer dry

Hound's tongue is a fall-dormant herbaceous perennial. More correctly, it begins to die back in late summer, the leaves wilting and turning dark before that. The new leaves, borne in basal rosettes, appear by late winter before spring fully arrives. They are one of the best features of the woodland garden at this time of year—their new bronze blades slowly unfurling. By early spring a stalk up to 18 inches has grown out of the broad, tongue-shaped leaves, and carries flowers in fiddlehead-like coils. Flowers open as the coil unwinds, the buds turning from pink-purple to sky-blue as they open. The flowers always charm with their forget-me-not-like collars in the center. They are followed by odd, wart-covered fruits which start new plants readily enough, but may be removed if considered unsightly.

Hound's tongue lives in open mixed forests or dense oak woodlands and will tolerate considerable summer drought, but looks worse for wear under those circumstances. It should always have good drainage, since its penchant is for steep, poison-oak-covered slopes. In the garden, plant it near ferns and other good foliage plants to hide the leaves in summer and fall. The flowers comple-ment milkmaids and redwood sorrel or shooting stars.

Hackelia. Mountain Forget-Me-Not, Stickseed. Borage family.

HT: in flower 18 inches to 3 1/2 feet   FLW CL: white, blue, pink-purple   FLW TM: June to August   PRPG: seeds   EXP: mostly light shade   WT: some summer water

HOUND'S TONGUE—*Cynoglossum grande.*

These are California's truly native forget-me-nots; the familiar garden forget-me-not is a European import. The several species all come from stout taproots and are winter dormant—the range is typical of the middle and subalpine zones of mountains throughout most of the state; common associations are the borders of shaded meadows or banks in coniferous forests. There are far too many species identified by technical detail to bother with here: some have relatively larger flowers (up to two-thirds inch across); some have white flowers, while others may be pink in bud and open blue or purple. All bear the flowers at the top of tall leafy stalks, the flowers coiled up in bud; flower shape is much like the typical forget-me-not, with a collar or corona around the entrance to the short flower tube. Flowers are followed by curious nutlets covered with various combinations of hairs and barbed spines (wonderful under the hand lens). These may be considered a detriment because they catch on clothing; most gardeners will prefer to cut back the stalks at this time.

Selection for the garden should be based on populations from the lowest possible elevations (down to around 4,000 feet) for lowland gardens and on the best flower color and size. Groupings of these charming flowers look wonderful mixed with other meadow flowers or along the edge of a woodland.

Mertensia. Mountain Bluebells, Lungwort. Borage family.

HT: in flower 3 to 4 feet   FLW CL: pink in bud, opening blue   FLW TM: June to August   PRPG: divisions or seeds   EXP: full sun (near coast) or very light shade   WT: summer water

Of all the mountain borage relatives, mountain bluebells are the most charming for meadow gardens. The rootstocks form large colonies which follow watercourses along brushy brooks and sloping meadows. The stems bear a number of broad, pale green leaves, ovate in shape; above are coiled clusters of delicate, graceful, bell-shaped pendant flowers. As is common in the family, pink buds change as flowers open to a pale sky blue. Mountain bluebells grow with other wet meadow lovers such as corn lily, fairy lily, butterwort, and meadow paintbrush.

Used in gardens in plantings much like those in nature—moist meadows—mountain bluebells continue to increase in size and beauty each year. Experimentation in coastal and lowland gardens will be necessary to determine adaptability; *M. ciliata* is the most widespread and reasonable candidate.

Oreocarya. Perennial Popcorn Flower. Borage family.

HT: in flower to 6 or 8 inches   FLW CL: white, cream, yellow   FLW TM: July to September   PRPG: seeds   EXP: full sun   WT: occasional summer water with excellent drainage

This group of 10 species used to be included in the cryptanthas, the latter being the common popcorn flowers which occur in such abundance they color foothill grasslands white like drifted snow. Oreocaryas, on the other hand, are short-

FORGET-ME-NOT—*Hackelia.*

lived perennials which form dense mats on barren rocks in the subalpine of the mountains or in high desert mountains. The leaves are closely tufted and covered with white to yellow, stiff bristly hairs; the nearly naked flowering stalks bear small coiled clusters of white, cream, or pale yellow forget-me-not-like flowers.

Because of habitat, the perennial popcorn flowers need a well-drained soil in full sun, and would go beautifully in rock gardens of hot climates. Other cushiony companions could include several of the buckwheats and bladderpod. The various species will not be detailed here since they're separated on rather subtle characteristics.

Brake Fern Family

(*Pteridaceae*)

A distinctive family of mostly small ferns, often connected with rocky habitats. The more common species have been included, although the common bracken fern (*Pterdium aquilinum*) is too invasive for garden use. Excluded also are the high-mountain species and especially the desert genera *Cheilanthes* and *Notholaena* on account of their specialized habitats.

Adiantum. Venus-Hair Fern, Maidenhair Fern, Five-Finger Fern.
Brake fern family.
HT: to 12 or more inches   PRPG: divisions or spores   EXP: light to deep shade   WT: varies

All three adiantums are lacy, delicate ferns worthy of a place in the garden. Their habitats range from seeps on rock walls and forest stream sides to desert oases and moss-covered banks of foothill woodlands. Two require moisture at the roots all year; one is summer/fall dormant. All need shade except along the immediate coast, and all are relatively small ferns seldom exceeding a foot. Adiantums are outstanding for their polished dark purple-black stipes and the light green triangular to broadly fan-shaped frond segments. Tiny forked and reforked veins create a distinctive pattern at close range.

Adiantums are valuable in the woodland garden, but vary in their adaptability:

A. capillus-veneris. Venus-hair fern, florist's maidenhair. Rare in California, the Venus-hair fern is similar in overall appearance to the California maidenhair, but grows by seeps, stream banks, or permanent desert oases where it mingles with brook orchid and the California fan palm. It is every bit as delicate when forming a cascade over a moist bank or edging a pond, but must have year-round moisture. Allow for a winter dormancy where winters are cold.

A jordanii. California maidenhair fern. This fern spills over rocky and mossy banks in open forests and woodlands, blending with spring flowers such as shooting stars, nemophilas, red larkspur, and clarkias. The first delicate new

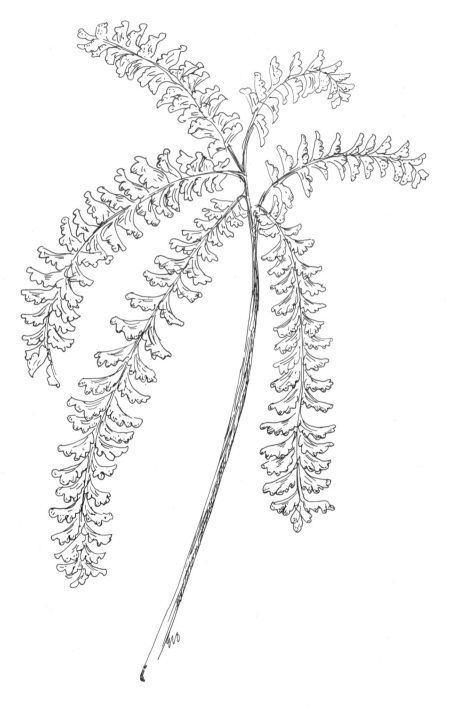

FIVE-FINGER FERN—*Adiantum pedatum.*

fronds appear soon after the winter rains start, and form small upright tufts by middle spring. According to the year, the fronds gradually dry and brown as soils lose their moisture and are dormant by summer. It is difficult to keep this species in the garden, whether from susceptibility to summer water or inadequate root system. Still, it is well worth the effort.

A. pedatum. Five-finger fern. Actually, the stipe usually bears a fan-like array of more than five fingers, each finger with several broad, fan-like pinnae. This pattern is unique and lends a special refinement no other fern has. This is also the tallest and boldest of the adiantums, with clumps two or more feet in diameter. Plant them, for best effect, around a pond or by a stream. Allow for the winter dormancy, when old fronds need to be removed.

Aspidotis. Cliffbrake, Indian's Dream Fern. Brake fern family.

HT: 4 to 6 inches   PRPG: spores   EXP: full sun (coast) to light shade   WT: once established, occasional summer water

This genus contains small rock fern gems with intricate frond designs. Habitats range from shaded stream sides to sun-baked serpentine and granite slopes. Elevations range from near sea level to the subalpine. Aspidotises have often been classified in various other genera, and the names are greatly confused—they are close relatives of pellaeas and cheilanthes. Both species have dark, polished, wiry stipes, and small fronds (less than six inches long) of a broadly triangular outline. Like other rock ferns, they are temperamental to transplant, require a full root ball, and must have summer water to become well established. Even then, they may not persist on truly dry soils, but respond well to pot culture.

These ferns are poorly known and not readily available, but add charm and interest to a well-designed rock garden, and make interesting potted specimens. Here are the two species:

A. californica. California lace fern or California cliffbrake. This is the rarer of the two, and clings to partially shaded rocky banks near streams or in steep ravines and gullies. It must have summer water to look its best. The fronds are lacier and more completely divided.

A. densa. Indian's dream fern or Oregon cliffbrake. This has the widest range. Fronds may die back in really hot, dry summers. It has evolved in nature to grow in some of the most inhospitable habitats, such as cracks between serpentine rocks. The bright green fronds are of a star-like design, with many long, delicate pointed segments.

Pellaea. Cliffbrake, Coffee Fern, Birdsfoot Fern. Brake fern family.

HT: to 12 inches or more   PRPG: spores   EXP: mostly light shade   WT: summer dry when fully established

Pellaeas are among the toughest and, once established, most drought tolerant ferns of the foothills. They live typically on rocky hillsides, often in company with goldback ferns and polypodies, and receive light shade or at least some afternoon shadow on long, summer days. They are most often associated with mixed-evergreen forests and oak woodlands. A few species grow among granite rocks in the high country, but are too delicate and temperamental to recommend for ordinary garden use. Pellaeas never completely lose their fronds at any one time, but under severe summer drought turn dark or purplish. The stipes are tough and wiry, the fronds much divided into small, rounded segments which curl under along their edges. The texture of the fronds is not typical of ferns, but is thick and leathery.

Pellaeas do not conform to the usual fern pattern, and for that reason are hard to accommodate into a natural setting. A mossy, rocky bank in part shade is ideal, or a protected corner of the rock garden, or use them as potted plants. Like the goldback ferns, they are difficult to establish and need summer water their first year, but once established increase in size and vigor each year. Here are the two common species:

P. andromaedifolia. Coffee fern. Fronds are a pale to bluish green but age to purplish or coffee brown. Old clumps may bear fronds to 18 inches.

P. mucronata. Birdsfoot fern. Easily confused with coffee fern, this kind has more finely divided fronds, each small segment ending in a minute, sharp point, or mucro. Once established, even tougher and more drought tolerant than coffee fern.

Pityrogramma triangularis. Goldback Fern, Silverback Fern. Brake fern family.

HT: 6 to 8 inches   PRPG: spores   EXP: light shade   WT: some summer water

This is the commonest of the small rock ferns and is found in a variety of habitats and forms. Habitats range from rocky banks in coastal forests to parched interior woodlands and desert mountains. Although goldback is capable of keeping some leaves all year, it becomes summer dormant when not watered during that period—the fronds roll up and finally die and new leaves appear after winter rains commence. The small leaves are divided like a snowflake, are triangular in outline, and have dark polished stipes, but are best distinguished by the gold or silver waxy powder which covers the backs. With age, this is overlain by the brown sori.

Goldback fern is difficult to move, and must receive summer water its first year to establish deep, well-branched roots. The fibrous roots must be kept moist. Large clumps eventually develop, and in amenable settings the spores grow into new plantlets on their own. Goldback fern is pretty in the front of an open woodland or on the rock walls of a partially shaded rock garden. Some forms would probably tolerate full sun in inland rock gardens, but some experimentation is necessary.

Buckwheat Family

(Polygonaceae)

This large important native family includes many annuals, often of desert environments, which are excluded here. Some genera—*Rumex* and *Oxyria*, for example—are unsuitable to garden culture because they are invasive weeds (the rumexes are also known as docks) or live in specialized habitats.

Eriogonum. Wild Buckwheat. Buckwheat family.

HT: 3 inches to 4 or more feet   FLW CL: white, pink, rose, red, yellow   FLW TM: June to October   PRPG: cuttings (some) and seeds   EXP: full sun for most   WT: varies

There is no more decorative or prolifically varied genus of natives; there is an eriogonum for every habitat except marshes and riparian woodlands. Most seek out openings in forests and are at home on rocky hillsides or sandy soils from seashore to timberline and on the deserts. For this reason, most need good drainage and are drought tolerant when fully established. Many luxuriate in hot summers; others accommodate well to freezing winters. Buckwheats vary from diminutive annuals to shrubby perennials; there is no hard line between perennial and true shrubbiness here, although at the end of the spectrum each category is clear. Accordingly, I cover here most of the perennial forms with which I am acquainted, although it must be emphasized that there await other garden-worthy species.

Eriogonums have tough, evergreen leaves which are frequently spoon shaped, curled under, and covered with close wooly felt underneath. These gray-leafed plants frequently add charm by their foliage texture. Flowers are valuable for their massing into flat-topped umbrellas or pompons, and for their long keeping qualities—they can be cut, dried, and used in bouquets as everlastings; on the live plant they frequently dry to a pretty brown, bronze, or red. Fresh flower color ranges from white through various shades of pink and rose to red, with several species in the cream range or brilliant yellow fading to red-orange. Since plant stature varies, garden use will also. The majority flower during summer; many continue into fall in the garden. They provide color at a slow time of year.

No single treatment of the eriogonums is complete, but here are some with garden merit:

E. arborescens. Santa Cruz Island buckwheat. This is one of the truly shrubby species. Multiple branches are covered with attractive, narrow, curled gray-green leaves topped by broad, flat-topped clusters of white-pink flowers. Excellent for large-scale planting in coastal gardens. Flowers beautiful dried. Tender.

E. X blisseanum. This is a hybrid between *E. arborescens* and *E. giganteum*. Combines attractive features of both parents.

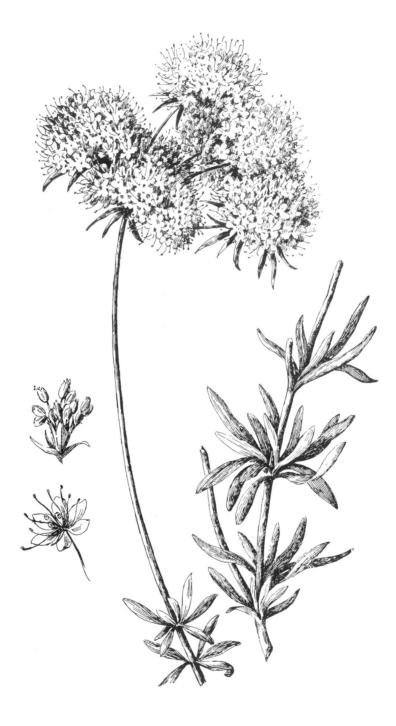

WILD BUCKWHEAT—*Eriogonum.*

E. compositum. Rock buckwheat. This species is quite similar to the last, but there is a single row of bracts on the flowering stalk. Broad, showy umbrellas of creamy flowers appear in mid-summer. This species seeks out some of the most inhospitable hot rocky slopes in the northern mountains. It should be a great asset in the dry garden.

E. crocatum. Conejo buckwheat. This originates along the edge of scrub and chaparral in the area of Conejo Grade, south of Ventura. It is closely similar to Pinnacles buckwheat, but the mounded bushes are completely gray and the showy flower clusters are bright, clear yellow. Very fine for a dry border or in the back of a rock garden.

E. elongatum. Wand buckwheat. This southern California species bears rather undistinguished leafy branches, woody at the base, clothed with narrowly spoon-shaped leaves, crinkled or wavy along their edges. It is the unfolding of the flowers which is the focal point; a nearly naked stalk grows taller, branches, then rebranches into several slender, wand-like stalks which eventually carry the small clusters of white to pink flowers.

E. fasciculatum. Flat-top buckwheat. Here is yet another widely ranging, varied species, mostly from the foothills and deserts of southern California. It is drought tolerant. Unlike most buckwheats, the stems are clothed in narrow, clustered, sometimes needle-like leaves. Flowers are borne on short stalks above the leafy branches in broad, flat-topped clusters, and are white to pale pink. A bee favorite, and excellent in front of chaparral shrubs. Flowers fade to rusty brown.

E. giganteum. St. Catherine's lace. This is the giant of the genus, a woody shrub from Catalina Island with repeatedly forked branches, large gray, wooly spoon-shaped leaves, and immense flat-topped clusters of white flowers which dry beautifully. This is a showstopper behind other drought-tolerant plants, and flowers persist long. Somewhat frost tender.

E. heracleoides. Giant buckwheat. The name refers to the rather large compound umbrellas of creamy flowers rather than the stature of the plant. This kind is distinctly woody at the base and bears flowering stalks to 18 inches tall with a couple of rows of leafy bracts up the stalk. From Modoc County.

E. inflatum. Desert trumpet. This curious species is often considered a desert annual, but the root may tap deeply enough to carry it over for a few seasons as a true perennial. The spoon-shaped leaves lie flat against the sandy desert soil and send up forked and reforked branches, the main branches conspicuously inflated as though they held water (they are actually full of air). The ultimate branchlets, often one or two or more feet high, bear small, graceful clusters of yellow-green flowers. This species should be grown for its curious appearance and is fine for a desert garden, or as a specimen plant in a hot inland garden. Dried plants make intriguing indoor arrangements.

E. kennedyi. Cushion buckwheat. Even the most extreme expression of cushions in alpine buckwheat hardly matches these cushions, which lie nearly embedded in the earth or among rocks and stones in high desert mountains. The branch systems beneath these mounds are truly miniature trees and show that some mats are quite old. The flowers are disappointing, being borne on slender leafless stalks with small clusters of scattered pale pink or whitish flowers. This plant commands attention in a special rock garden for its form alone.

E. latifolium. Coast buckwheat. This complex has been reworked several times, and now the strictly coastal bluff/dune form is considered a species on its own. It forms low rounded mounds with broad, wooly spoon-shaped leaves which are a nice foil to leaf shapes of other coastal plants. In summer, pompons of flowers arise on stalks to six or nine inches. Flower color is often a disappointing faded white, but forms from Humboldt Bay bear pink to rosy flowers, and these are preferred for the garden. Lowland rock gardens.

E. lobbii. Lobb's buckwheat. Another gem for the rock garden, this species hails from the subalpine and alpine of the east slope of the Sierra, where its broad wooly leaves lie against rocks, and the flowering stalks plaster themselves flat along rock surfaces. The showy flower clusters extend way beyond the leaf rosettes and vary from white to rosy pink.

E. mariifolium. False sulfur buckwheat. This species mingles frequently with the true sulfur buckwheat on dry, sandy mountain soils, but differs in technical features. Flowers do not recurve in this species with age as do those of *E. umbellatum.* Otherwise, stature, habit, and habitat remain similar.

E. nudum. Naked buckwheat. This is closely related to coast buckwheat, and like the sulfur buckwheat, has numerous varieties. It grows from middle and inner Coast Range foothills across the Sierra to timberline. Leaves are in low rosettes, spoon shaped, usually green above and wooly below, and bear naked flowering stalks to a foot or two high with small, rounded clusters of white or pinkish flowers. By itself, the true species is seldom showy enough for serious consideration in the garden, but some varieties are quite fine:

var. *grande.* Listed by many as a separate species from the Channel Islands. Plants are more robust and flowers generally larger. Of this kind, the so-called var. *rubescens* bears deep pink to red flowers and is the choice form for the garden. Tender in winter cold areas.

var. *saxicola.* Similar to var. *sulphureum,* but flowers are pale yellow in quite large clusters. From the desert edge of the eastern Sierra.

var. *sulphureum.* Sulfur-yellow pompons of flowers. Showy and nice mixed with other pink or white buckwheats.

E. ovalifolium. Alpine buckwheat. Here is another gem for the mountain rock garden. Exceedingly tight tufts of silver gray leaves cover the nearly hidden or buried branches (like a miniature ming tree). From these, inch-high stalks bear round pompons of white, pink-and-white, pink, or rose-red flowers. Some color forms are striking, such as the deep red ones from the White Mountains. Needs perfect drainage.

E. parvifolium. Small-leaf buckwheat. This also has leafy branches, but the branches sprawl or are half-decumbent. It grows along coastal bluffs of the central and south coast. Leaves are spoon shaped but tightly curled and consequently appear narrow. Modest, round balls of white to pink flowers fade a lovely red-brown. Good in coastal rock gardens.

E. saxatile. Pinnacles buckwheat. The gray leaves of this species cover low cushiony clumps along the chaparral edge in several parts of the inner south Coast Ranges. Flowers are borne in rounded clusters and vary from white to pink to pale yellow. Pleasant but not so spectacular as Conejo buckwheat.

E. sphaerocephalum. Yellow-ball buckwheat. This comes from the high desert lava country of northeastern California, from Lassen and Modoc counties. It is hardy and drought tolerant. Matted leaves and flowering stalks to a foot high bear tight, showy balls of white to pale yellow flowers.

E. umbellatum. Sulfur buckwheat. Few species are more variable than this, and I shall not attempt to specify all of the characteristics. They vary in plant height, leaf hairs, and other details, but all make loose mats of leaves often green above and gray-wooly beneath, with six-to nine-inch flowering stalks with rounded to flat clusters of sulfur yellow flowers, which fade orange or red. Some races come from rather low elevations in rocky places to the north; others climb to timberline in the Sierra. Source material should be chosen on the basis of matching garden climate to habitat. Choice for rock gardens.

E. umbellatum var. *dicrocephalum.* This variety stands out for its closely matted gray leaves and the lovely white flower clusters, sometimes tinted pink. Very choice, but from the upper Canadian zone of the Sierra. Seems garden adaptable.

E. wrightiii. Wright's buckwheat. Another cushiony buckwheat from the dry side of the Sierra and other desert mountains. Leaves are entirely clothed in white hairs and are narrowly elliptical. From these mats, forked flowering stalks carry small clusters of pinkish flowers. Easy for the rock garden.

Polygonum. Knotweed, Bistort, Smartweed. Buckwheat family.

HT: 2 inches to 5 or more feet   FLW CL: white, green, pink   FLW TM: June to September   PRPG: divisions or sections (some) and seeds   EXP: full sun to light shade   WT: varies

The genus *Polygonum*, although diverse, is poorly known amongst native plant enthusiasts. Perhaps it is because of the small, unshowy flowers or weediness of some. Nonetheless, there are interesting and attractive species to try. Polygonums vary from minute annuals to tall, vigorous herbaceous perennials and aquatic plants, and are found from sand dunes by the ocean to timberline. Most prefer open habitats, but water requirements run the gamut from drought tolerant to constantly wet. Leaves are characterized by sheath-like papery stipules (the ochrea), but leaf shape is quite variable. Flowers are borne singly or in small clusters in the axils of leaves or in terminal panicles and are green, white, pink, or red. Here are a few worthy of consideration for the garden:

P. bistortoides. Bistort. Here is one of the midsummer dominants of Sierran meadows. Tall, graceful stems to two or three feet carry spike-like clusters of white flowers. A picture of yellows, white, and blues is created by massing bistort with sneezeweeds, yarrow, St. Johnswort, potentillas, and whorled penstemons in the meadow garden.

P. davisae. Davis's knotweed. This plant is noteworthy for the color of its young shoots, which emerge as plump pink asparagus after snows melt in the high mountains, and for the leaves and stems, which dry red, making pretty contrasts with neighbors such as gray sagebrush and yellow-flowered rabbitbrush. The fully developed stems sprawl and branch to form clumps with pinkish stems, broad green leaves, and inconspicuous axillary green flowers.

P. paronychia. Dune knotweed. This is a rather unassuming dweller of coastal sand dunes, with low, branched wiry stems, clusters of narrow leaves with edges curled under, and small clusters of white to pinkish flowers. It is a pleasing addition to a coastal rock garden, where its interesting form complements coast buckwheat, seaside daisy, coast goldenrod, and others. Use it also as a sort of sandy-ground cover.

P. phytolaccaefolium. Meadow knotweed or meadow polygonum. This is a striking plant from shaded meadows at middle elevations, with tall stems to four, five, or six feet and airy panicles of white flowers. It may become invasive in the garden, but is a worthwhile addition to the back of a watered mixed border when late summer bloom is called for.

P. shastense. Mountain knotweed. Here is an alpine form of the dune knotweed— low, woody mats and white flowers. Attractive draped over granite rocks.

Buttercup Family
(Ranunculaceae)

This is an important family in California, and most of the major genera have been included. A few are too rare (for example, *Trautvetteria* and *Coptis*), or are unshowy (*Isopyrum* and *Myosurus*).

Aconitum columbianum. Monkshood. Buttercup family.

HT: in flower to 4 feet   FLW CL: purple or nearly white   FLW TM: June to August   PRPG: divisions or seeds   EXP: light shade   WT: summer water

The aconites are well known throughout the northern hemisphere for their interesting flowers and poisonous properties. Our native is winter dormant and grows from mid to high mountains, along shaded streams and watercourses that meander through high meadows. The broad, palmately lobed leaves remind one of the closely related larkspurs and buttercups. By summer a tall leafy stalk ends in racemes of curious flowers. Color varies from white to vivid blue-purple. Each flower has an upper hooded sepal that gives the genus its common name.

Monkshoods from the middle elevations should accommodate themselves to lowland gardens, especially behind a pond (the stalks reach four or five feet), along a stream, or at the back of a lightly shaded, watered woodland garden. The cheerful flowers are bee favorites, and combine well with red columbine, fairy lily, common corn lily, and giant larkspur.

Actaea arguta. Baneberry, False Bugbane. Buttercup family.
HT: in flower to 18 inches   FLW CL: whitish   FLW TM: May to July   PRPG: divisions or seeds (acid treatment)   EXP: shade   WT: some summer water

Here is another attractive foliage plant. Baneberry is found throughout the moist forests of both coast and middle mountains, through the great yellow pine belt, where it seeks shade and grows near seeps or springs. It is winter dormant, and the new foliage is reminiscent of a coarsely cut fern whose pinnae are bright green and pointed at their ends. These leaves do not stand nearly so high as those of meadowrue, and the flowers are borne in spikes just above them. Flowers lack petals and call attention to themselves only through the clusters of white stamens. By fall, the flowers are replaced by vivid red berries, poisonous but beautiful, with a shiny, waxy coat.

Baneberry should be used in the garden for its foliage and berries. It does well in the watered woodland garden where it can stand above ground covers such as redwood sorrel or wild ginger, or be mixed with small ferns.

Anemone. Anemone, Windflower. Buttercup family.
HT: 4 to 12 inches   FLW CL: mostly white   FLW TM: varies   PRPG: divisions   EXP: light to full shade   WT: some summer water

Like the aconites, the anemones are known throughout the northern hemisphere. The habitats vary from limestone outcroppings in the high eastern desert to alpine tundra to cool, moist northern forests. Only the forest species are amenable to garden culture, and the desert species is more curious than horticulturally attractive. All have short, ternately divided leaves which arise from creeping rootstocks, but some travel more than others. All bear delicate but conspicuous flowers on separate stalks, one flower to a stalk with colored sepals but no true petals. Flowers are nearly always white. Bunches of stamens decorate the center of the flower, and our alpine species is made extra showy by the large bunches of plumed fruits (much like *Clematis*).

In the garden, the western rue and forest anemones lend special refinement and grace to the woodland setting. Since they grow rather low, they should be given a place where they will show to advantage; in fact, *A. deltoides* can be used as a seasonal ground cover (the leaves disappear in winter). The high alpine species might be tried in a very well drained rock garden where it receives summer

MONK'S HOOD—*Aconitum columbianum.*

irrigation, but it is doubtful how well it will adapt to the lowland garden. Here are three species:

A. deltoides. Forest anemone. This is the most adaptable and showy. The stolons range widely to form carpets and bear broad, dark green leaves. In middle to late spring there is a fine show of large white flowers.

A. occidentalis. Western anemone or pasque flower. In scree above timberline. Finely divided, ferny leaves are light green. The uncommonly large flowers are cream color with numerous stamens in the center and white plumes in fruit.

A. quinquefolia. Western rue-anemone. This is a delicate, rather uncommon forest species. The leaves are divided into at least five segments, and the flowers, borne higher on the stalks, are small and white to pale bluish.

Aquilegia. Columbine. Buttercup family.

HT: 15 to 36 inches   FLW CL: white or pastel shades or red and yellow   FLW TM: May to September   PRPG: seeds (may self-sow)   EXP: light to full shade   WT: some summer water

All columbines are attractive garden subjects, and California does not lack for attractive species. They come from moist coastal forests, stream sides and seeps, subalpine meadows, and rock scree above timberline. All are taprooted perennials with basal clusters of ternately divided pale green to rather glaucous leaves, the divisions often three-lobed or redivided in a pretty fashion. From late spring through summer, tall flowering stalks carry a succession of showy, horizontally held or hanging flowers characterized by brightly colored sepals, cup-like petals which end in long nectar spurs, and long bunches of stamens. Old flowering stalks need to be removed, although allowing them to seed is a good way to increase the population. Different species often hybridize, so that if seedlings of pure parentage are wanted, the different kinds should be planted far from one another. Columbines need ample moisture during their flowering and are not drought tolerant. In most lowland gardens, all species grow best in light shade or with indirect sun during hot, summer days.

The woodland columbines look elegant at the back of a woodland garden, where their bright red and yellow flowers light up the scene and attract hummingbirds. They are particularly nice nodding over a stream or the back of a pond. The alpine columbine is a good candidate for the back or middle part of a rock garden, although it flowers poorly in the foothills because of the lack of winter cold. Here are three species:

A. eximia. Sticky columbine. Closely related to *A. formosa* but the stems are covered with glandular hairs. It needs year-round moisture and light shade.

A. formosa and varieties. Red columbine. This is the common, woodland columbine with red sepals, yellow petals, and red spurs with hanging flowers. It is easy to grow, and blooms and seeds abundantly with summer water.

A. pubescens. Alpine columbine. A true alpine gem from alpine scree. Flowers, held horizontally, are pale yellow, purple, or white with long spurs. Rock gardens.

Caltha howellii. Marsh Marigold. Buttercup family.

HT: in flower to 15 or 16 inches   FLW CL: blue in bud; creamy when open   FLW TM: June to August   PRPG: divisions or seeds (stratify)   EXP: full sun   WT: wet all summer

Marsh marigold is not a marigold at all, but rather a close relative of the buttercups. Unlike them, however, it lacks true petals, substituting for them showy sepals which are blushed blue in bud and open flat to a beautiful cream color with bunches of creamy stamens in the middle. These are followed by upright follicle-type seed pods, which themselves are rather decorative. Also exclusive to the calthas are the distinctive, kidney-shaped basal leaves. These are true harbingers of mountain spring, pushing through soggy sedges and grasses just as the snows melt. Unfortunately they grow in the subalpine and alpine zones, and may not be fully adaptable to lowland gardens.

A clustering of marsh marigolds is extremely attractive toward the front of a pond or in a moist meadow. Although they put on a show all by themselves, companions can include buttercups, elephant snouts, and shooting stars.

Clematis. Clematis, Virgin's Bower, Pipe-Vine. Buttercup family.

HT: climbs to many feet in one season   FLW CL: cream   FLW TM: April to September   PRPG: cuttings, root sections, seeds   EXP: full sun to light shade   WT: varies

Like the wild sweet peas and morning glories, the clematises are true vines. Each winter they die back to the woody growth, and in one season may grow many feet from this. In fact, in garden care, it is best to cut them back severely to promote plenty of new growth the following year. They climb by the twisted petioles of the compound leaves, clinging to fences or festooning bushes. One of their most striking means of display—in nature or the garden—is when they form true bowers between chaparral shrubs in protected canyons. In addition to the attractive foliage and pliable, rope-like stems, the flowers and fruits are both attractive. Flowers are relatively small compared to the cultivated Asiatic species, but are produced in great profusion, each flower a small four-pointed creamy star with numerous stamens or numerous pistils. By fall, the pistils have grown into white plumes of great beauty and are often as showy as the flowers.

In the garden, clematises almost have to be restrained because they grow so well, but are ideal for climbing an arbor or up a deck, hiding a rock wall, or as in nature festooning bushes (be sure in this case they don't completely smother the foliage of the bush). Different locales have different flowering times, and species differ somewhat in this respect, too. We have three rather similar species: *C. pauciflora* (southern California), *C. lasiantha*, and *C. ligusticifolia*. All three come from chaparral and open woodlands of the foothills, but there are differences in number of leaflets per leaf and the grouping of flowers. Of the three, *C. ligusticifolia* is the showiest with somewhat larger, creamier flowers and would be first choice for gardens.

Delphinium. Larkspur. Buttercup family.

HT: in flower 8 inches to 6 or more feet   FLW CL: white, pink, purple, blue, yellow, scarlet   FLW TM: varies   PRPG: seeds   EXP: full sun to light shade   WT: varies

The delphiniums are little appreciated in native gardens, yet offer some of the best spring and early summer color. They differ from the garden larkspurs in having less finely dissected leaves and being longer lived, and from the Pacific hybrid delphiniums in being more delicate and subtle of form, yet with a fine range of colors. As with other large genera, it is difficult to generalize, but all species grow from either woody rootstocks or clusters of tubers, and die back part of the year (the foothill and desert kinds are summer/fall dormant). All make clusters of basal leaves which are palmately divided, sometimes ternately secondarily lobed or toothed much like buttercup leaves. The height of the flowering stalk has wide range, and flower color does also, although blues and purples dominate. All have five showy sepals; the upper forms a long tapered nectar spur; inside there are four smaller, two-lipped and sometimes bicolored petals. One of the problems most larkspurs have is predation by snails and slugs. Another is the tendency to rot, or alternatively, the roots dry out too much in shallow pots during their rest, and shrivel. At least they should not be disturbed by gophers, since they're poisonous to most animals.

Since larkspurs vary, it is hard to point to one use in the garden. The taller kinds (usually wet-growers) are fine for the back of a watered border; the shorter kinds can fit in elsewhere in the border if it is summer dry; some are good for woodland settings; and all can be accommodated in large pots where they can be stored away for their dormancy. Here are some attractive species:

D. cardinale. Cardinal larkspur. Another of the large species, this comes from deep, woody roots and sends up stems to six feet on hot slopes near chaparral in southern California. Unlike most foothill species, this does not flower until late spring or early summer, and will take a rest later, but to thrive, it needs heat during the growing period. The tall stalks bear dozens of bright red, long-spurred flowers. Spectacular at the back of a border and a good hummingbird flower.

D. decorum/patens. From clusters of tuberous roots. Both grow from one to two feet tall, have simple racemes of dark blue (purple) flowers, and grow in grassy areas or by brush. Some forms of both species occur at high elevations in the coastal mountains and should be handled accordingly. Very attractive.

D. glaucum. Giant or tower larkspur. This is a very tall larkspur from a winter-dormant, stout woody rootstock, and can grow up to six feet or more. It lives in wet meadows in the middle to high Sierra. Flowers are blue-purple. Beautiful in a wet meadow, behind a pond, or in the back of a well-watered border.

LARKSPUR—*Delphinium.*

D. gypsophilum. White larkspur. This one comes from stout, branched rootstocks and bears flowering stalks to three feet, the leaves withering early as the flowers begin to develop. They are pure white, and the petals bearded. Restricted to the southeastern corner of the San Joaquin Valley in full sun and often alkaline soils. Excellent for the dry mixed border and especially welcome in poor soils.

D. hesperium. Western larkspur. This is a large-flowered dark blue-purple species from the inner foothills around the Great Valley. It needs full sun, summer rest, and fairly mild winter temperatures. It springs from a rootstock and the stems reach one to two feet.

D. luteum. Yellow larkspur. A rare species from coastal bluffs near Bodega Bay. Closely related to the red larkspur, but generally no more than a foot high with light yellow flowers. Choice for the coastal rock garden.

D. nudicaule. Red larkspur. This kind flowers in early to mid spring, mostly in the foothills of central and northern California. Its rootstocks penetrate rock crevices on steep mossy banks where it may grow with sedums, various saxifrages, and mist maidens. The stalks rise one to two feet and bear orange-red flowers visited by hummingbirds. Little or no summer water.

D. nuttallianum/depauperatum. A couple of closely related species with tuberous roots and flowering stalks to about a foot. Both have varied flower color—often dark blue—and both grow by edges of chaparral and woods in the middle to high northern Sierra. The latter should have plenty of summer water.

D. parishii. Desert larkspur. From woody roots with stems one to two feet, which carry a number of rather delicate light blue to purple flowers. Since it is adapted to deserts and grows well through brush, it can be used accordingly in the garden. It needs a definite summer rest, plenty of light and warmth in the spring, and some winter chill. Ideal for interior valley and desert gardens.

D. parryi. Southern larkspur. From woodlands of coastal southern California. Grows from a deep, woody rootstock with scapes from one to almost three feet with blue-purple sepals and bicolored petals (blue and white).

D. polycladon. Alpine larkspur. Stems rise to two or more feet from slender rootstocks which travel between rocks along the edge of wet places: meadows and rushing mountain streams. Since it is from the high mountains, it may not adapt to lowland gardens. Blue flowers. Excellent drainage and summer water.

D. purpusii. Pink larkspur. An unusual kind from the foothills of Kern County at the southern extremity of the Sierra. Rose-purple sepals and stalks to three feet. Summer rest.

D. trolliifolium. Giant larkspur. This large species sprouts from stout woody rootstocks and bears very large leaves and flowering stalks to five feet with violet-purple flowers. It lives in seeps in the forests of extreme northwestern California, and must have shade and summer water in the garden. A fine backdrop for the shaded pond or woodland garden.

D. variegatum. Royal blue larkspur. A foothill species which is variable, and hybridizes with others. From clustered thick roots, one- to two-foot flowering stalks with unusually large flowers, the sepals royal blue, the petals white. This should be used to develop superior garden forms.

Ranunculus. Buttercup, Crowfoot. Buttercup family.

HT: 4 to 15 inches   FLW CL: yellow or occasionally white   FLW TM: variable   PRPG: divisions (some spp.) or seeds (may self-sow)   EXP: mostly light shade   WT: variable

This rather cosmopolitan genus does not lack for native representatives, which range from coastal prairies to the alpine scree of the Sierra: some even grow in ponds. Most are charming in the wild, but some are less than good horticultural subjects, and the introduced kinds are downright weedy (for example, the shade-loving, creeping buttercup, *R. repens*). Although it is hard to characterize requirements, all buttercups prefer open to lightly shaded habitats which are moist through the flowering/fruiting period. High-elevation kinds need winter rest and flower in summer just after snowmelt, while foothill kinds are often the first flowers to open after heavy winter rains. These latter will stand a dry rest period in summer, although their growing/flowering is extended significantly by some water. Buttercups in general bear palmately lobed leaves in basal clusters with reduced leaves up the flowering stalks, and a succession of cheerful bright yellow flowers whose petals look lacquered. There are some exceptions.

Some foothill buttercups are best naturalized in a native grassland or meadow setting, and a couple lend an interesting note to ponds. Here is a sampling of some to try:

R. alismaefolius. Meadow buttercup. This is one of the prettier buttercups of mid to high mountain meadows. The leaves are simple and elliptical rather than palmately divided, and the flowers showy and bright yellow. For a meadow setting or by a pond.

R. aquatilis/lobbii. Water buttercups. These are both aquatic species—the difference being that Lobb's buttercup has floating leaves as well as the narrowly divided, filmy, submerged leaves. Both bear myriad white flowers, like drifted snow, just above the surface of ponds and lakes. Lobb's buttercup is annual.

R. bloomeri. Vernal pool buttercup. This one comes from low fields which are temporarily wet in spring, such as vernal pool areas. It adapts well to the garden with spring bloom, and will continue to grow in summer if watered.

R. californica/occidentalis. California/western buttercups. These two are of such similar appearance, they're grouped together. Both occur in foothill grasslands near the coast or inland, on the edge of mid-elevation meadows or open woodlands. They are the very first spring flowers. They grow rapidly in the garden and freely reseed: the old flower stalks need to be removed to prevent the plants from looking rangy. They are best planted in mass and could be the feature of the front of a border in early spring or in a natural grassy meadow. Good companions include blue-eyed grass and shooting stars.

R. eschscholzii. Alpine buttercup. One of the best, but very exacting in its native environment, where it grows near timberline at the base of scree and blooms just as snowmelt irrigates the roots. The flowers are large, carried well above the leaves, and are pale yellow. This is one to experiment with in the garden; it may not make the adjustment to lowland situations.

R. hystriculus. Waterfall buttercup. Growing on dripping rocks in middle elevations of the mountains, this is a small but charming buttercup with white petals. Nice next to a pond or on a moist mossy rock wall.

Thalictrum. Meadowrue. Buttercup family.

HT: 18 to 36 inches FLW CL: green FLW TM: varies PRPG: divisions or seeds EXP: light shade WT: some summer water

The California thalictrums are not like the showy kinds from Asia; rather, the flowers are greenish and inconspicuous and wind pollinated. But the foliage has merit and lends an air of graceful, fern-like quality to a woodland setting. The leaves first appear in early spring (for the lowland kind), and unfurl in a most beautiful way from tight purplish shoots. As they expand, each leaf reveals itself as divided into ternate segments which are redivided. Mature leaves reach a foot in length and look like a finely divided bright green columbine. They last as long as there is moisture but usually die back by summer. Thalictrums grow where their thick clusters of roots reach beneath rocks for moisture—on stream banks, or north-facing slopes of woodlands; the mountain kinds frequent sloping meadows, stream sides, and dripping rock faces. Flowers are generally unisexual and on separate plants: the female bears sepals and small clusters of greenish pistils whereas the male has sepals with long, dangling stamens. The latter are showier.

Thalictrums may be used in woodland gardens or, with the high-elevation kinds, in a meadow garden. The graceful leaves look particularly fine overhanging a stream or pond. *Thalictrum polycarpum* (foothill meadowrue) is the most amenable to gardens and grows throughout the central and northern foothills; *T. fendleri* is the common kind from high mountains.

Deer Fern Family
(Blechnaceae)

This is a small family of interesting ferns; our two genera, each with a single species, are described below.

Blechnum spicant. Deer Fern. Deer fern family.

HT: to 2 feet PRPG: spores EXP: shade WT: moist at all times

The single species is circumboreal. In California, deer ferns are most often seen on moist mossy banks near the coast, along swales and stream sides, or even on the hummocks of sphagnum bogs. They seem to require a constant water supply and partial shade rather than the deep shade which common sword fern tolerates so well. The fronds are once divided, tapered at both ends, with distinctive sterile outer fronds and stiffer upright brown, central fertile fronds. Fronds go partially dormant in winter and the new spring flush of sterile fronds is very pretty.

Deer ferns are small compared to many woodland ferns and seldom exceed 18 inches. To move them, you need to dig deeply to get the whole root system and to keep them moist at all times. Once established, they can pass through summer without excessive moisture, although the plants will be far more vigorous if the roots are deeply watered. Deer ferns are best used in front of other ferns, and along the borders of ponds and streams. Natural companions include Labrador tea, western azalea, bayberry, and fringed corn lily.

Woodwardia fimbriata. Chain Fern. Deer fern family.

HT: to 7 or 8 feet   PRPG: spores   EXP: shade   WT: moist all year

This is the giant of native ferns. It grows by seeps, springs, swales, and stream sides, where fronds may attain eight feet in length. These plume-like fronds are striking but lack the delicacy of lady or wood ferns: the segments are coarser and larger. The chains of worm-like sori on the underside of the frond give this fern its name. Sometimes it grows in the open within the fog belt, but it is most at home in partial shade. Because of its size, chain fern is a fitting companion for other giant forest plants such as elk clover and skunk cabbage.

Chain ferns may be transplanted when they are quite young, and allowed to grow steadily and slowly to full size over several years. Their fronds, like those of lady fern, become unsightly and tattered toward year's end, and should be cut off to make way for the new flush of spring fronds. Chain ferns can be the focal point in the wet parts of a woodland garden. Lilies growing up through the fronds make an alluring combination.

Dogwood Family
(Cornaceae)

Most dogwoods are deciduous shrubs or small trees in the single genus *Cornus;* the one exception is given below.

Cornus canadensis. Bunchberry, Creeping Dogwood. Dogwood family.

HT: 4 to 6 inches   FLW CL: white   FLW TM: May to July   PRPG: root divisions   EXP: shade   WT: summer water

Bunchberry is distinctive as our only nonwoody dogwood, and is relatively rare within our borders but much more typical of moist conifer forests in Oregon and Washington. It grows from widely traveling stoloniferous roots, in time

BUNCHBERRY—*Cornus canadensis.*

forming a carpet of many stems. The short stems bear typical dogwood leaves: ovate, borne in pairs and entire; above them a single "blossom" is carried. The blossom actually turns out to be four showy white, petal-like bracts surrounding a tight button of true greenish flowers which ripen later into bright orange-red berries. In the garden, give this charming plant summer moisture, a rich, humusy soil, and shade. Bunchberry makes a fine ground cover in the woodland garden, where it might be combined with vanilla leaf, twinflower, and anemones. It is twice showy—in late spring for its flowers and in late summer for its berries. An unusual combination would be to grow it under its showy brother, the tree-like Pacific flowering dogwood (*C. nuttallii*).

Evening Primrose Family
(Onagraceae)

This important family is represented by several genera with perennials, although the family also contains a wealth of annuals, such as the genera *Clarkia* and *Gayophytum*.

Camissonia. Suncups, Golden Eggs. Evening primrose family.
HT: 2 to 5 inches   FLW CL: yellow   FLW TM: varies   PRPG: seeds   EXP: full sun on the coast   WT: some summer water

The camissonias used to be in the genus *Oenothera*, but most are not properly evening primroses since their flowers open wide at midday. Many are annuals, but at least two perennials deserve mention. These are low growing, and as it turns out, both come from coastal situations—one from sand dunes, the other from coastal grasslands. Both have a long growing season, although *C. ovata*—suncups—dies back to its taproot in late summer/fall. The plants are moderately drought tolerant, and succeed where temperatures are moderate in summer. With water, their flowering season is extended. Neither is likely to be cold hardy.

Camissonia ovata—suncups—grows from a stout taproot, sending up a low rosette of broad, bright green leaves after the rains begin. From these, circles of flowers appear in spring, bright yellow and saucer-shaped and nestled just above the leaves. Suncups is best in a coastal bluff garden, or as the lowest edge of a mixed border, but cannot tolerate competition from taller plants. *C. cheiranthifolia*, or beach evening primrose, starts life from a taproot in much the same way as suncups, with a circular mat of leaves, but these are narrowly spoon-shaped gray-green to silvery green, and later send out stolons to make new rosettes or as flowering branches. These are tinted red, and have alternate leaves and a long succession of yellow, slightly smaller flowers. This species flowers almost any month where temperatures are cool, but the older plants become untidy as they develop odd, twisted brown seed pods. It's best to start this one new each year.

Circaea alpina. Enchanter's Nightshade. Evening primrose family.

HT: 6 to 8 inches   FLW CL: white   FLW TM: May to July   PRPG: divisions   EXP: shade   WT: all year

Few know the diminutive, delicate enchanter's nightshade, although it occurs in many areas where there is moisture and shade. Look for it in seeps of coastal forests and in the cool shade of willows or alders by mountain meadows. It cannot stand much competition, but once established forms a closely knit colony from branched rootstocks. The paired leaves are broad and light green, and the tiny flowers are white, delicate, and summer flowering. This plant will not overwhelm, but is an altogether charming addition to a natural garden.

Enchanter's nightshade would be best along the front of a partially shaded pond, spring, or stream bank. It should be given room to expand, and not planted with aggressive mints or monkeyflowers. Other delicate companions include the bladder or fragile fern, tinker's penny, and shooting stars.

Epilobium. Fireweed, Willow Herb. Evening primrose family.

HT: 3 inches to 4 or more feet   FLW CL: rose to purple   FLW TM: June to September   PRPG: root divisions or seeds   EXP: sun to light shade   WT: some summer water

This genus is successful nearly everywhere in the lowlands, and is probably familiar for the short-lived perennial and annual weeds. These have opposite leaves the shape of which suggests willows, and open racemes or panicles of small white to rose-purple flowers with notched petals, followed by long, four-parted seed pods which produce tiny seeds wafted on winds by their tufts of white hairs. Some perennial epilobiums have showy flowers. These vary from the tall-stalked fireweed, so common in the Sierra and Pacific northwest, to the low ground cover rockfringe from rocky meadows in the mountains. Here are three species:

E. angustifolium. Fireweed. This is the beautiful wildflower of the common name. It moves into areas after forest fires, where it takes advantage of the abundant light. This plant spreads by underground rootstocks and requires moisture, especially during summer, to succeed. It will accept partial shade, especially inland, but will not grow so tall or flower well with too much shade. The shoots bear numerous narrow, willow-like leaves and are topped by long racemes of pink-purple flowers and red flower buds. The whole stem may attain four or five feet, and so this plant is best for the back of a watered, mixed border or edge of a woodland, where its summer flowers light up the scene. With less generous water, the invasive roots wander less.

E. obcordatum. Rockfringe. This is a low, mat-forming species from the subalpine and alpine Sierra. Its roots spread in sandy soils between rocks and the stems creep over adjacent rocks to form broad, circular mats. These are smothered with pink-purple flowers with notched petals from mid to late summer. When grown from seed this plant will adapt to lowland gardens, where it is stunning in the front of a rock garden.

E. rigidum. Siskiyou rockfringe. This is very close to *E. obcordatum*, but grows a bit taller (still only inches high) and has gray-felted leaves. The flowers are a paler pink or purple. The advantage of this restricted species is that it grows below 3,000 feet and so is even more adaptable to lowland gardens. It comes from sandy, nutrient-poor soils, hot summers, and very wet winters. Start it from seed and plant the seedlings in a rock garden with excellent drainage.

Jussiaea repens. Water Primrose. Evening primrose family.

HT: 4 to 6 inches   FLW CL: yellow   FLW TM: summer   PRPG: rooted sections   EXP: full sun   WT: wet all year

Few know this attractive aquatic, yet it is not altogether uncommon. The creeping stems root as they go in shallow water on marsh borders and ponds in full sun. They do not appear in the dense growths of tules or cattails. An evergreen herb, its stems are attractively red-tinted, bearing a profusion of simple, rounded, dark green leaves. In summer, the whole plant is liberally sprinkled with open, showy yellow flowers, with five petals, an exception to their family where four petals are the rule.

   Knowing the habitat for this plant dictates its garden use: the edge of ponds or permanently wet spots. It is attractive, but like so many marsh plants, grows rapidly and invasively, and needs to be held in check. This is not difficult: the rooted sections are easily pulled out.

Oenothera. Evening Primrose. Evening primrose family.

HT: 1 to 6 feet   FLW CL: white or yellow   FLW TM: varies   PRPG: seeds   EXP: full sun   WT: at least some summer water

The oenotheras are a varied bunch and some have recently been re-classified as *Camissonia.* The latter open their flowers at mid-day and have ball-shaped stigmas; the former are truly flowers of the late afternoon and evening hours and bear cross-shaped, four-armed stigmas. Some oenotheras are annual, but a few are short-lived perennials or biennials. They bear rosettes of leaves atop taproots their first year, then flowering branches their second and third years. The flowers are uncommonly large, some several inches across, and either yellow or white fading pink. A long succession of flowers is produced on the racemes; it is usual to have buds, open flowers, and seed pods at the same time. Oenotheras are notorious seeders, and may have to be discouraged from taking over the entire garden. Cultural conditions are according to species, but all need full sun. Here are two species:

Oe. deltoides howellii. Antioch dunes evening primrose. This variety is now rare and endangered in its restricted habitat at the Antioch dunes, but grows easily from seed and is grown in several botanical gardens. It is closely related to the widely distributed desert annual species, but differs by being a short-lived perennial with wavy, gray-green leaves. The flowering stems branch widely

CALIFORNIA FUCHSIA—*Zauschneria californica.*

close to the ground, less than a foot high. The flower buds are reddish, the open flowers white, but fading to soft pink. Altogether this is a stunning flower, but the plant is rangy out of flower, and should be planted with other plants in the mixed border. It is best treated as an annual for cultural purposes.

Oe. hookeri. Hooker's or yellow evening primrose. This is a common sight along wet ditches, swales, and seeps from the coast to the middle elevations of the mountains. Flowering stalks reach six feet or more with a long flowering. This kind is ideal for the back of the mixed border, and thrives with summer watering. It will also look good around the back of a pond.

Zauschneria. Hummingbird Fuchsia, Hummingbird Trumpet, Wild Fuchsia. Evening primrose family.

HT: in flower 6 to 24 inches   FLW CL: normally scarlet red   FLW TM: July to October   PRPG: seeds, root divisions   EXP: full sun   WT: occasional summer water

All zauschnerias are denizens of rocky slopes, often along stream banks, or situations where the wandering roots can tap unseen moisture. They grow rapidly and spread from branching deep-seated rootstocks, so they should be accorded ample room in the garden. They die back in winter, the shoots renewed in spring. Growth is rapid through summer, and by summer's end the low, multiply branched stalks show flower buds. Flowers often last until the first frosts, and lend vivid color at a time when few other plants flower. Add to this the great beauty of the scarlet trumpet-shaped flowers, the bonus of attracting hummingbirds, and the pleasant foliage and you have a fine group of natives for the fall garden. Zauschnerias need good drainage, thrive in heat, and are drought tolerant once established, but need removal of the old branches, and some containment.

Since these are of only moderate height, they are best for the middle part of a mixed border, as a rank ground cover, in front of drought-tolerant chaparral shrubs, or in an expansive rock garden. Here are three species:

Z. californica. The widest ranging species, of low foothills throughout California. Leaves are pale green to gray-green, narrowly lance-shaped. Pink and white cultivars are sometimes available and make a pleasing contrast to the usual red.

Z. cana. This kind, from southern California foothills, is particularly drought tolerant, has nearly linear gray-white leaves. Nice contrast with the red flowers.

Z. latifolia. An especially low growing kind, from habitats moister than those of *Z. californica* and lightly shaded. The leaves are green, somewhat broader, and the brilliant flowers larger in proportion to the rest of the plant. This is the showiest bloomer.

Figwort Family
(Scrophulariaceae)

This large and characteristic native family has many perennials of ornamental value, although there are numerous annuals, as well. Some genera, such as *Parentucellia* and *Verbascum*, are excluded because they are introduced.

Castilleja. Indian Paintbrush. Figwort family.

HT: 6 inches to 5 feet   FLW CL: yellow, orange, red, pink, red-purple   FLW TM: varies   PRPG: seeds sown near host plants   EXP: full sun   WT: varies

Castillejas are well known to wildflower enthusiasts throughout the west, but are seldom mentioned for the garden. The many species are mostly herbaceous perennials; there is one shrubby kind, and two are considered annuals. The many kinds are often bewildering to identify, and we will not attempt to enumerate them all here. The habitats range from coastal bluffs and dunes to chaparral and coastal scrub to subalpine meadows, alpine scree, and desert oases. Always, they seek full sun, tend to live in well-drained rocky soils, and—most important—their roots hook to roots of host plants for nourishment otherwise unavailable in the soil. Without this link, the plants will not survive, and this accounts for the rarity of information on garden culture. The host plant is often a grass or shrub (frequently some kind of *Artemisia* or chamise); some species may be more specific than others to their host. They appear not to significantly harm the host. The connection can only be made by planting seeds in the appropriate place. Foothill species might be tried with native bunchgrasses and small shrubs such as California sagebrush or buckwheats. The seeds should be sowed in late fall after the rains have begun, and thickly so that some will find the appropriate roots. The plants should have the same water regime as their hosts.

If this seems hardly worth the trouble, recall that the paintbrushes are among our most colorful flowers—from green and pale yellow through the bright end of the spectrum, mostly centered around flame orange, scarlet red, and rosy pink. Those species with variable color will show great variation from seed, and the less desirable color forms can be eliminated. The paintbrushes also grow from a few inches high to over three or four feet for one annual kind, with leaves which are long, narrow, and simple to broad and much slashed, and carrying torch-like spikes of colorful flowers. The actual flowers are partly hidden inside the bracts, and it is these and the sepals which bear the brilliant colors rather than the green petals. Flowers appear from late spring for the coastal species through the summer into fall for the high-mountain kinds, and are usually visited by hummingbirds. Paintbrushes work well in the coastal rock garden, in front of drought-tolerant shrubs, or in the middle zones of mixed borders. Here are some outstanding kinds:

INDIAN PAINTBRUSH—*Castilleja.*

C. affinis. This is a foothill and middle-elevation species from the interior with bright red flowers.

C. applegatei. Mountain paintbrush. Low-growing species from dry, rocky soils. Mostly orange. Good with mat phlox, asters, and sulfur buckwheat in a mountain rock garden.

C. chromosa. Desert paintbrush. This comes from middle and high deserts, most often associated with sagebrush (*Artemisia tridentata*). The saturated, brilliant colors include electric pink and scarlet red. Very striking and good for hot, dry climates.

C. foliolosa. Chaparral paintbrush. This is a strictly hot chaparral species which grows with chamise. The leaves are a striking white or wooly gray. Low growing. Interior rock gardens.

C. lemmonii. Alpine paintbrush. This is a wet meadow kind from high mountains. Color is an arresting magenta-pink.

C. miniata. Meadow paintbrush. From wet mountain meadows in vibrant colors of orange, red, and pink. Relatively tall.

C. stenantha. Annual paintbrush. This "annual" is included because it is similar in terms of culture to the others. Very narrow leaves and tall stalks with flame-red flowers. Grows in wet places.

C. wightii/latifolia. Coast or bluff paintbrushes. These two similar species are best adapted to coastal situations with good drainage, and colors range widely from yellow through red. Some have wonderful combinations of yellow streaked with orange or red. Low growing. Coastal rock gardens.

Diplacus. Bush Monkeyflower, Sticky Monkeyflower. Figwort family.

HT: from 1 to 3 feet   FLW CL: yellow, buff, orange, red, and other warm shades for selected hybrids   FLW TM: summer and early fall   PRPG: tip cuttings or seeds   EXP: full sun to light shade   WT: better with some summer water

Again we are crossing the line into true shrubs, but most diplacuses are at best subwoody and not especially tall as shrubs go. In addition, they are best treated as bedding plants or short-lived perennials. They are easily started anew by tip cuttings, and need reshaping because of the tendency for old growth to become leggy and brittle. The diplacuses are very close to the true mimuluses, which are strictly herbaceous, but all the former have a bush-like growth pattern. The leaves on all are lance shaped, with tiny teeth, arranged in pairs; they curl and become quite sticky on hot days. Without summer water, these leaves shrivel, and in particularly dry, hot summers, the plants look dead. Even though they revive with winter rains, they look better if they receive some summer water, which also prolongs the flowering. Near the coast, bush monkeyflowers may have some flowers at almost any time, but the real peak of flowering is the summer months. Most live on rocky hillsides as companions to other coastal scrub or coastal sage plants—coyote bush, buckwheats, salvias, artemisias, and the like. The flowers are borne in profusion with the usual whimsical monkeyface appearance, and range from yellow through red. Hybrids are easily made, and from these, superior color forms have been selected for the garden, including bronze, rose-purple, and near white. Many of these hybrids are called Verity hybrids.

Bush monkeyflowers are among the most showy of summer perennials, especially when the hybrid forms are used. They are ideal at the front of chaparral shrubs, in the middle of a mixed border, or toward the back of a coastal rock garden. Here are some true species:

D. aurantiacus. This is the common species of the central and northern coast. The flowers have a pure orange color throughout. Smaller-flowered than some.

D. bifidus. Azalea-flowered monkeyflower. Of all the true species, this is the finest, with large flowers of great beauty. The shrubs are quite low with glossy foliage, weak branches, but myriad azalea-like flowers, each petal deeply notched. The basic flower color ranges from near white to apricot with darker splotches of orange and yellow toward the throat. Choice. Partial shade inland.

D. longiflorus. This is the southern equivalent of the first species, with somewhat larger flowers, and longer flower tubes. The colors tend more toward apricot and buff.

D. puniceus/flemingii. This species pair is from southern California, the first from San Diego County, the second from the Channel Islands. Both have shiny leaves and rather small orange-red to brick-red flowers. Good for hybridizing to introduce pure red color.

Galvezia speciosa. Island Snapdragon. Figwort family.

HT: 2 to 3 feet   FLW CL: red   FLW TM: February to May   PRPG: stem cuttings or seeds   EXP: light shade   WT: occasional deep summer watering

Island snapdragon belongs to the borderline category of subshrub, being green-woody. It is a handsome, much-branched plant, reaching three feet in height with triplets of leaves, simple and dark green. Since our species is restricted to open coastal scrub and the edge of chaparral on the Channel Islands, it is adapted to mild winters and is not frost tolerant. Nor is island snapdragon fond of very hot summers; it is best grown in open spots near the coast. The best feature is the bright red snapdragon-shaped flowers, another hummingbird favorite.

Island snapdragon is relatively drought tolerant and can be planted in the front of other, taller drought-tolerant shrubs, such as the ceanothuses, bush poppies, and manzanitas, or it can be used in the middle to back of a mixed border. The summer-blooming, red flowers should be considered in the context of what they blend well with—white, purple, and blue flowers are the most pleasing.

Keckiella. Shrubby Penstemons. Figwort family.

HT: 12 inches to 6 or more feet   FLW CL: white, yellow, red, orange   FLW TM: May to August   PRPG: half-woody cuttings; layering; seeds   EXP: full sun to light shade   WT: once established, little summer water

The keckiellas have been recently removed from the penstemons because of their woody, shrubby habit, together with some differences in flower structure. As such, they do not strictly belong here, but most are such low shrubs or are sufficiently green-woody that they can be considered perennials. They are widely scattered, generally in foothills to middle elevations, one on the desert edge, others in woodland and forest openings, and still others in chaparral or coastal sage scrub. Most live where the light is plentiful, the summers hot, and the soils rocky. All are more or less evergreen, but the lanky, leggy kinds need severe pruning to keep a semblance of good shape. Most are drought tolerant, but do not mind some extra summer water.

Because of the variation in species, the interesting kinds are described here separately. Most can be used in front of large drought-tolerant foundation shrubs; a few are suitable for the middle or back of a mixed border.

K. antirrhinoides. Bush snapdragon or yellow beard-tongue. Although similar in size to *K. breviflorus*, this species is more densely branched and can be shaped into a rather nice rounded form; it bears numerous short, narrow leaves. The feature of interest is the succession of summer flowers, gaping (again like *K. breviflorus*) but of a cheerful yellow and quite showy. Good for a mixed border or in front of chaparral shrubs.

K. breviflorus. Gaping penstemon. This is a low subshrub to three feet high with lax, often wandering branches and small, narrow toothed leaves. The flowers consist of curious white petals fused into short tubes and a gaping, open "mouth" marked with purple lines. More interesting than beautiful.

K. cordifolius. Climbing penstemon. This species is technically a woody climber when given the right setting. It can be planted to climb through tall chaparral shrubs, such as ceanothuses and rhamnuses. The bonus is that the shrub seems to flower twice; once in spring and again in summer, since the penstemon produces its profusion of bright red-orange flowers only when the stems have reached light at the top of its support. In full flower, these two-lipped, gaping flowers are superb, and good attractants to hummingbirds. A yellow form also exists. Both are tender in areas with heavy frosts, but often recover from their roots.

K. corymbosus. Red foothill penstemon. This close relative to *K. cordifolius* behaves in a more predictable way: clones may form sprawling woody mats where wind trims them, but otherwise grow into low, spreading bushes two to three feet high. Lustrous, dark green rounded leaves clothe the stems, and corymbs of bright red flowers appear in summer. It is fine in a large rock garden, and can stand plenty of summer heat. Good companions include the purple monardellas and yellow eriophyllums.

Mimulus. Monkeyflower. Figwort family.

HT: 3 inches to 3 feet   FLW CL: yellow, pink, red, purple   FLW TM: varies   PRPG: divisions or seeds (may self-sow)   EXP: mostly light shade   WT: summer water

In this treatment we reserve the genus *Diplacus* for the semiwoody, subshrubby monkeyflowers, and talk about mimuluses as strictly herbaceous. Although California has an impressive number of these mimuluses, the majority are tiny annuals. Among the perennials, there are some real gems of easy culture. All like moisture, summer and winter, and would soon die in dry soils. They vary as to the need for shade; some come from fully lighted mountain meadows, while others prefer the shade of forests. Most readily adapt to the garden when given these conditions, and flower prolifically there. Many have a relatively short life since they burn themselves out. Fortunately, they are easily increased through root divisions of the ever-enlarging clumps, or they reseed freely. Monkeyflowers are mostly summer bloomers and some, such as the cardinal monkeyflower, extend into fall. Here are the important species:

M. cardinalis. Cardinal or scarlet monkeyflower. This robust plant has a habit similar to the golden monkeyflower's, growing at least as tall, but favors partially shaded stream banks throughout the foothill and middle mountain country. The flowers are large, carried high above the leaves and of a peculiar shape, the lower lip swept backwards, the stamens extending beyond the upper lip, and all of a brilliant red-orange hue. This is a good hummingbird flower and striking beside a pond or stream, but the older flowering stalks need to be trimmed back periodically or the growth becomes floppy and unsightly.

M. dentatus. This is a north coast forest monkeyflower, superficially like a moderately tall golden monkeyflower, but the leaves are narrowly lanceolate and evenly toothed, and the golden flowers have a shape between that of a snapdragon and the musk monkeyflower. Fine for the woodland garden in moist places.

M. guttatus. Golden monkeyflower. This variable species comes in annual as well as robust perennial forms. The latter can grow in full sun or light shade, and under favorable conditions the leafy flower stalks carry flowers to two or three feet. The leaves have their own special pattern, broadly rounded and sharply toothed. The showy flowers look much like golden snapdragons with purple or brown dots on the lower lip leading into the throat. Reliable around a pond or in a mixed border with plenty of water.

M. lewisii. Pink or mountain monkeyflower. This is a robust herb of mountain meadows and seeps, but some forms are quite amenable to lowland gardens. The leaves are almost exactly the shape of those of the cardinal monkeyflower, broadly lance shaped, toothed, and light green, but the flowers are penstemon-like in appearance, with two lips and a definite opening into the throat. Flower color is an intense pink-purple in the best forms with a golden throat. Same cultural requirements as *M. cardinalis.*

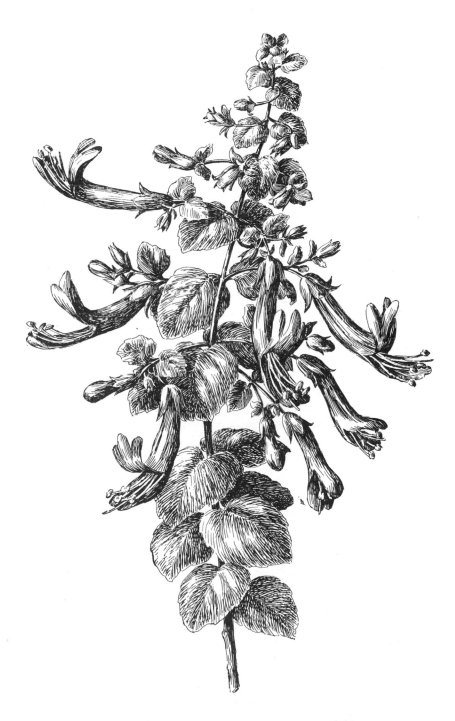

CLIMBING PENTSTEMON—*Pentstemon cordifolius.*

M. moschatus. Musk monkeyflower. Some clones are said to retain their musk odor, but none that I have ever examined do. This is a wide-ranging species, particularly common in northern mountains, and follows streams from lowland to subalpine forests. The rootstocks wander widely, sometimes poking up where the surface soil is dry. The leaves are unique—they feel slimy to the touch. The flowers are produced freely from the ends of each leafy branch, carried only a few inches high, and are a cheerful yellow with nearly regular petals. Naturalizes well around ponds and streams.

M. primuloides. Primrose monkeyflower. Here is a diminutive species, the whole plant sometimes no more than an inch high. The distribution is from middle to subalpine meadows, but is amenable to lowland gardens. The little leaf rosettes are light green and crowded one against the next, and the edges are lined with white hairs which catch the late afternoon light or reflect dew droplets. Exquisite primrose-shaped yellow flowers are carried singly at the ends of naked stalks just above the leaves. Since the plants are so small, they are suitable only for mass planting in front of ponds (with the similar tinker's penny), or in dish gardens.

Pedicularis. Lousewort, Indian Warrior, Elephant Snouts. Figwort family.

HT: in flower 8 to 18 inches   FLW CL: red, purple, or rose   FLW TM: varies   PRPG: seeds sown near host plants   EXP: light to full shade   WT: some summer water

The louseworts are close relatives to the Indian paintbrushes, and like them are root parasites. The host plants are frequently members of the heather family such as madrone and manzanitas, or for the high-mountain kinds, meadow sedges and grasses. Although the genus is of modest size, there is considerable variation in habitat and horticultural merit. Most have fern-like leaves, often tinted red or purple when they first push out of the soil after their winter rest. Some have obscure and drabbly colored flowers, while others are brilliantly cloaked in red or pink-purple, and have curious flower shapes which invite close inspection. Nonetheless, most are probably not appropriate to the garden because of habitat (high-mountain meadows) and the host-root connection. Establish them by sowing seed near host plants. Here are three showy species:

P. attolens. Baby elephant snouts. Much like *P. groenlandica* and in similar habitats, but shorter and the flowers with only a partially twisted snout.

P. densiflorus. Indian warrior, wood betony. This has the greatest likelihood of success, since its habitat is coastal forests and woodlands where large patches grow next to their host—usually some heather relative which itself is ornamental in gardens. The creeping rootstocks send up coarsely divided leaves in early spring, and are followed by short spikes of dark red to red-purple flowers. A display of a large colony of these is arresting. Indian warrior blends well with hound's tongue, milkmaids, and fritillaries.

P. groenlandica. Elephant snouts. Even though this lives only in subalpine mountain meadows, it is so interesting that it is worth a trial. Shortly after snowmelt, purplish leaves come up through short grasses and sedges. A little later, spikes to 18 inches carry curious pink-purple flowers which look like animal faces, the upper petals twisted and curled into a long "snout."

Penstemon. Penstemon, Beard-Tongue. Figwort family.

HT: in flower 4 inches to 4 feet   FLW CL: white, pink, purple, blue, red   FLW TM: varies   PRPG: half-woody cuttings or seeds   EXP: full sun (for most)   WT: varies

Penstemons are renowned throughout the garden world for their many ornamental forms. So varied are they that there is even a Penstemon Society which devotes exclusive attention to them. Yet, all considered, there are many species deserving cultivation which are seldom seen. Obviously, with such a widely varied lot, it is impossible to generalize about culture for the group as a whole; penstemons range from deserts to meadows to chaparral to alpine scree. Few, however, are found near the coast. Flower colors run the gamut of blues, purples, pinks, and reds with occasional white-flowered and yellow-flowered kinds. Sizes run from inches high to splendidly tall kinds with five to six foot flowering stalks. Fortunately, many kinds do well in the garden, although the life span is inclined to be short. This is offset by the ease of starting new plants from cuttings or divisions of clones. Here is an incomplete synopsis of worthy species:

P. anguineus. Somewhat like *P. procerus* and other whorled penstemons, but with taller flowering stalks, larger individual flowers, and from drier habitats, such as shaded banks in pine and fir forests in the northern corner of the state. Flower colors vary through the blues and purples. Floriferous and fine for a partially shaded mixed border or woodland edge.

P. azureus/laetus. These fine penstemons grow at middle elevations in the conifer belt of northern mountains, where they eke out a living on dry, rocky banks in full sun, or on loose talus and scree. The basal stems are subwoody and much branched with narrow, blue-green leaves, and the flowering stalks carry many large, strongly two-lipped blue to purple flowers which are yellow in bud. The color variation at any site may include light blue to deep red-violet. Floriferous and excellent for the front or middle of a mixed border. Better blooming and short-lived when watered. Closely related to *P. heterophyllus.*

P. bridgesii. Mountain scarlet penstemon. Here is another red penstemon from the high and dry slopes of the Sierra, especially along the eastern side. Low, much-branched subwoody stalks have narrowly spoon-shaped, yellow-green leaves from which arise two- to three-foot-high stems with conspicuously two-lipped, scarlet red flowers in mid to late summer. Handsome for the back of a border or in the background of a rock garden.

P. centranthifolius. Scarlet bugler. Another of the tall penstemons, this comes from the hot chaparral in south-central California and further south. The basal leaves

SCARLET BUGLER—*Pentstemon centranthifolius.*

are arrayed on many subwoody branches and are broadly spoon shaped and gray-green, and the flowering stalks soar in early summer to three or more feet with dozens of showy, trumpet-shaped bright red flowers. This is an excellent hummingbird flower and contrasts well with blue flowers toward the back of the mixed border.

P. davidsonii. Alpine penstemon. This is much like mountain pride, but grows lower to the ground, with greener leaves and uncommonly large purple flowers on stems two inches above the leaves. This is a true alpine, and is suitable only for a well-drained rock garden, but most lowland gardens do not provide the needed winter chill.

P. deustus. This is more curious than anything else. It is a rock grower in the mid to high dry parts of the Sierra, and makes subshrubby branches with toothed, light green leaves and short whorled clusters of yellowish flowers, marked purple. Nice for close viewing in a rock garden.

P. heterophyllus. Blue bedder penstemon. This is the foothill equivalent of *P. azureus*, with many of the same attributes, including yellow buds and similar height and habit. It lives on steep rocky banks next to chaparral or coastal scrub and is quite drought and heat tolerant. It is also short lived in the garden, but easily started from cuttings. One of the best for borders or edging in front of large shrubs. Beautiful with golden eriophyllums and orange diplacuses.

P. labrosus. Southern scarlet penstemon. Another bright hummingbird flower, this hails from middle elevations in the conifer zone of southern California mountains. The basal leaves are thick and bright green, narrow to oblanceolate, and the flowering stalks, to two and a half feet, bear a series of strongly two-lipped bright red flowers. Use in the middle or back of a mixed border.

P. newberryi. Mountain pride. Here is a subwoody mat-forming penstemon which often grows out of pure rock from middle to subalpine places in the mountains. The thick glaucous leaves are rather broadly ovate, and the flowering stalks seldom top twelve inches, but bear flowers so close together as to cover the plant with sheets of rose-purple. A real showstopper, especially combined with sulfur buckwheat, mat phlox, and Indian paintbrush. There are two varieties which may be even more amenable to gardens: ssp. *berryi* from the high, inner north Coast Ranges, and ssp. *sonomensis* from Sonoma, Lake, and Napa counties, where some populations live at less than 1,000 feet. These should not need the winter rest the mountain forms do.

P. palmeri. Palmer's penstemon. This is a sensational penstemon from high desert mountains of eastern California. The subwoody branched stems bear oblong grayish leaves which ascend the stalks in fused pairs. It is among the tallest kinds, with racemes extending more than four feet and bearing showy, fragrant, inflated flowers of white with pink or lilac shadings and beautiful nectar guides in the throat. Fine at the back of a mixed border.

P. procerus/cinicola/oreocharis/heterodoxus/shastensis. Whorled penstemons. This series consists of five very closely related, difficult-to-distinguish species which can be treated the same way horticulturally. They wander about in mountain meadows from short rootstocks, and can be cloned, and they have short, leafy stems with broad, rounded leaves. The flowers are borne in whorls of several tiers, usually less than a foot high, and the individually small flowers are blue or purple. The effect of a massing of these is lovely; they can be used in meadows and the front of mixed borders. Summer water. Winter rest preferable.

P. purpusii. Purpus's penstemon. A rather local and not well known penstemon from the high mountains of the inner north Coast Ranges. There it grows in nearly alpine settings, on loose talus in the red fir zone where it has little competition. The stems lie nearly flat against the ground. The overlapping leaves are broad and short, but strongly curled up to prevent water loss. The flowers hug the ground, only a few inches above the leaves, with red buds and uncommonly large (in proportion) gaping, blue or blue-purple flowers. Deserves an honored place in the rock garden or front of a dry border.

P. rupicola. Related to *P. newberryi* and *P. davidsonii*, with mats of glaucous leaves and close clusters of lavender to red-purple flowers. Fine for rock gardens.

P. speciosus. Showy penstemon. Here is a truly spectacular subalpine to alpine species on the dry side of the Sierra and other high mountains. It grows on sandy or rocky slopes in forest openings with low subshrubby branches covered with narrow spoon-shaped leaves. The racemes of flowers, borne many to each plant, carry close wands of gaping blue flowers. In nature this combines with sulfur buckwheat and Lyall's lupine, or complements blue flax and scarlet gilia. Plant it in the front of a mixed border or rock garden.

Scrophularia. Bee Plant, Figwort. Figwort family.

HT: 2 to 3 1/2 feet   FLW CL: maroon-brown   FLW TM: April to August   PRPG: divisions   EXP: full sun to light shade   WT: occasional summer water

The few species are herbaceous perennials from widely branching and rapidly spreading rootstocks. They grow in open spots of the coastal scrub and woodlands where they are excellent colonizers. In the garden, they become invasive with summer water, but are not too difficult to control. The best feature is the purplish-red new leaves and shoots in the spring (they're winter dormant), and the handsome pattern of mature leaves. These are large, broadly triangular, arranged in pairs on tall stems with coarse teeth. The open spikes of dull, maroon-red flowers with gaping throats are curious, but not beautiful.

One species, *S. villosa* or shaggy bee plant, is handsome even in flower, owing to the flowering stalks being decorated with stiff, white whisker-like hairs, which take on special luminescence in back-lit situations. Shaggy bee plant is drought tolerant but requires mild temperatures for best growth—it comes from the Channel Islands. Use it for contrast in a mixed border.

Synthyris reniformis. Grouse Flower. Figwort family.

HT: in flower to 4 inches   FLW CL: white to purple   FLW TM: March to April   PRPG: divisions   EXP: shade   WT: some summer water

This is the only species in the genus readily obtainable; it hails from moist mossy banks in coastal forests of northern California. The leaves are shaped much like and even confused with the saxifrages such as fringe cups and alumroot, being rounded and scalloped and attractively net-veined. The plants increase vegetatively by slender stolons, but not nearly so prolifically as many other forest denizens. In early to mid spring, short stems arise from the leaves with racemes of charming blue, purple, or nearly white flowers. The darker colors are much more striking. The flowers are narrowly cup shaped and are scarcely irregular, as are most figworts. The plants are easily grown in the garden, provided they have shade, mild winters, and summer water.

Grouse flower makes a charming addition to the woodland garden as a slow-growing ground cover, and should be used where its low flowers can be seen to advantage. It combines well with other ground covers such as violets, redwood sorrel, various saxifrages, and anemones, but remember it is not so vigorous as they are.

Veronica. Veronica, Speedwell, Brook-lime. Figwort family.

HT: seldom more than a few inches   FLW CL: white to blue or purple   FLW TM: summer   PRPG: divisions or sections of rooted stems   EXP: mostly light shade   WT: summer wet

Veronicas are a diverse group throughout the world, perhaps best known as weedy annuals in lawns and as stiff-leafed shrubs from New Zealand (now called *Hebe*). Our own natives seek out permanently wet spots: stream sides, seeps, and wet mountain meadows. There are two basic habits of growth: the common kinds range greatly in elevation, have creeping stems which root as they grow, periodically throwing up a cluster of blue flowers from the leaf axils (*V. americana*). A second group is found in high-mountain meadows, where the leaves form a tight clump on the surface of the soil and the creeping stems are underground; from the leaf cushions arise demure stalks which carry small racemes of graceful light purple to deep blue flowers (*V. cusickii* and *V. alpina*).

As garden subjects, only the last-mentioned mountain species are worth the trouble, and these are lovely in the front of a pond, in a planter dish with the diminutive tinker's penny and primrose monkeyflower, or in a mountain meadow near the front. The widely ranging *V. americana* is simply too invasive to be worth keeping under control.

Flax Family
(Linaceae)

The majority of our native flaxes are diminutive annuals; only one species is truly perennial and is discussed below.

Linum lewisii. Blue Flax, Mountain Flax. Flax family.
HT: to 30 inches   FLW CL: sky blue   FLW TM: June to September   PRPG: seeds   EXP: full sun or light shade   WT: some summer water

All other flaxes are ephemeral annuals, or are introduced. The mountain blue flax is a pretty perennial from a woody root. Its favored habitat is middle to subalpine slopes in dry meadows or sandy soils on the edge of low sagebrush. The stems branch low and wide, bear short, narrow leaves, and are topped by large, delicate, wide-open sky blue flowers. There is a succession of buds for prolonged bloom; individual flowers are short lived. This is a summer bloomer because of its habitat. In the garden, it is short lived, often succumbing to winter wetness, but is easily restarted from seed.

Blue flax grows to 12 or 18 inches but is rangy out of flower, so it should be combined with other heavily leafed plants in the middle of a mixed border. The clear blue color is a good foil for purple or red-purple flowers. Cut back after flowering.

Four o'clock Family
(Nyctaginaceae)

The four o'clocks are by and large from sandy and desert habitats; there are several genera which are scarcely showy, and are not discussed here (among them *Acleisanthes*, *Boerhavia*). A few of the sand verbenas are annual and so also not included.

Abronia. Sand Verbena. Four o'clock family.
HT: 3 to 6 inches   FLW CL: rose, purple pink, yellow   FLW TM: late spring through summer   PRPG: seeds (scarify)   EXP: full sun on the coast   WT: some summer water

The spectacular desert sand verbenas are annual, but the coastal kinds, draping over the first dunes back from ocean beaches, are perennials with a long growing season. Mature plants have deep, stout taproots which serve as reservoirs for food and water. From these, prostrate stems are renewed each year in a more or less circular pattern, spreading several yards to bind and cover sand. Leaves are broadly rounded, thick, fleshy, and often sticky. The plants fill an important niche in dune ecosystems. From middle spring through summer (and often sporadically throughout the year), the plants produce umbels of fragrant, brightly colored verbena-like flowers. Some are yellow, others pink-purple, white, or deep red-purple. All do best in deep well-drained soils and summer-cool conditions. They are salt and wind tolerant.

WESTERN BLUE FLAX—*Linum perenne.*

Sand verbenas fill a special niche in the garden: a sandy bank or exposed slope near the coast where they bind the soil and produce a decorative ground cover. They are difficult to establish, and are sought out by snails, slugs, and other pests. Here are the three common species:

A. latifolia. Yellow sand verbena. Very succulent leaves from the central and northern coast.

A. maritima. Southern sand verbena. Deep red-purple flowers in tight clusters and thick, fleshy leaves from the southern coast and Baja California.

A. umbellata. Pink or purple sand verbena. Pale pink, purple, or almost white flowers and thinner, dull green leaves from the central and southern coast.

Mirabilis. Four o'clock, Wishbone Plant. Four o'clock family.

HT: 6 to 12 inches   FLW CL: white, purple, rose   FLW TM: spring   PRPG: seeds (scarify or stratify)   EXP: full sun   WT: summer dry

The old fashioned four o'clock has been in gardens for a long time, and comes from Mexico. But few know of our own native species, many of which might be tried in dry, hot gardens. All are from stout, thick woody roots which often grow deeply between rocks. The stems, sometimes woody at the base, are branched and rebranched in a forked, dichotomous pattern, hence the name wishbone plant. The leaves are simple and oval, and the flowers are produced in large numbers from branch ends in curious "involucres," cup-shaped rows of green bracts that look like sepals. Each involucre contains one to several flowers, their "petals" white to deep red-purple. After flowering, the stems eventually lose leaves and by fall and early winter go into dormancy. All four o'clocks grow on hot, dry slopes in full sun, either in desert mountains or near chaparral and coastal sage scrub. Some enter northern California, but only in the hot interior foothills in the rain shadow of the high Coast Ranges.

Altogether four o'clocks provide a profusion of flowers and handsome foliage in a low sprawling bush form that lends itself to the middle of a mixed border, or a spot in front of drought-tolerant chaparral shrubs. Here are four species:

M. bigelovii. Desert four o'clock. This is a low, widely branched plant to two feet with small white to pale purple flowers. Best for a desert or inland garden.

M. greenei/froebellii. These two similar species differ in small details, but both produce large flowers of deep red-purple. Very handsome in flower, with flowers to two inches long. The former comes from the hot interior north Coast Range foothills; the latter from the deserts of southern California.

M. laevis. Coast four o'clock. Similar to *M. bigelovii* with red-purple flowers, from the coastal mountains of southern California. Somewhat frost tender.

YELLOW SAND VERBENA—*Abronia latifolia.*

Fumitory Family
(Fumariaceae)

We have two native genera: *Corydalis*, whose petals are backed by a single spur, and *Dicentra* or bleedingheart whose petals end in two inflated sacs.

Corydalis. Corydalis. Fumitory family.

HT: up to 3 feet in flower   FLW CL: white to pale pink-purple   FLW TM: June to August   PRPG: root divisions, seeds (stratify)   EXP: light shade   WT: summer water

The corydalises are relatively rare in California, and little known. The two species are restricted to rather remote parts of the northern corner of the state. They bear racemes of curious and striking irregular flowers, whose petals end in one-sided spurs. Coarsely divided, ferny leaves form basal clusters below the flowers.

Of the two species, only *C. caseana* is perennial; the low-growing *C. aurea*, with bright yellow flowers, is normally annual. *Corydalis caseana* is a striking multi-stemmed herb from brushy mountain meadows with attractive bluish green leaves and racemes of flowers to three feet tall. Flowers are held at an angle such that they tilt downward, and are white to pale pink-purple, the petals tipped purple.

Corydalis caseana is such a striking plant that it deserves trial in the back of a wet meadow garden, or toward the back of a pond. Its lightly colored flowers should illuminate a site that's in dappled shade in summer.

Dicentra. Bleedingheart, Golden Eardrops, Steer's Head. Fumitory family.

HT: 2 inches to 5 feet   FLW CL: flesh, cream, yellow, pink   FLW TM: variable   PRPG: root divisions and seed (fire treatment or stratification for some)   EXP: sun to shade   WT: all year with good drainage; some summer dormant

All dicentras are perennial from horizontal rootstocks or tubers which progressively expand the size of the colony. Some are long lived, but a couple are notoriously short lived under garden conditions. Leaves are deeply slashed, divided into fern-like segments; most have a slight to pronounced glaucous green color. Some are low plants with flowers on separate stalks at or just above the leaves. Others bear tall flowering stalks from the center of their leaf rosettes. Flower color varies with species. Habitats also vary from moist forest floors to alpine scree or hot chaparral slopes.

With such diversity, different dicentras get different treatment in the garden. Here is a description of the different kinds:

D. chrysantha and *D. ochrolecua*. Golden and creamy eardrops. Both are short-lived perennials which appear in abundance after chaparral fires. They live on hot

BLEEDING HEART   *Dicentra formosa.*

slopes in southern California and are very susceptible to rot from overwatering or poor drainage. They seem to do best in large pots rather than directly in the ground, although both kinds are handsome in the back of a mixed border. Flowering stalks grow to four or more feet under ideal conditions with dozens of upright hearts. Showy, choice, and difficult.

D. formosa (and the closely related var. *oregona*). Western bleedingheart. This is the most commonly cultivated kind, and easy, even invasive once established. It thrives in shaded places, where the ferny foliage blends nicely with small ferns, wild ginger, various saxifrages, trilliums, and similar plants. Summer water improves performance. The flowers on *D. formosa* are borne in short racemes and hang like upside down hearts. Color varies from pale fleshy pink to deep rosy-purple. The superior forms are sometimes available and are worth obtaining over the ordinary pale forms. *D. oregona* has blue-green foliage and white hearts, and needs especially good drainage. Winter dormant.

D. uniflora and *pauciflora*. Steer's head. These are rare and difficult. They come from scree on high mountains and should only be attempted in a well-drained rock garden with winter chill. They are utterly charming, especially *D. uniflora* with its single leaf and fleshy pink flower with the look of a steer's horns and head.

Gentian Family
(Gentianaceae)

The gentians are renowned for their beauty; unfortunately not all are amenable to garden culture. There also remain some rather shy gentians (for example, in the genus *Swertia*) with little ornamental value, as well as annuals in the genera *Centaurium* and *Microcala*.

Frasera speciosa. Green Gentian, Deer-Tongue, Monument Plant.
Gentian family.

HT: in flower 2 to 5 or more feet   FLW CL: green with purple spots   FLW TM: June to August   PRPG: seed (3 or more years to flower)   EXP: full sun   WT: some summer water

This is a striking plant from mountain meadows, unlike any other. A stout tap-root produces large rosettes of light green tongue-shaped leaves. In summer a huge flowering stalk arises from the rosette, reaching up to six feet. It carries numerous starry, four-pointed green flowers, dappled with purple spots and double, purple nectar glands. In fruit, it is nearly as showy with its pale green seed pods carried high. For best results, this plant needs full light, plenty of summer water, and a winter rest. The forms from mid-elevations are most adaptable to lowland gardens.

Because of its striking form, green gentian can be used as a specimen plant in a large container, or at the back of a summer-wet mixed border. It should be started from seed, and the seedlings will require several years to reach full blooming size.

Gentiana. Gentian. Gentian family.

HT: 4 to 12 inches   FLW CL: blue or blue-purple; occasionally white   FLW TM: July to October   PRPG: seeds (stratify)   EXP: full sun to light shade   WT: summer water

The gentians are renowned among late summer flowers, especially for the intense blues of some species. Many are already in cultivation from eastern North America and the Alps. Of our dozen species, half are perennial, and of those, some have a restricted range and are in wet meadows. The shiny, opposite leaves are entire and the stems either stand upright or creep close to the soil. All bear showy deep, cup-shaped flowers of great beauty from late summer to early fall. They need winter rest and plenty of summer water.

In the garden gentians work best in a meadow or by a pond: the taller kinds could be used in the middle of a well-watered border. Here are four worthy species:

G. calycosa. Explorer's gentian. This is another fine species with large, intensely blue flowers and stalks to about one foot. The rootstock makes ever-expanding clumps. It occurs above 4,000 feet and may be difficult to establish satisfactorily in lowland gardens. Choice.

G. newberryi. Alpine gentian. From subalpine and alpine meadows, low mats bear uncommonly large flowers. The flowers are unusual in that the petals are white or light purple sprinkled with green dots. Choice, but difficult for lowland gardens.

G. oregana. Oregon gentian. A sprawling to semidecumbent plant from northern prairies and brushy spots close to the coast. Easy for garden culture, but the flowers are smaller and rather pale blue compared to others.

G. sceptrum. King's gentian. This fine species has upright stems to two or more feet and grows in bogs along the northern coast. Flowers are showy and bright blue. Excellent for lowland gardens with summer moisture.

Menyanthes trifoliata. Buckbean, Bogbean. Gentian family.

HT: 6 to 8 inches above the water   FLW CL: white or pale purple   FLW TM: June to August   PRPG: rooted sections   EXP: full sun or light shade   WT: soggy soil to standing water at all times

Here is one of the rare aquatic plants with garden possibilities. Buckbean is a frequent companion of other bog plants in the Sierra, and more rarely in a few coastal locales in the north. From the latter it would be most amenable to lowland gardens. The plant grows by the main stem creeping through the muck of shallow water, rooting as it goes, and bearing, in most ungentian-like fashion, alternate compound leaves with three bean-shaped leaflets. The flowers rise on separate stalks several inches, in short racemes, and are truly beautiful at close

GENETIAN—*Gentiana.*

range. Each flower is a five-pointed pale purple star heavily fringed with hairs.

Buckbean can grow where the soil is merely soggy all the time, and thus has slightly greater range than pond-lily or arrowhead, but is probably most effective edging a pond where it may join the latter two. (Another plant of similar habit and ecological niche is the purple-flowered *Potentilla palustris*, which is tolerant of very acid soils.)

Geranium Family
(*Geraniaceae*)

Aside from the familiar garden "geraniums," there are a number of weedy plants in the genus *Geranium* itself and in the genus *Erodium* (filaree or clocks), not described here. Only a few are truly native perennials.

Geranium. Cranesbill, Wild Geranium. Geranium family.
HT: to about 1 foot   FLW CL: rose, purple, pink, white   FLW TM: June to August   PRPG: division of large clumps or seeds   EXP: full sun to light shade   WT: some summer water

Most think of garden pelargoniums or the weedy wild geraniums when this group is mentioned, but California has several species of nonweedy, perennial geraniums—most of them from meadows and open forests in the mountains. Typically, the plants slowly form clumps, the clumps characterized by rosettes of broad, palmately lobed and toothed leaves. The flowers are open, of modest size, and carried above the foliage. The flower detail is most appealing; delicate white, pink, rose, or lavender petals with a tracery of dark purple veins. Wild geraniums need little special care, but some summer moisture, and removal of old seed-bearing stalks.

In the garden, wild geraniums blend well toward the front of a watered border, or in a meadow. I detail only a few species here; others might be tried.

G. oreganum. Northern geranium. Only from open forests of modest elevation in the far northwestern mountains. Flowers are a lovely rose-purple color. Choice.

G. richardsonii/concinnum/californicum. Mountain geraniums. All in this trio of species are quite similar, differing in minor details only. All live at middle to subalpine elevations in wet meadows and bear showy flowers: the first has nearly white flowers, the others pink to purple flowers.

Ginseng Family
(*Araliaceae*)

The aralias and ginsengs are an important subtropical and tropical family, but poorly represented in our native flora. Discussed below is the only native, *Aralia californica*.

RICHARDSON'S GERANIUM—*Geranium richardsonii.*

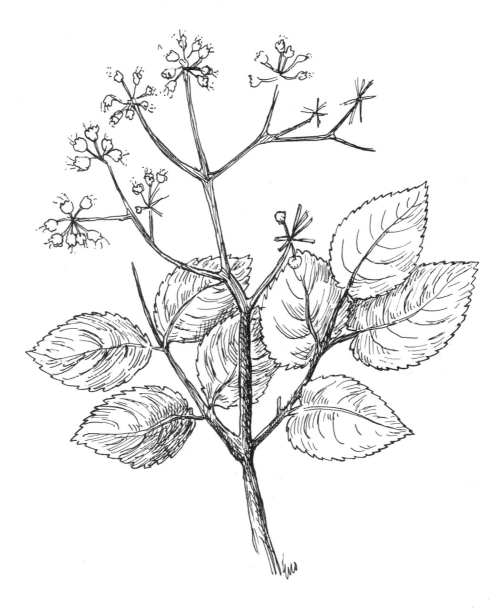

CALIFORNIA SPIKENARD—*Aralia californica.*

Aralia californica. Elk Clover, Spikenard, california Aralia. Ginseng family.

HT: up to 7 or 8 feet   FLW CL: greenish white   FLW TM: June to August   PRPG: seeds (2 to 3 years to full size)   EXP: shade   WT: wet all year

Here is an herbaceous perennial which grows with and blends well with the skunk cabbage. Actually, elk clover is more versatile, and will tolerate most soils as long as they are not alkaline and never dry out completely. It can also tolerate soggy soils (but with drainage), though it does not require them. Like skunk cabbage, elk clover is winter dormant, and leaves a gap in the garden then.

Elk clover produces enormous clusters of tropical, pinnately compound leaves which first appear in spring, and culminates in summer by tall flowering stalks of unshowy whitish flowers. It is much more handsome in fall when leaves turn yellow and flowers are replaced by shining red-purple berries. This is a plant for the shade garden, and it does well by a stream or pond, where it needs ample room. Individual leaves can reach more than six feet in length!

Honeysuckle Family
(*Caprifoliaceae*)

The honeysuckles are important throughout the northern hemisphere, but the vast majority are woody shrubs and small trees. Our single perennial is detailed below.

Linnaea borealis. Twinflower. Honeysuckle family.

HT: 2 to 3 inches   FLW CL: pale pink   FLW TM: May to July   PRPG: rooted sections   EXP: light shade   WT: moist all year

This is the only nearly herbaceous member of the family, although the older stems become a bit woody. Twinflower is a creeping ground cover which hugs mossy banks in moist forests of northwestern California. It ranges from the edge of the redwood country in Humboldt and Del Norte counties into the middle elevations of the pine belt in the Siskiyous and Klamath Mountains. Its glossy evergreen leaves spread on trailing inch-high stems, and its pairs of hanging pale pink bell-shaped flowers lend it great charm. It grows naturally with other woodland flowers such as mountain anemone, Oregon boxwood, creeping dogwood, and violets.

Twinflower is beautiful draped over a shaded bank or edging a fern garden, and its leaves remain attractive all year. The added bonus of the delicate flowers makes it especially desirable. It could complement other ground covers such as modesty and yerba buena, although its vigor does not match that of modesty. This plant takes time to establish itself, and it does not grow well unless conditions are to its liking. It is not a candidate for the dry shade garden, but needs to be kept cool and moist.

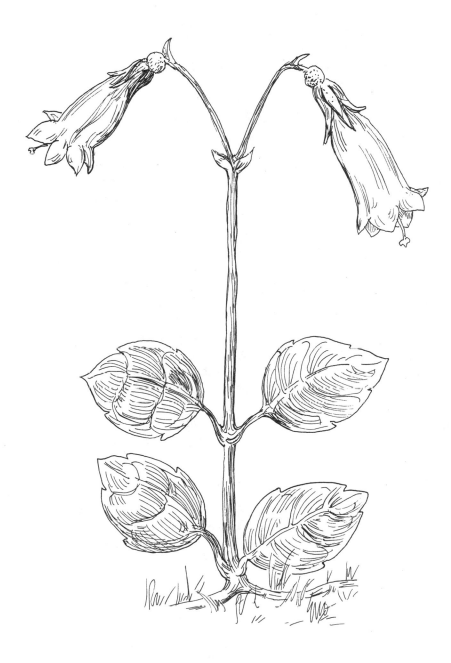

TWINFLOWER—*Linnaea borealis.*

Horsetail Family

(Equisetaceae)

The horsetails and scouring rushes represent an ancient lineage of perennials harking back to the earliest land plants on the face of the earth. Although there is a small number of species, most behave vigorously, even invasively, when given the right conditions. The single genus is detailed below.

Equisetum. Horsetail, Scouring Rush. Horsetail family.
HT: 1 to 6 or more feet   PRPG: divisions of rhizomes   EXP: light shade   WT: some water all year

The horsetails are the most ancient of living land plants commonly grown in gardens. Although frequently referred to as fern relatives, they are, in fact, on an evolutionary sideline all their own. They are winter dormant to widely spreading, invasive rhizomes. From these, new shoots spring each year; in some species the first are whitish fertile shoots with spore-bearing cones; in others the only shoots are the green vegetative shoots which later produce cones. The vegetative parts are put together in a rather curious way: sections of hollow stems jointed at the nodes, the nodes having sheaths of brown or black scaly leaves. In many species there are also whorls of green side branches. The main stems themselves are ridged and furrowed, the ridges stiff with silica and green to carry on photosynthesis. Those species with whorled side branches are referred to as horsetails; those with few are no side branches are the scouring rushes. Equisetums grow readily if given supplemental summer moisture and soon form extensive colonies. New shoots are strong enough to push up asphalt; thus, horsetails should never be planted where they can't be contained.

In the garden, the horsetail-type species are quite attractive, adding a note of feathery green beside ponds, streams, or seeps. Because they are so invasive, however, the roots must be containerized. There are two species with these horsetail-like stalks, the common horsetail (*E. arvense*) and the giant horsetail (*E. telmateia*).

The unbranched "scouring rushes" are also attractive in colonies, but with the roots still contained. They may grow to six or more feet with an effect similar to dark green, jointed bamboo stems. New shoots are particularly attractive, first arising as pink or purplish stalks. *E. hymale* is the best of this group.

Iris Family

(Iridaceae)

Our native irises and their relatives are mostly rhizomatous plants, belonging to the two important genera given below. Most species have garden potential and so are given treatment here.

GROUND IRIS—*Iris macrosiphon.*

Iris. Wild Iris. Iris family.

HT: 8 to 30 inches or more   FLW CL: blue, purple, white, cream, yellow, rose pink, red-brown   FLW TM: March to July   PRPG: divisions or seeds (for variation in offspring)   EXP: full sun to light shade   WT: some summer water

There are few peers for the wild irises. They spread readily, start easily from seed or root divisions, and require minimal care, but should have occasional summer water. They grow from creeping rhizomes which rapidly increase the clump each year, and bear evergreen sprays of fan-like, sword-shaped leaves in the manner of other irises. Leaf color and width varies considerably with the species. Most flower in mid-spring and put on a reliable show every year. The typical iris-type flowers are borne a few to a stalk, one opening at a time, and the range of color and delicacy of the lines of the nectar guides give the irises a beauty hard to match. Most set seed prolifically, but hybridization is common; for pure stock one has to be careful about isolation. Irises are best moved and established in the wet winter months, and should have supplemental water all year to maintain their attractive leaves.

The several species range from coastal bluffs to the edge of wet meadows in the high mountains, and through most forests and woodlands in the central and northern part of the state. Most can be used widely in the middle zone of the mixed border or in a woodland setting and are not disturbed by gophers, because they are poisonous. A description of several species follows.

I. chrysophylla. Restricted to Del Norte County and adjacent Oregon. The flowers are delicate and white to pale yellow with purple veins. Woodland garden.

I. douglasiana. Douglas or coast iris. This is the most varied of all. It grows both on the edge of coastal forests and on bluffs and prairies overlooking the sea. The leaves are large, broad, and bright to dark green and quite attractive by themselves. They transplant easily. Flower color ranges from the palest purple or near-white to rich, deep blue-purple. Good for the border or the woodland garden. Many forms have been crossed with this species to produce a number of select, named cultivars. These crosses run the gamut of colors, including red-violet, bright yellow, rusty orange, and pure white, and are available in the trade. Clumps increase readily.

I. fernaldii. Fernald's iris. Forests and woods of the middle Coast Ranges of central California. Leaves narrow and flowers pale yellow. Good for woodland gardens. Hybridizes readily.

I. hartwegii. Rainbow iris, Sierra iris. This variable species is a consistent feature of the ponderosa pine belt in the Sierra and high Transverse Ranges of southern California. The leaves are narrow, pale green, and the flowers light yellow with golden or purple veins. Woodland gardens. Difficult to establish.

I. innominata. Del Norte iris. Restricted to Del Norte County and adjacent Oregon. This is a miniature iris with very narrow leaves and showy flowers. Flowers are brilliant yellow or intense purple, and this species has been used in a number of selected garden crosses. Very fine for shaded spots, ideal for shaded rock gardens. Choice.

I. longipetala. Long-petaled iris. This iris is restricted to swales and moist spots in coastal grasslands from San Francisco south to Monterey. It is not common. It combines the best features of *I. missouriensis* with slightly wider, greener leaves, and more flowers per stalk, and once established is a fine addition to any garden. Meadows, wet borders, or by ponds. Choice.

I. macrosiphon. Ground iris. Variable species from the foothills of the inner north Coast Ranges and Sierra, mostly in open woods. Somewhat drought tolerant when established. Very narrow leaves which exceed the flowering stalks. Flowers may be pale purple, pale yellow, or more often blue to blue-purple with some deep tones. Fine floral display. Woodland garden or border. Hybridizes readily.

I. missouriensis. Mountain iris. A wet-grower of meadows from middle to high elevations, mostly in the Sierra, but also in other high mountains. The grayish-green leaves are relatively broad, and the large flowers are a fine sky blue with beautiful white and yellow veining. This iris does not seem to adapt well to the lowland garden, but is worthy of cultivation for the moist border, around a pond, or in meadows. Tolerant of mildly alkaline soils.

I. munzii. Munz's iris. This is one of the finest and least known, and is restricted to the Tule River drainage in the southern Sierra foothills. The flowers are large and usually in shades of light blue or purple. Woodland garden or border.

I. purdyi. Purdy's iris. Coastal forests of the north Coast Ranges. Leaves narrow and flowers pale yellow, often tinted purple or veined with purple or brown. Hybridizes readily. Woodland gardens.

I. tenuissima. Ranges across the northern mountains in open woods. The cream colored flowers are attractively veined with purple or brown.

Sisyrinchium. Blue-Eyed Grass, Gold-Eyed Grass, Grass Widows.
Iris family.

HT: 6 to 18 inches   FLW CL: yellow, blue-purple, or red-purple (yellow centers); rarely white   FLW TM: varies   PRPG: divisions or seeds (may self-sow)   EXP: full sun (coast) or light shade   WT: some summer water

Sisyrinchiums look and behave vegetatively like miniature irises. The fan-like sprays of small, sword-shaped leaves are borne by creeping rhizomes which enlarge the colony each year. Unlike irises, the flowers are small and borne in umbels and each flower has six colored tepals which spread wide, and three stamens forming a short cone in the center. They prefer open grassy areas, some inclined toward boggy or wet spots. Flowers are blue-purple, red-purple, or bright yellow, but occasional albino forms are known in the blue-flowered kinds. The low-elevation species bloom through the spring, taking a summer rest, but mountain kinds flower in summer; their roots should not dry out. Sisyrinchiums are very satisfactory if given some summer water, and frequently reseed themselves. Although the flowers are individually small, they make up for it by a profusion of bloom.

The wet-growing sisyrinchiums are best suited to meadows, edges of ponds, and the like, but can get by on less water than they appear to need in nature. The dry-growers are fine in a coastal rock garden, or massed together in the front of the mixed border. They blend well with their relatives the wild irises, and complement buttercups and bulbous liliaceous plants. Here are five species:

S. bellum. Blue-eyed grass. This is the nearly ubiquitous foothill kind which lights up many grasslands and coastal prairies with starry blue-purple flowers. The tepals are prettily veined wtih darker purple and there is a yellow eye in the middle of the flower. There are many forms: some are white, others low-growing with uncommonly large flowers (from coastal bluffs), and one named form (*macounii*) is both dwarf and with large white flowers. The latter is fine for the rock garden. Will tolerate some drought.

S. californicum. Gold-eyed grass. This foothill species stays close to the coast and seeks out seeps, springs, and edges of marshes. The leaves are pale gray-green and dry black, and the flowers are golden yellow. Seeds readily, and should have some summer water for best results.

S. douglasii. Grass widows. This rare kind is found only in the extreme north of the state, in moist spots in openings of woodlands at middle elevations. The flowers are almost an inch across, the largest of our sisyrinchiums, and red-purple. Needs late summer/fall rest without water. Choice.

S. elmeri. Mountain gold-eyed grass. Similar to *S. californicum*, but the leaves are brighter green and do not turn black. It inhabits middle-elevation wet mountain meadows and adapts to gardens with summer water.

S. idahoense. Mountain blue-eyed grass. This is a shy flower of wet mountain meadows, the flowers similar to but smaller than *S. bellum*. It adapts well to lowland situations, but should have summer water.

Lily Family
(*Liliaceae*)

The lilies are a large, important family both from the standpoint of numbers of species and plants with horticultural merit. The majority come from rhizomes, tubers, corms, or bulbs. A few rare or inconspicuous genera have been omitted here, such as *Streptopus* (twisted stalk), *Leucocrinum* (sand lily), *Stenanthium*, and *Hesperocallis* (desert lily).

Calochortus. Mariposa Tulip, Globe Tulip, Star Tulip, Pussy Ears. Lily family.

HT: 3 inches to 2 feet   FLW CL: white, pink, rose, red, yellow, red-purple, and numerous other shades   FLW TM: April to July   PRPG: offsets or seeds (3 or more years to flower)   EXP: full sun to light shade   WT: most, summer dry

There is no other genus in the lily family with so many fine ornamental species. The plants spring from bulbs, are mostly dormant in summer and fall (rest comes later for high-mountain kinds), and often start life in spring with a single long leaf followed by a flowering stalk with smaller leaves. All leaves are narrow and grass-like, and the edge often curls under slightly. The flowers vary considerably, falling into three groups. 1) The mariposas have large, deep, cup- or bowl-shaped flowers and beautiful markings on the inside petals around and above the uniquely-shaped nectar gland, the latter often covered with hairs of various sorts and colors; seed pods are long, narrow, and upright. 2) The globe tulips or fairy lanterns have hanging flowers whose petals overlap at the tips to form a closed globe; seed pods are broad, fat, and pendant. 3) The star tulips or pussy ears have somewhat smaller, daintier, upright flowers of a shallow bowl shape; petals are sometimes decorated by colorful hairs inside; seed pods are broad and pendant. All calochortuses need excellent drainage, a definite rest, and protection from gophers and moles. Some seek light shade, and some need wet soil at flowering; others are dry-growers in full sun. A few come from areas so winter cold they need winter chill. Regardless of species, calochortuses are worthy of time and effort for a place in the garden. Great potential is awaiting the hybridizer for superior forms and colors; nature has provided the raw materials in abundance.

In general, the mariposas are excellent as specimens in deep planters or for the middle of a mixed, summer-dry border. One high-mountain species would go well in a montane rock garden. The globe tulips are best in a woodland garden, but will fail in deep shade. The star tulips vary, but many look nice in a meadow or as special rock garden subjects—they are low growing. Here is a brief listing:

Mariposa Tulips

C. catalinae. Catalina mariposa. From the coastal mountains of southern California. Blooms early to middle spring in grasslands. Flowers white or tinged with purple; inside purple spot at base of sepals; petals without special markings except for dark gland. Stamens lilac color. Fine in groups and an early bloomer.

C. concolor. Goldenbowl mariposa. Stout stems to two feet high. Large flowers of bright yellow with red splotch at base of each sepal and a small round gland on each petal. From low to middle elevations in the ponderosa belt of the southern California mountains. Choice for chaparral gardens.

C. kennedyi. Flame mariposa. Leaves wavy, and the stem sometimes winding. In late spring to early summer brilliant flowers of purest red-orange, or in the eastern part of the range, an intense waxy yellow-orange. A dark spot often at the base of each petal, and the gland is round. From the low to middle deserts of southern mountains in the Mojave desert. Very difficult to cultivate, but well worth the trouble. Give plenty of sun and heat and excellent drainage.

C. leichtlinii. Sierra mariposa. Scree and gravel soils of middle to alpine zones in the Sierra. Large flowers often borne on short stalks (sometimes less than two inches high). Flowers white, smoky gray outside, and the ovate gland with a dark spot above it, and yellow below. Fine for rock gardens.

C. luteus. Golden mariposa. One of the most common. In foothills throughout the Coast Ranges and Sierra. Flowers bright yellow, usually pencilled inside with dark brown lines and/or spots. Gland crescent shape. Often hybridizes with *C. superbus, C. vestae,* and *C. venustus.*

C. macrocarpus. Bigpod mariposa. Stout stems with one to three handsome flowers. Petals are purple with a central green stripe and often a purple band above the gland. Middle elevations of the sagebrush country of northeastern California. Choice for desert gardens.

C. palmeri. Palmer's mariposa. From meadows wet in early spring at middle elevations in the mountains of the Transverse Ranges. Flowers white to lavender, a brown spot above each rounded gland, which is covered with yellow hairs.

C. splendens. Lilac mariposa. Lovely lilac-purple flowers with a purple spot on each sepal and petal. Stamens dark. From foothills of coastal central and southern California.

C. superbus. Superb mariposa. Similar to *C. venustus,* but the gland is an upside down V. Northern Sierra foothills. Choice.

C. venustus. White mariposa. Actually, this species has a greater color range than all others, but is most often white. Other colors include deep red, bronze, pink, purple, and light yellow. The square gland has incredible spots, blotches, and markings above and around it. Choice. From hot foothills of the central/southern Sierra and central/south Coast Ranges.

C. vestae. Similar to *C. superbus,* but the gland is an upside down W. North Coast Ranges.

Globe Tulips or Fairy Lanterns

C. albus. White fairy lantern. The most widespread and variable. Found in woodlands from San Francisco Bay south and through the Sierra foothills. There are two races: the Sierran with pure white globes, and the Coast Range kinds with petals and sepals flushed with green and pink, reaching an extreme in var. *rubellus* with rosy sepals and deep pink petals. Choice for woodland gardens.

C. amabilis. Golden globe tulip. Common throughout the wooded foothills of the north Coast Ranges. Lower growing than *C. albus* (less than eight inches

FAWN-LILY—*Erythronium giganteum.*

high) with perky-looking deep golden yellow globes. Goes nicely with red ribbons clarkia and California fawn lily. A similar species, *C. pulchellus*, occurs around the Mt. Diablo area.

C. amoenus. Pink globe tulip. This is a more restricted species, from the southern Sierra foothills, with flowers of deep pink-purple. Very fine.

Star Tulips or Pussy Ears

C. coeruleus. Beavertail grass. Similar to *C. tolmiei*, this species is from the coniferous belt of the Sierra and extreme north Coast Ranges. Flowers are pale blue, petals fringed, and hairs occur inside above the gland.

C. monophyllus. Yellow pussy ears. From the red clay zone of the lower ponderosa belt in the northern and central Sierra. This perky flower grows only inches high with bright yellow starry flowers, the petals covered with yellow fur. Grows with rainbow iris and California Indian pink. Choice for the shaded rock garden.

C. tolmiei. Pussy ears, purple pussy ears. Another charming plant, this one for the coastal rock garden. The flowers are white to pale purple and thickly bearded inside with bright purple hairs. Several variants. Grows in scree or coastal meadows.

C. umbellatus. Oakland star tulip. This diminutive star tulip has pretty white to pale purple petals which lack hairs. It grows on serpentine soils around the San Francisco Bay. Fine for coastal rock gardens.

C. uniflorus. Meadow star tulip. This lives in temporarily wet prairies and meadows in the central and north Coast Ranges. Flowers pale purple, often with a dark purple spot. Pretty for a meadow garden.

Camassia. Camass, Camass-Lily. Lily family.

HT: in flower 18 to 30 inches   FLW CL: blue   FLW TM: May to July   PRPG: offsets or seeds (3 to 4 years to flower)   EXP: full sun   WT: all year

Our two camasses are closely similar—one has slightly irregular flowers; the other does not. Both are bulbous plants with basal clusters of narrow, grass-like bright green leaves, and flowering racemes to two or more feet with dozens of showy, star-like sky- to deep-blue flowers. A meadow of these is a sight seldom forgotten. They flower late in spring (near the coast) or into middle summer (in the mountains) and favor wet, boggy meadows. Although the leaves look superficially something like the related death camass, the bulbs of this kind were considered among the best edible root foods of the Indians. Camasses eventually go dormant and should then have less water, but not fully dry soil.

Camasses provide excellent color in the blue range and have fine form. They may be used in bunches in the middle of a mixed border or around a pond or wet meadow. They are among the easiest and showiest of native bulbs. Combine with Jeffrey's shooting star and bistort.

Chlorogalum. Soap Plant, Amole. Lily family. Liliaceae.

HT: in flower 8 inches to 2 feet   FLW CL: white or purple   FLW TM: May to June   PRPG: offsets or seeds (several years to flower)   EXP: full sun   WT: summer dry

The chlorogalums are bulbous plants best known for the properties of their large fibrous-coated bulbs: Indians lathered these in water for soap. Only one species, *C. pomeridianum*, is well known, but there are several others all from foothill prairies and grasslands. Most produce basal rosettes of attractive and distinctive, often wavy leaves from late winter through early spring. Only by late spring do the widely branched flowering panicles appear, and even then few see the flowers because these mostly open in late afternoon and evening. Flowers are rather delicate, with widely spreading petals which give a graceful, delicate air to the plants. By early summer, capsules have shed their seeds, and plants take a summer/fall rest.

Chlorogalums are easy subjects, and don't seem particularly bothered by gophers. Their curious leaves are an attractive addition to foothill meadows and near the front of borders, and the flowers are a plus for those who wander in the garden late in the day. Here are three species for consideration:

C. angustifolium. Narrow-leaf soap plant. From the hot northern Sierra foothills. Leaves narrow, bright green and *not* wavy. Flowers in small panicles, white.

C. pomeridianum. Common soap plant. Leaves robust and bluish green; flowers white. Easy culture.

C. purpureum. Purple amole. Rare and restricted to the south-central Coast Ranges. Leaves bright green and wavy; flowers a rich blue-purple, opening early in the day.

Clintonia. Beadlily, Bride's Bonnet. Lily family.

HT: 6 inches to 30 inches   FLW CL: pink-purple or white   FLW TM: May to July   PRPG: seeds (3 to 4 years to flower)   EXP: shade   WT: summer water

Clintonias dwell on mossy banks in cool coastal forests, or in middle-elevation coniferous forests. The two kinds both spring from deep-seated rootstocks with clusters of fleshy roots. The rootstocks grow slowly horizontally to make more shoots, and with time, a colony is established. Beadlilies are fall/winter dormant. They begin in spring with basal rosettes of broad, shiny bright green leaves. From late spring to early summer flowering stalks arise, one per rosette. Flowers are followed by lovely deep blue berries which are eagerly browsed by forest animals.

Because clintonias live in cool forests, they prosper with some summer water and are suitable only for the shaded, woodland garden. The coastal beadlily, *C. andrewsiana*, shows well behind low plants such as redwood sorrel, small ferns, wild ginger, and mitrewort. The racemes rise to a foot or more with red-purple flowers. *C. uniflora* serves best as a ground cover and requires more summer moisture since that is its major growing period. It spreads widely, each leaf rosette bearing a short stalk with one or two open, bell-shaped white flowers. Use with twinflower or anemone.

Disporum. Fairy Bells, Fairy Lantern. Lily family.

HT: 1 to 2 feet   FLW CL: white or green   FLW TM: April and May   PRPG: root division   EXP: shade   WT: water till end of summer

Fairy bells are winter-dormant woodland/forest plants from deeply seated fleshy rootstocks. They are interesting in many seasons: asparagus-like new shoots in early spring, the delicate unfolding of broad leaves on low, horizontally branched stems, the dainty, bell-shaped flowers which hang under the leaves, and the orange berries in late summer. They prefer cool, foggy coastal forests or middle-elevation pine forests. They are not for hot, exposed places.

Fairy bells, although not spectacular of flower, are charming in a woodland garden with other spring lily relatives: trilliums, Solomon's plumes, beadlilies. They slowly colonize, rewarding with larger patches each year. There are two species: *D. hookeri* has small greenish flowers; *D. smithii* has larger white bells and shinier dark green leaves; it is the better of the two.

Erythronium. Fawn Lily, Glacier Lily, Adder's Tongue, Dogtooth Violet. Lily family.

HT: 6 to 12 inches   FLW CL: white, purple, yellow, rose-purple, pink (often yellow centers)   FLW TM: April to July   PRPG: offsets or seeds (3 or more years to flower)   EXP: light to full shade   WT: some, summer dry; some need summer water

Erythroniums are closely related to true lilies, as revealed by the showy, pendant flowers, but they grow from slender corms rather than bulbs and bear two or three basal, broadly tongue-shaped leaves. The one to three flowers are borne on separate stalks, and are large in proportion to the plant. The entire plant is low and best used in the forefront of gardens. As with other lily relatives, gophers are fond of these plants and the corms need protection. There are two groups of erythroniums horticulturally and habitat-wise: 1) those from foothill woodlands and forests with mottled leaves (hence the name fawn lily), spring flowers, and summer dormancy (light summer water is okay); and 2) those from montane meadows and willow thickets with solid green leaves, summer flowers, and winter dormancy (summer wet). Flower colors include pink-purple, white, cream, and bright yellow. There are several species, all of which are fine ornamental subjects for the woodland or meadow garden (or as specimens in containers).

E. californicum/helenae/multiscapoideum. A trio of closely related plants from similar habitats and with similar cultural requirements. All live on rocky slopes in the openings of forests, where they receive lots of moisture in early spring then dry completely by summer. The first two are from the north Coast Ranges—*E. helenae* local around Mt. St. Helena—and the third is from the Sierra foothills. All have mottled leaves and showy white flowers with yellow-green base, and are excellent early spring flowers for the rocky or woodland garden. Adapt well to gardens.

E. citrinum. Similar habitat and range to *E. howellii*; flowers white with yellow-green base.

E. grandiflorum. Glacier lily. Our California variety occurs in the high mountains of the north Coast Ranges, where it grows on the edge of meadows. It should have partial shade in the garden. Bright yellow flowers in early summer as snows melt.

E. hendersonii. Henderson's fawn lily. Unusual species with mottled leaves from the far northern forests at low elevations. Flowers pink-lavender with dark purple base rimmed with yellow and/or white. Choice.

E. howelii. Howell's fawn lily. Rare, local species in Del Norte County and southern Oregon with mottled leaves and white flowers barred yellow, or with orange base. Handsome.

E. purpurascens/klamathense. From meadows of the Sierra and Siskiyou Mountains and differing only in small details. The leaves are bright green, and the smallish flowers are white with yellow bases. The former has flowers which age purple.

E. revolutum. Bog fawn lily. Forest plant which grows on the edge of bogs—should have summer water but good drainage. Mottled leaves, flowers rose pink with yellow bands near the base. Choice.

E. tuolumense. Tuolumne lily. One of the handsomest, a wet grower from the foot hills of Tuolumne County. The shiny leaves are solid green, and the large flowers golden yellow, but the plants often skip years in flowering. Easy to grow, but needs occasional summer water.

Fritillaria. Fritillary, Checker Lily, Mission Bells, Adobe Lily, and Others. Lily family.

HT: In flower from 4 inches to 3 feet   FLW CL: yellow, scarlet, checkered brown/purple/green, white, pink, rose-purple   FLW TM: varies   PRPG: rice grain bulblets or seeds (4 or more years to flower)   EXP: varies   WT: varies

This close ally of the lilies differs mainly in the stamen attachment: on lilies the pollen sacs swing (are versatile), and on fritillaries, they're fixed in place. Many fritillaries have smaller bulbs with a circle of tiny "rice grain" bulblets around the base from which new plantlets can be started. And many fritillaries have a checkered color pattern on the petals. Even so, many species look convincingly like true lilies. This is a genus which has seldom been used in the garden except for the regal crown imperial (*F. imperialis*) from the Near East. The flowering stalks bear whorls of leaves, but are generally not so tall as lily stems, and bear few to several open, hanging, bell-shaped flowers. Habitats range from coastal forests and grasslands to hot interior foothills to subalpine forests; flower colors include yellow, red-orange, pink, white, mottled brown/green/purple. Each kind has its own special merits. In the garden, fritillaries are often finicky, the bulbs are eaten by gophers, and the foliage is devoured by snails and slugs. In addition, plants often take a year or two "off" from flowering—during this time they make a single broad tongue-shaped basal leaf. In order to assure good flowering, one needs a colony of several bulbs. All need good drainage, and some a summer rest, but many species are not harmed by small amounts of summer water. Some are shade lovers; others require full sun. Like the lilies, fritillaries make good specimen plants for tubs and planters. Here are some superior species:

F. biflora. Chocolate lily, mission bells. This is a grassland or woodland species of the central and southern Coast Ranges with stalks to about a foot, and a few hanging chocolate maroon-brown bells with a satiny sheen. Unusual subject for highlighting. Summer rest.

F. glauca. Serpentine fritillary. Another rare, unusual kind, this grows on scree, often serpentine, in the high inner north Coast Ranges. Its leaves are near the ground and are glaucous blue-green: the one to three hanging bells are yellow dotted with purple and green fading yellow-orange. A wonderful plant for the well-drained rock garden.

F. lanceolata. Checker lily, mission bells. This is the most common fritillary and also the most variable. The leafy flowering stalks reach up to four feet and carry a dozen or more bells. The flowers are beautifully checkered with brown and green, sometimes with purple and yellow inside, and are a study in subtle patterns. Some have more green in them; others are nearly black-purple (near the coast). Work is needed to select the forms with superior color and size. This is a woodland grower and combines well with trilliums, Solomon's plumes, ferns, and similar plants. Occasional summer water.

F. liliacea. White fritillary. This rare species is from coastal prairies near the Bay Area. The stalks seldom exceed 12 to 18 inches, and they carry a few nodding whitish flowers, tinted or striped green, and yellow inside in the center. This is one of the easiest to grow and flowers reliably in lowland gardens. Use plants as container specimens or naturalize in meadows. Summer rest.

F. pluriflora. Adobe lily. Lives in the hot interior foothills of the northern Sacramento Valley in heavy adobe soils. Locally occurs in large fields in early spring—a fine sight. The stalks reach 18 inches and carry a few nodding, waxy, pink-purple bells (occasional white flowers). Choice for the middle border or rock garden. Summer dry.

F. pudica. Golden bells. Lives in the sagebrush country east of the northern Sierra crest and across the lava country of the extreme northeastern corner of the state. Stems grow to a foot with a few yellow (fading orange) hanging bells. Lovely but difficult to grow. Rock gardens.

F. purdyi. Purdy's fritillary. Another rare and choice scree species, again from serpentine or loose talus in the inner north Coast Ranges. It often grows with *F. glauca.* The leaves are bright green, near the ground, and the stalks are up to a foot high carrying one to several bells checkered white, purple, and yellow. Waxy flowers. Choice for rock gardens. Flowers late; give late summer rest.

F. recurva. Scarlet fritillary. This is the showiest of all and the most lily-like. The narrow glaucous leaves are borne well up the stalk and are topped by several bright scarlet flowers, the petals often recurved (although one variety has straight petals) and flecked with yellow inside. This is a good hummingbird flower. A robust specimen reaches three feet. This species grows on rocky brush-covered slopes, often in light shade. A colony is a sight not soon forgotten. Good for the edge of woodland gardens or shaded rock gardens. Choice. Late summer rest.

F. striata. Striped fritillary. A rare species, restricted to adobe soils in the foothills of the southern Sierra near the Greenhorn Mountains. It grows no more than a foot tall with a few hanging white or pink bells, striped red. Very choice for the rock garden.

Lilium. Lily. Lily family.

HT: in flower from 12 inches to 5 or more feet   FLW CL: orange, yellow, red, pink, rose, white   FLW TM: May to August   PRPG: bulb scales and offsets or seed (four or more years to flower)   EXP: mostly light to full shade   WT: some water throughout the year; some need special attention to summer water

There is no finer genus of bulbous plants than the true lilies, and although there are already numerous hybrids, cultivars, and Asiatic species available for the garden, the west Pacific coast is notable for its beautiful kinds. Many are rare or poorly known. All fall into two horticultural groups and habitats: 1) those with large single bulbs which grow on hillsides (soil may be wet part of the year, but dries in summer)—these need a summer or late-summer rest; and 2) those with creeping rhizomatous bulbs which grow along bogs, streams, and wet meadows—these must have moisture all year, and generally, some shade. Lilies have whorled leaves and flowering stalks from a foot to over six feet. Flower colors range through most of the warm shades or are white. Most have pendant flowers, but in a few the flowers are held horizontally or even nearly upright. All have beautiful flowers in summer.

Lilies may be used in several settings: behind ponds (wet-growers), at the back of a woodland garden (especially nice through ferns), and at the back of a mixed border (for the dry-growers, or those tolerant of full sun). They are favorite food for gophers, so in gopher country they must be placed in wire baskets, tubs, or raised planters, where they can serve as specimen plants. Here is a brief synopsis of many species:

Dry-Growers

L. bolanderi. Bolander's lily, turk's cap lily. This is another rare, little-known lily living on impoverished stony soils in chaparral or open forests. Restricted to Del Norte County and adjacent Oregon. It is an unassuming lily with a maximum height of three feet, blue-green leaves, and a few horizontal to nodding flared, bell-shaped flowers of dull, dusky red with purple spots. Good for rock gardens.

L. columbianum. Columbia or Oregon lily. This is the "tiger" lily seen through the northern redwood country, often growing up through banks of ferns and rhododendrons and azaleas. It belongs to the category of dry-growers, since the bulbs occur on slopes with good drainage. Stems may reach five or six feet, and under favorable circumstances carry a dozen or more nodding light orange flowers, spotted maroon. A fine lily for the woodland/fern garden.

L. humboldtii. Humboldt lily. This lily is often confused with "tiger" and leopard lilies, but it differs by having a single often-large bulb. At its best this Sierra foothill lily reaches enormous size—up to six, seven, or eight feet with dozens of flowers carried above the leaves. Flowers have the typical tiger pattern; reflexed yellow-orange petals dotted liberally with brown or red spots. Varieties also occur in southern California in moist coastal canyons. Give partial shade and occasional summer water. Choice.

L. kelloggii. Kellogg lily. This little-known lily comes from rocky openings of coastal forests in the northwestern corner of the state. Flowering stalks are usually shorter than the first two, and bear fewer flowers, but the hanging flowers are exquisite close up: recurved petals which open pale pink with dark spots and a central yellow band, and which age rose-purple.

L. rubescens. Redwood, chamise, or chaparral lily. Closely related to the first. From brushy slopes or hills on the edge of coastal forests from central and northern California. Its flowers are less fragrant, and considerably smaller than *L. washingtonianum*, and open a delicate pink and fade deep rose-purple. Very choice.

L. washingtonianum. Washington lily. Grows in open forests or through montane chaparral at middle elevations. One of the finest, with stout stalks carrying several large, flaring white flowers, dotted with purple and very fragrant (like cloves). Stalks may top six feet under ideal conditions.

Wet-Growers

L. maritimum. Coast lily. This rare species is confined to the immediate coastal fog belt in Sonoma and Mendocino counties, where it grows up through berry bushes and ericaceous shrubs on forest edges or boggy spots. The stems seldom exceed three feet, and carry a few, horizontally held intensely red-orange, bell-shaped flowers of great beauty. Give this one acid soil on the edge of a woodland garden, and plenty of moisture. Blends well with ferns, Labrador tea, and salal.

L. pardalinum. Leopard or "tiger" lily. The true tiger lily is Asiatic, but many call ours by that name. It is the most widespread of the wet-growers extending through the Coast Ranges and lower to middle elevations of the Sierra. Its typical habitat is stream sides in forests, but in at least one coastal area it grows in an open seep. This is one of the most graceful and charming of the spotted orange lilies, and is of easy garden culture. In time, the creeping rhizomes establish sizable colonies. Use it with golden and scarlet monkeyflowers, western azalea, spicebush, and stream orchid.

There are two other species of close affinity: *L. vollmeri* from northwestern bogs and *L. kelleyanum* from wet meadows of the high southern Sierra.

L. parryi. Lemon lily. This is now a very rare lily of the middle and high mountains of southern California, where it borders streams in coniferous forest. It is especially desirable because the three- to four-foot stalks carry fragrant, horizontal clear lemon yellow flowers (some forms may be spotted), a color rare in our lilies. Choice.

L. parvum. Fairy or alpine lily. This is the common lily of the middle to subalpine central Sierra, where it grows along stream margins and boggy spots on the edge of forests, often in willow or alder thickets. The flowers are smaller than other lilies, vivid orange, held horizontally, and have a flaring bell shape; robust specimens may produce a dozen or more flowers on stalks to six feet. This exquisite lily is fine in back of a pond or a stream in a woodland with monkshood, tower larkspur, and red columbine.

Maianthemum dilatatum. Mayflower, False or Wild Lily-of-the-Valley. Lily family.

HT: in flower 6 to 8 inches   FLW CL: white   FLW TM: April to June   PRPG: root divisions   EXP: shade   WT: some summer water

Mayflower spreads widely by shallow, underground rootstocks which quickly colonize borders of coastal forests in northern California. It is fall/winter dormant. In spring, each node of the subterranean rootstock produces a broad, heart-shaped glossy green leaf with conspicuous parallel veins. These attractive leaves last through summer. By May, separate, short stalks bear spikes of tiny white flowers, delicate but not showy. More attention-getting are the red-speckled berries in summer or fall.

When established, mayflower makes a thick ground cover whose interesting texture complements redwood sorrel, wild ginger, and saxifrages. Without summer water the leaves disappear early and vigor diminishes.

Smilacina. Solomon's Plume, False Solomon's Seal. Lily family.

HT: 10 to 18 inches   FLW CL: white   FLW TM: April to June   PRPG: root division
EXP: shade   WT: water till end of summer

Smilacinas are frequently confused out of flower with fairy bells. Their leaf shape and pattern is similar, as are their habits, cycle of growth, and roots. They colonize more quickly, however, and are more dependable with less water, although they do their best with occasional summer water. They are found in cool coastal forests and middle-elevation pine woods, and frequently grow with fairy bells. The stems never branch and the flowers are smaller, but are massed into showy clusters of white stars at the ends of the leafy branches. They are followed by round marble-like speckled or red-striped berries.

Like fairy bells, Solomon's plumes are perfect for a natural woodland garden, where they colonize readily and complement other spring flowers. There are two species: fat Solomon's plume (*S. racemosa*) is a stouter plant with deliciously fragrant panicles of tiny cream-colored flowers. An old plant may bear dozens of flowering stems, and when all are in flower at once the odor and effect are stunning. Slim or starry Solomon's plume (*S. stellata*) is a slender, more delicate, lower growing plant with darker green leaves and simple racemes bearing few white, star-shaped flowers. Although less showy, they have a delicate bearing, and are quicker to spread.

Trillium. Trillium, Wake-Robin. Lily family.

HT: 8 to 24 inches   FLW CL: white, rose, maroon, pink, green   FLW TM: March to May   PRPG: divide clumps; seeds (4 years to flower)   EXP: shade   WT: water to end of summer

Of all the spring forest lilies, trilliums are among the best. They spring from deep-seated rhizomes which slowly increase the size of the clump, starting with a single stalk. An old clump may bear more than a dozen flowering stalks at once. Like the clintonias, they are fall/winter dormant, the new leaves unfurled from a rolled-up shoot in early spring. The scientific name *Trillium*, "in threes," is appropriate since there are always three broad leaves on flowering-size plants. In their seedling stage, trilliums have one leaf. A single showy flower arises from the middle of the leaves in middle spring and is followed by a six-ridged seed pod. Trilliums have the same habitats as clintonias, excepting that they may also live in dense brushy areas in the higher mountains. They thrive with summer water and shade.

Trilliums are striking when massed together. They blend beautifully with sword and lady ferns, lower ground covers, clintonias, and for a background, western azalea, rosebay rhododendron, or thimbleberry. The following are the three natives:

T. chloropetalum. Wake-robin. The flowers rise directly out of the leaves. The original species was described from the green-flowered races found near San Francisco Bay, but these are not particularly attractive for the garden. Other colors include deep maroon-red, pink-purple, and pure white. White forms from the north Coast Ranges have large flowers, and are stunning in a massed planting.

T. ovatum. Coast trillium. Distinguished by the flower rising on a short stalk above the leaves. Flowers open pure white, then fade deep rose at the end of a week. Large-flowered forms come from the Siskiyous of northwestern California.

T. rivale. Siskiyou trillium. This rare species is more curious than ornamental and lives on brushy scree slopes. Its small pinkish flowers are borne on stalks, as are the three leaves. Difficult to obtain.

Veratrum. Corn Lily, False Hellibore, False Skunk Cabbage. Lily family.

HT: in flower to 5 or 6 feet   FLW CL: white or green   FLW TM: July to October PRPG: root divisions or seeds (several years to flower)   EXP: varies   WT: summer wet

LITTLE ALPINE LILY—*Lilium parvum.*

The most familiar of the corn lilies is *V. californica* from Sierran meadows. At every stage they're distinctive: as snow melts, fat asparagus-like shoots appear; these turn into leafy stalks with large, conspicuously pleated, ovate leaves later topped by showy panicles of white flowers. The flowers, star-like in design, are borne by the dozens and are among the showiest sights of meadows in midsummer. Veratrums frequent the wettest spots, often lining rushing brooks next to aconites, fairy lily, larkspurs, and willow thickets. In the garden, the old growth needs to be cut back as soon as it turns brown; the food has then been carried to the roots for storage. The mountain species do best with winter rest.

Veratrums are bold specimen plants in mountain meadow gardens, behind ponds, or along partially shaded stream sides. They are poisonous, and so are not bothered by gophers or deer. Here are two species:

V. californicum. Common corn lily. The most typical large plant of mountain meadows. Flowers white, greenish in the middle.

V. fimbriatum. Fringed corn lily. Rare and restricted to the Sonoma and Mendocino coasts in shaded boggy places. Flowers white with yellow base; petals prettily fringed. Flowers in fall. Choice for the woodland garden.

Xerophyllum tenax. Beargrass, Squaw Grass. Lily family.

HT: in flower to more than 4 feet   FLW CL: white   FLW TM: May to August   PRPG: seeds (several years to flower); use burn treatment or stratify   EXP: full sun to light shade   WT: occasional deep summer water

Beargrass makes large fountains of curved, grass-like leaves to three feet and is handsome without flowers. It is a tough evergreen with masses of deeply-penetrating fibrous roots. The central flower stalk rises a foot or more above the leaves: a dense plume of hundreds of tiny cream-colored flowers. This should be cut off later as it browns. Beargrass ranges from the borders of coastal forests, on poor sandy and granitic soils, to brushy and meadowy slopes of the northern mountains. In the coastal locales it seldom flowers, and may disappear as taller plants shade it out; it moves in after fires, flowers, then declines. But in mountain meadows, plants flower by the hundreds in early summer, a truly magnificent sight.

It is unlikely that beargrass can be counted on to flower reliably in the home garden, although it is certainly worth experimenting with different kinds of soils and exposures. A shaded situation will not promote flowering, but the leaves are handsome on the edge of a woodland garden or around a pond. The leaves also lend texture to the mixed border and are green when others have died back.

Zygadenus. Zygadene, False Camass, Death Camass, Star-lily. Lily family.

HT: 8 inches to 3 feet   FLW CL: white or cream   FLW TM: March to June or July   PRPG: offsets or seeds (3 to 4 years to flower)   EXP: light shade (sun near coast)   WT: most, summer dry

The zygadenes have relatively large, poisonous bulbs. For this reason they are unlikely to be consumed by gophers in the garden as are so many of the other native bulbs. Zygadenes live in open woods and forests, on serpentine and talus slopes, or in wet meadows from sea level to the subalpine. Most do well in nearly full light as long as other requirements are met; these vary according to species. All need moisture through flowering, but then go dormant with a summer/fall dry period. (With pot culture, this means placing the pots in a cool, shaded, dry spot after the foliage has turned brown.) Some species tolerate summer water. All need good drainage and start life from basal clusters of several narrow, somewhat upfolded leaves. The inflorescence is either a raceme or panicle of cream-colored star-like flowers with curious yoke-shaped, yellow-green nectar glands at the base of the petals.

Only the showiest species are worthwhile. They may be displayed in potted arrangements with other native bulbs or by themselves, or in the middle to front of a mixed border. The small-flowered *Z. micranthus* (tiny-flowered zygadene) is on a scale for rock gardens, where it could be massed. Here are the best species for the garden:

Z. exaltatus. This is a robust species from the central Sierra foothill forests. Its flowers are not so large as those of *Z. fremontii*, but put on a good show; the inflorescence may branch and grow to four feet.

Z. fontanus. Fountain star-lily. Restricted to wet serpentine meadows, mostly to the north of San Francisco Bay. It blooms into June and is tolerant of summer water. It needs wet soil through flowering. The size of the inflorescence is comparable to that of *Z. fremontii*, but the individual flowers are somewhat smaller and with heart-shaped petals.

Z. fremontii. Fremont's star-lily. Common and reliable. Its star-like flowers are displayed for several days as the panicle opens buds from bottom to top. Robust specimens reach three feet or more at the peak of bloom. Summer dry.

Liveforever Family
(Crassulaceae)

This well-known family of succulents is represented in California by two genera worthy of garden culture. Many would combine with Mexican species of *Echeveria* and *Sedum* in a succulent garden.

Dudleya. Bluff Lettuce, Liveforever, Wild Hen-and-Chickens.
Liveforever family.

HT: with flowers, to two feet   FLW CL: white or yellow   FLW TM: May to July   PRPG: stem cuttings and divisions; seeds (very fine)   EXP: full sun, or light shade inland   WT: some summer water for best appearance

Dudleyas are universally admired leaf succulents closely related to the Mexican echeverias or hen-and-chickens. Most grow from rootstocks which penetrate rock crevices on bluffs and cliffs of interior foothills, coastal promontories, and desert mountains. All bear rosettes of fleshy leaves whose shapes range from broadly ovate to almost linear and from bright green to chalky white, often tipped red. Flower stalks grow from leaf axils and are from a few inches to two feet tall with candelabra-like clusters of starry white, pale yellow, bright yellow, or orange-red flowers. On some species, the flowers are hardly worth the notice, while on others the vivid colors complement the foliage. Dudleyas are evergreen, but the oldest leaves become brown and ragged and the older rootstocks elongate and become unsightly. Brown leaves should be trimmed off for best appearance.

Dudleyas are ideal for a succulent or rock garden. They are at home on a rock wall, in the interstices between rocks or along the top edge, and complement other leaf succulents such as the native sedums. They are surprisingly intolerant of drought in sandy soils; there the leaves shrivel in hot summer exposures. For best performance, they should get occasional summer water. They also do well as potted specimens in a well-drained potting soil top dressed with pebbles.

The many species listed in Munz are difficult to describe in detail. A few grow from underground corms and go dormant in the summer; others are too rare for consideration. Here are a few well-known species:

D. brittoni. This plant enters southernmost San Diego County and so is included. It grows on coastal cliffs of northern Baja, where its handsome rosettes adorn rock walls by the hundreds. The large rosettes are broad and green to gray with star-like pale yellow flowers.

D. cymosa. Grows on hot, interior cliffs with short rosettes of broad, drab-green leaves. The outstanding feature is the bright red-orange flowers in late spring.

D. farinosa. Bluff lettuce. The typical species of bluffs in central and northern California; leaves are lanceolate, often red-tipped, and either bright green or gray. The two forms make nice contrasts planted side by side. Flowers are small and light yellow.

D. pulverulenta. Chalk lettuce. This is the giant of the genus with rosettes of broad, chalky white leaves up to two feet across. The tall inflorescences bear small red flowers. A handsome specimen plant.

Sedum. Sedum, Stonecrop. Liveforever family.

HT: 3 to 8 inches   FLW CL: yellow, white, cream, deep red   FLW TM: varies   PRPG: cuttings, rooted sections, or seeds   EXP: full sun to light shade   WT: some summer water

All sedums are leaf succulents with pretty star-like flowers. Many are already well established in gardens, both for showy flowers or for their curious leaves. Most of the cultivated kinds come from the Old World and Mexico, leaving few of the natives in demand. All seek rocky slopes and cliff faces where roots cling to bits of moss and soil. They require good drainage, but look better if they are

CHALK DUDLEYA—*Dudleya pulverulenta.*

watered even during the dormant period. Otherwise, the leaves tend to shrivel, and in extreme cases, the whole plant dies. The tight rosettes of leaves, their patterns, and colors are reason enough to grow them, but sedums also add seasonal color with their yellow, white, or rosy flowers from late spring in the foothills to summer in the mountains. Most grow best in light shade; inland, they should never get full sun.

Because they grow low, sedums are best for edging borders, between stepping stones, in the fore of rock gardens, or along the edge of woodland gardens. Here are some likely candidates for the garden:

S. lanceolatum and *stenopetalum*. These two look so much alike, I'm including them together. Both form low, multibranched clumps of short upright leafy stalks, the leaves narrow and pointed and turning red-purple in the sun. As soils dry, each stalk sends up a cluster of showy yellow flowers but the leaves wither. With extra water, these leaves remain and plants look better but tend to be short lived. The first kind comes from lowland areas, and is sure to succeed in the ordinary garden, while the second comes from the subalpine and alpine where winter chill makes for healthier plants. Both are nice for a shaded rock garden with saxifrages and small ferns.

S. laxum. Pink stonecrop. From northwestern mountains. Bears such a profusion of pink flowers, it seems worthy of trial in the garden, although I have never grown it.

S. obtusatum. Sierra stonecrop. Grows in the subalpine on granite outcroppings, making low mounds of very fleshy, purple-green leaves. Flowers are less showy, being pale yellow, although a form from the northwest bears white flowers veined with red. Easy in the garden.

S. purdyi. Purdy's sedum. From the mountains of the northwestern corner of the state comes this little-known species. The pale green leaf rosettes look as though they had been compressed into a thin wafer, and the stems spread out close to the ground. Should be excellent in rock gardens.

S. rosea. Rosecrown. Another high-mountains species which grows among mossy rocks where snows linger long. Stout roots produce new upright bunches of stems each year with broad, bright green, rounded leaves topped by flat clusters of starry red-purple flowers. This is pretty even in fruit when the seed pods turn red-purple, imitating the flowers. Possibly not reliable in foothill gardens, but excellent in mountain rock gardens.

S. spathulifolium. Common stonecrop. This widespread species appears in many forms along rocky walls throughout the foothills and middle elevations. Near the coast, the leaves may be chalky white, or even white edged with red-purple, and some have been selected and grown under cultivar names. These are choice for leaf color and texture in the rock garden. In the central Sierra, forms with vivid green leaves were once called *S. yosemitense*. For a stunning effect in the garden, grow different leaf colors side by side. All bear open cymes of bright yellow star-like flowers.

Lizardtail Family
(Saururaceae)

This curious, little-known family is represented by a few disjunct, relict genera from North America and Asia; we have but a single species in California.

Anemopsis californica. Yerba Mansa. Lizardtail family.
HT: in flower to 8 inches   FLW CL: white, green center   FLW TM: May to July   PRPG: rooted stolons   EXP: mostly light shade   WT: summer wet

This is a curious plant, one of only 12 species in the entire family. It occurs in southern California along seeps, stream edges, and wet meadows, especially where the soil is slightly alkaline. The light green, rounded leaves form handsome low rosettes which send out, in strawberry fashion, long bright red runners. Soon a whole colony is established. But yerba mansa really shines when the single "flowers" are carried above the leaves in great numbers in late spring. Each "flower" is, in fact, a collection, the base surrounded by large, showy white bracts with a central cone-like spike of tiny greenish flowers.

Yerba mansa comes from such a specialized habitat that it would seem to have limited use in the garden, but the roots do not require an alkaline pH (decidedly acid soil will slow the spread of the plant) and once established are surprisingly amenable to ordinary watering. Yerba mansa is attractive in front of a pond, as a coarse ground cover where it is not trampled, or in a meadow of short grasses. It is definitely an asset where soil pH is above 7.

Loosestrife Family
(Lythraceae)

There are many attractive loosestrifes native to North America, but in California we have but one worthy species, below. Other natives in the family are weedy or are not particularly attractive.

Lythrum californicum. California Loosestrife. Loosestrife family.
HT: in flower to 3 or 4 feet   FLW CL: purple   FLW TM: April to October   PRPG: divisions or seeds   EXP: full sun   WT: wet all year

The lythrums are a widely varied group, but few people know of our California species. At least one is an introduced weed which is especially bothersome in gardens with temporarily wet soil: *L. hyssopifolium*. But our true native lives in seeps, springs, and oases throughout the state, often accompanying brook orchid and sticky columbine. Its roots send up several long, wand-like stems, clothed with short ovate leaves below and with spikes of attractive purple flowers above. As is common in the family, petals have a crinkled appearance.

CALIFORNIA LOOSESTRIFE—*Lythrum californicum.*

California loosestrife is easy with plenty of moisture and may be somewhat invasive, but is easily controlled.

Plant loosestrife in the back of a watered border or behind a pond or moist meadow. Other good companions include annual Indian paintbrush, wild roses, and goldenrods.

Mallow Family
(Malvaceae)

There are many ornamental mallows in the world, some perennial and some, such as the hibiscuses, woody. The number of natives is limited here because so many are shrubs (genera *Malacothamnus* and *Lavatera*, for example), or are annuals (such as *Malvastrum* and *Hibiscus californica*).

Sidalcea. Checkerbloom, Wild Hollyhock. Mallow family.

HT: 6 to 18 inches   FLW CL: purple or pink   FLW TM: varies   PRPG: divisions   EXP: full sun   WT: mountain kinds need summer water

Sidalceas come in two forms: annuals of foothills and perennials of grasslands and meadows. Although there are several species of the perennial kind, most are difficult to identify, and some have restricted habitats (and are rare and endangered). The perennials have creeping rootstocks or rhizomes to which they go dormant from summer through fall according to locality. Rhizomes bear dense tufts of dark green, rounded, shallowly palmately lobed leaves, from which rise the flowering racemes from spring to summer—again according to locale. Leaf shape changes dramatically up the stalk, the higher cauline leaves deeply lobed or digitately divided, like fingers on a hand. The flowers are showy, of typical mallow or hollyhock construction, and of various shades of purple or pink. Most species grow low to the ground and should be placed in the front of a mixed border and given room to spread. Here are a few:

S. glaucescens. Mountain checkerbloom. Common component of dry meadows of middle to subalpine zones. The open racemes are pale purple and flower in summer. Summer moisture.

S. malvaeflora. Common checkerbloom. Common species of coastal grasslands and prairies, and a reliable middle spring flower which accompanies poppies, baby-blue-eyes, cream cups, and blue-eyed grasses. It can get by with little summer water. The flowers are pink-purple but different races vary as to flower size. The bisexual flowers are bigger and showier than the male sterile kinds (without pollen-bearing stamens).

S. rhizomata. Pt. Reyes checkerbloom. This rare species might be perpetuated in a wet garden, such as by a pond. The rhizomes range widely and bear handsome pink flowers in late spring.

S. spicata. Mountain hollyhock. The other common mountain species, favoring

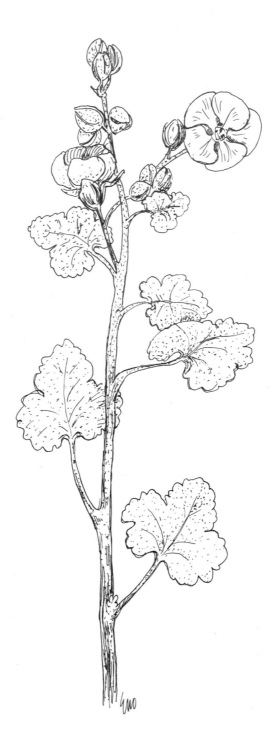

WILD HOLLYHOCK—*Sidalcea malvaeflora.*

wet meadows and stream margins. Its flowers are in tight spikes and are deep pink-purple. Very striking with paintbrushes and whorled penstemons.

Sphaeralcea ambigua. Apricot Mallow. Mallow family.

HT: to 3 feet   FLW CL: apricot orange   FLW TM: April to May   PRPG: seeds   EXP: full sun   WT: summer dry

Most of the bushier mallows are true shrubs, but this one is so weakly woody—the majority of stems greenish—that it can be considered a perennial. Apricot mallow is a stunning bush of middle to high deserts, blooming according to elevation from April through May. The weak stems range widely, some sprawling, the whole plant seldom exceeding three feet. The broad, rounded leaves are closely felted with hairs, and the branches end in wand-like racemes of apricot-orange flowers. In full bloom, it is stunning. It must have sandy soil, plenty of sun and heat, but needs periodic summer water its first summer. It is unlikely to thrive in a coastal garden, and will be short lived in cultivation.

Give apricot mallow plenty of room in the middle or mid-high zone of the mixed border with lots of sun and a loose soil. The unusual flower color contrasts well with bright yellow and blue-purple flowers such as desert aster (*Machaeranthera tortifolia*) and Panamint daisy (*Enceliopsis*).

Milkweed Family
(Asclepiadaceae)

The milkweed family is well represented around the warmer parts of the globe, but California's only notable native genus is *Asclepias*, given below.

Asclepias. Milkweed. Milkweed family.

HT: 1 to 4 feet   FLW CL: purple, red-purple   FLW TM: May to August   PRPG: seed   EXP: full sun to light shade   WT: late summer to early fall, dry; winter dormant

Milkweeds are herbaceous perennials with a winter dormancy. There are several kinds, most of which grow in hard, rocky soils from open forests to desert washes. Many thrive where there is little competition such as on talus slopes near watercourses. All spring from thick, perennial rootstocks which are difficult to transplant; they should be started from seed. In the garden, they must have well-drained soil. It is important to note that some are invasive with summer water and spring up in unexpected places by widely wandering roots.

Not all milkweeds are attractive, although most have interesting leaves. They go well in mixed borders, although *A. cordifolia* needs light shade. Some have furry, silver-gray leaves which contrast nicely with bright green leaves of neighbor plants. Some have showy umbels of white to purple flowers which are especially attractive to bumblebees and butterflies. In addition, some serve as food for the caterpillars of the beautiful monarch butterfly. Here are a few handsome species:

COMMON MILKWEED—*Asclepias.*

A. californica. California milkweed. Has broad, wooly white leaves. It should have excellent drainage, dry summers, and full sun, and grows best inland. Umbels of purple flowers complement the leaves in May or June.

A. cordifolia. Heartleaf milkweed. Has broad heart-shaped, glaucous leaves which are a beautiful red-purple when they first come up. The umbels bear many red-purple and white flowers in May and June. Light shade.

A. speciosa. Showy milkweed. Has broad pale green leaves and wandering roots. It does well in full sun and bears showy clusters of large purplish flowers through summer.

Mint Family
(Labiatae or Lamiaceae)

This is an important family in areas with a Mediterranean climate, and many of our culinary herbs belong here. Since California's climate is Mediterranean, it goes almost without saying that the state is richly represented by them. Several are chaparral shrubs, not included here.

Agastache urticifolia. Horsemint. Mint family.

HT: 18 inches to 3 feet   FLW CL: white to purple with red-purple bracts   FLW TM: June to August   PRPG: divisions or seeds   EXP: light shade   WT: through the year

This is an altogether delightful member of the mint family, increasing steadily by underground rootstocks but neither overly aggressive nor shy. The leafy stems rise to two or three feet with glossy green, toothed, and pleasantly aromatic leaves which end in whorls of purple or pink-purple mint-like flowers. These plants live in wet meadows and stream sides in the mountains, but some may grow as low as 3,000 to 4,000 feet and thus are amenable to lowland gardens. They are winter dormant and need full light and summer water.

Horsemint would be attractive in the middle of a mixed border. It is especially pretty in bud with the red-purple bracts surrounding the flowers. It is also fine massed with other mountain meadow flowers, such as mountain bluebells, columbine, butterwort, and larkspurs.

Monardella. Western Pennyroyal, Coyote Mint. Mint family.

HT: 6 to 18 inches   FLW CL: purple, white, red   FLW TM: June to September   PRPG: cuttings or divisions or seeds   EXP: full sun   WT: drought tolerant

Monardellas are seldom mentioned as garden material, yet many are of easy culture and flower profusely. The genus is characterized by flowers borne in dense heads surrounded by bracts, the individual flowers with slender tubes and narrow petal lobes—like a colorful pincushion. Bees and butterflies are both fond of these flowers. The species range from ephemeral annuals to subwoody, branched perennials, and several are so rare as to be inappropriate for discussion here. Leaves are elliptical and rounded, borne in pairs and highly fragrant, and may be brewed as an herbal tea. Monardellas are typically found on sunny, rocky slopes in chaparral, open woodlands, or on sand dunes, and range from sea level to timberline. In the garden, they are drought tolerant, preferring sunny warm to hot exposures, and rot in winter if they have poor drainage. The leaves are evergreen, but the old flower heads need to be removed and the branches pruned back to keep a neat, compact appearance.

Monardellas work nicely in the herb garden, in the middle section of a mixed border, in a large-scale rock garden, or in front of drought-tolerant shrubs. Their profusion of bloom is an asset in summer months, and may continue into fall. The blue- and purple-flowered kinds blend well with eriophyllums, and later with hummingbird fuchsias. Here are five ornamental species:

M. crispa. Nipomo coyote mint. This is a rare endemic of the gigantic sand dunes between Pt. Conception and Pismo Beach. It is mentioned because it deserves to be perpetuated in the garden as well as saved in the wild. It is a low bushy plant with fleshy, aromatic leaves, and attractive purple flowers. It is also wind and salt tolerant.

M. macrantha. Hummingbird mint, scarlet coyote mint. This striking species has creeping rootstocks and eventually creates sizable colonies. It must have excellent drainage. The leaves stay close to the ground, are glossy green, and the large flower heads have long, tubular red-orange flowers. Outstanding if you can find a good color form (some have a weak, washed out orange). A hummingbird flower, and easy in containers.

M. odoratissima. Mountain pennyroyal, mountain coyote mint. Another variable species with many subspecies. It grows in sandy soils in the openings of coniferous forests from the middle to subalpine elevations. The stems form large mats about a foot high. In summer these are covered with flower heads whose color ranges from near white to bright blue-purple. The darker colors are showier, but the pale ones contrast well with other blue and purple flowers. True to its name, the leaves are highly fragrant.

M. villosa. Common coyote mint. This variable species is found throughout the foothill country and has several subspecies. The stems branch to form a small subshrub to two feet with fuzzy leaves. Flowers are purple to blue-purple and bloom a long time. Use in the mixed border or in front of shrubs.

M. viridis. Inhabits hot dry foothills of the inner north Coast Ranges and is especially appropriate for inland gardens. The stems rise only to one foot with leaves green above and white and hairy below. The showy flowers are rose-purple. Blooms late summer.

Salvia. Sage. Mint family.

HT: 8 to 18 inches   FLW CL: blue, rose-purple   FLW TM: March to June   PRPG: divisions, rooted sections, or seeds   EXP: full sun to light shade   WT: varies

We are lucky to have many attractive native sages; most are shrubs, and a few are annual. Only two kinds qualify as perennial herbs, but since their habitats differ, they will be described separately below. Salvias are characterized by aromatic leaves, the smell varying from overpowering to rather pleasant. Their leaves have interesting textures, and the flowers are borne in tiered whorls. Sage honey is tasty and is an added feature for growing salvias for the bee-keeper. The two perennials are:

S. sonomensis. Sonoma sage. This interesting sage has long, trailing stems bearing numerous short, upright leafy stems. In its native habitat it seeks out rocky slopes where the stems drape down and festoon precipitous banks. This species must have good drainage and should not be over-watered once established. Plants have a tendency to rot otherwise. Sonoma sage proves excellent for checking soil erosion and prospers in soils low in nutrients. The dusky green leaves have a wrinkled texture and are strongly scented; the flower spikes bear tiers of blue-purple flowers to about a foot. Excellent for the foreground of drought-tolerant shrubs, as a coarse ground cover, or in the herb garden.

S. spathacea. Pitcher sage, hummingbird sage. This species has creeping rhizomes, in lightly wooded areas of central and southern California coastal mountains. It is frequent in oak woodlands. The upright stems bear several pairs of broad, beautifully quilted light green leaves of pleasant aroma. Flower spikes appear in middle to late spring, rising above the leaves to two or three feet. The rather large flowers are protected by robust sepals, and have long, tubular, rose-pink petals which are hummingbird favorites. In the garden, the woodland setting is best except near the immediate coast, where this sage could be used in the middle of a mixed border. Better with light summer water. Flowering stalks tend to be weak and sometimes need support.

Satureja. Yerba Buena, Wild Savory. Mint family.

HT: 1 to 12 inches   FLW CL: white or red   FLW TM: April to October   PRPG: rooted section or cuttings   EXP: light shade   WT: some summer water

Yerba buena is the famous trailing mint relative which used to be so plentiful in San Francisco that the city bore that name. It prefers the interface between forest and scrub, or forest and coastal prairie, not far from the sea. The plant is slow to become established and requires moisture through the first summer. Once it is settled in, it forms a pretty ground cover for low foot traffic. The bright green, rounded leaves have tiny scallops along their margins and have a delicious mint fragrance and make a good herbal tea. The flowers are tiny white two-lipped affairs borne in the axils of leaves. A second species of *Satureja* occurs along creek banks in the mountains of southern California; it has orange-red flowers and is a clump-forming perennial.

   Yerba buena (*S. douglasii*) makes a marvelous ground cover for the coastal shade garden. It combines well with other low growers such as modesty and woodland strawberry. The red-flowered wild savory (*S. mimuloides*) is poorly known, and deserves a trial in the woodland garden or by a shaded pond.

Scutellaria. Skullcap. Mint family.

HT: in flower 3 to 12 inches   FLW CL: blue, purple, white   FLW TM: varies   PRPG: offsets (some spp.) or root divisions   EXP: light shade to full sun   WT: some summer water

The skullcaps are a charming group of native mints, little known in gardens. They are low herbs from creeping, underground rootstocks or tubers, and spread to form loose colonies, but are seldom invasive. The leaves lack the usual strong odor associated with mints, and die back during the short days of the year. The colorful snapdragon-like flowers are borne in leaf axils from late spring through summer. Most have white or purple petals. In fruit, the sepals form an old-fashioned skullcap around the nutlets; hence the common name. Skullcaps grow along the edge of open woods or brushy areas on steep banks where they have few competitors. One species lives in swamps and wet meadows, but the others receive little summer water, although their season in the garden will be prolonged with water.

Because of their low stature (seldom over one foot), the skullcaps are best suited to the front of a lightly shaded border or in the rock garden. Allow space for the colony to spread, since the flower show is better that way. *S. californica* and *S. tuberosa* might also be nice on a mossy bank of a woodland garden with small ferns and saxifrages. Here is a brief listing of species:

S. antirrhinoides. Much like *S. californica*, but with blue-purple flowers.

S. austinae. Another blue-purple flowered species from foothill and middle elevations of the southern California mountains and Sierra.

S. bolanderi. Rhizomatous with thin, triangular leaves and white flowers. Foothill woodlands of the Sierra.

S. californica. Taller than most with attractive white snapdragon flowers. From dry, rocky soils in open foothill and middle elevation forests.

S. galericulata. Pretty blue flowers from stoloniferous rootstocks. Middle elevations in northern mountain meadows and swamps.

S. siphocampyloides. Rather tall with sticky stems and deep violet-purple flowers. From open, dry woods of the Sierra foothills and inner Coast Ranges.

S. tuberosa. Tuberous roots, fuzzy, sticky foliage, and showy, fuzzy purple flowers. From foothill woods of central and northern California.

Stachys. Woodmint, Hedge Nettle. Mint family.

HT: 8 inches to 5 or 6 feet   FLW CL: purple, white, rose-purple   FLW TM: varies   PRPG: root division   EXP: most, light shade   WT: some summer water

The several species are aggressive mint relatives from woodlands and forests throughout the foothill and middle elevations. Many are difficult to identify

SKULLCAP—*Scutellaria.*

without the aid of a good hand lens. As a group, they are fall/winter dormant, and increase in size rapidly from creeping rootstocks. They may be controlled by digging out the unwanted pieces or sections, but some are quite invasive when given summer water. The opposite leaves are fuzzy with a quilted pattern of veins, and with a distinctive odor all their own. In fact, they share this odor with a European species in cultivation, the lamb's ears (*S. olympica*). They range from low ground-cover-like plants less than a foot high to robust kinds up to six feet tall. Although the leaves may look nettle-like, they do not sting. The flowers, two-lipped and decorative at close range, are borne in circular whorls above the leaves.

Woodmints are good for naturalizing in areas receiving little care, and add a pleasant note to the woodland garden. They will never win renown for spectacular flowers but a couple of species are noteworthy for certain special features. The commonest species, *S. rigida*, *S. ajugoides*, *S. bullata*, and *S. quercetorum*, follow the comments above.

S. albens. Wooly woodmint or hedge nettle. This is a tall native version of lamb's ears with soft wool-covered stems and leaves of a gray-green color. These are attractive in spring when they first emerge from the ground. Whorls of white flowers top two- to three-foot stalks in summer. Full sun. Stake when in flower and cut back after.

S. chamissonis. Coast woodmint or hedge nettle. This is the tallest and rankest of all, but excellent for naturalizing quickly in constantly wet, shaded spots. It must be kept from getting out of hand, but in containers is nice with native lilies, aralias, and azaleas. The five- to six-foot flower stalks bear uncommonly large red-purple flowers.

Morning Glory Family
(Convolvulaceae)

Here is a well-known family of subtropical and tropical vines; our familiar garden morning glory is of such origin. Unfortunately, wild morning glories have earned an unsavory reputation because of the particularly aggressive introduced bindweed, but the genus below has some real horticultural possibilities.

Calystegia. Wild Morning Glory. Morning glory family.

HT: vines to many feet   FLW CL: white, cream, purple   FLW TM: May to September   PRPG: seed (soak first)   EXP: mostly full sun   WT: some summer water

The old name for the wild morning glories was *Convolvulus*, and many books still refer to them by that name. Calystegias are basically vines, but there is considerable difference in habitat and the way in which the vininess manifests itself. These vines grow rapidly and wind themselves around other plants, but they are

MORNING GLORY—*Calystegia.*

easily subdued; in contrast the European pestiferous bindweed springs from deep rootstocks which divide and redivide, making eradication almost impossible. The native viny species have a discrete central root; the ambitious stems may be pruned back to their woody bases.

Calystegias range from seashore to middle elevations, most often as seekers of light on the edge of woodlands and chaparral. The climbing kinds grow swiftly in order to reach the sun. Several bury or partially bury their main stems, forming wide-ranging ground covers instead of climbing vines; these grow in open, fully lighted situations. All go dormant in winter, and the old unsightly growth must be then removed. New sprouts appear the following spring, and plants are in full flower by late spring or early summer. The prolific flowering, large flower size, and attractive morning glory shape suggest a wider use in wild gardens, but allowances must be made for the growth cycle, the vigor of the plants, and the period without foliage. Climbing species are effective in the way of garden morning glories—up trellises, over cottages, and against walls. Creeping kinds fill spaces between stepping stones, spill over a rock wall, or front a rock garden.

There are several climbing calystegias with closely similar habits and flowers. These include *C. occidentalis* from north and central California, *C. cyclostegius* from central to southern California, and *C. macrostegius* from the Channel Islands. The latter two are superior in flower size and abundance of bloom; some forms have white flowers flushed with pink. Ground cover types include *C. malacophyllus* and *C. subacaulis*, both with large white to cream flowers, the former with wooly gray leaves. Both need frequent watering for establishment. The most distinctive is *C. soldanella* from coastal sand dunes—it has nearly round, dark green leaves and decorative flowers of pale purple striped with deep red-purple. This latter kind must have excellent drainage and is unlikely to prosper in summer hot areas.

Mustard Family
(Cruciferae or Brassicaceae)

This large family is well represented in California, but horticulturally many of the species are less than showy. For this reason, the genera included are only those felt to have garden merit. To be sure, some of the mountain members such as *Draba* might have been included, but their specialized requirements make them seem undesirable.

Arabis. Rockcress. Mustard family.

HT: most from a few inches to 18 inches   FLW CL: purple, rose, or white   FLW TM: variable   PRPG: divisions or seeds (stratify high-elevation species)   EXP: full sun to light shade inland   WT: some summer water

Arabises are mostly plants of rocky situations: coastal bluffs, exposed rocks in the chaparral, or rock pockets in the high mountains. They are anchored by taproots which penetrate between rocks; these are topped by leaf rosettes from which spring one or more flowering stalks a few inches high. The stalks may be leafless or the leaves are gradually reduced as they ascend. Flowers are in loose to dense racemes, individually small. Few bear showy enough flowers to merit a place in the garden, although some have interesting seed pods which are often showier than the flowers. Seed pods are long and narrow, but vary from straight to broadly arched, and from strictly upright to widely spreading.

The coast rockcress, *A. blepharophylla*, is exceptional for its large spring flowers of intense pink-purple. It is ideal for the front of a rock garden or for low edging of a mixed border, but performs best near the coast. Inland, it needs summer water especially in well-drained soils. It can also be grown as a potted plant.

One rockcress relative deserves mention here—the spear-pod (*Phoenicaulis cheiranthoides*), with low, woody crowns covered with gray-green leaves. Its flower stalks reach 12 inches in summer, with attractive light purple flowers followed by flattened, lance-shaped, sharply pointed pods. Propagation is as for arabis.

Dentaria. Milkmaids, Toothwort, Pepper Root. Mustard family.

HT: with flowers to 12 or 15 inches   FLW CL: white to purple   FLW TM: February to June   PRPG: offsets or seeds   EXP: mostly shade   WT: some summer water

Milkmaids are among the earliest of flowers, often appearing in late winter woods or forest edges on mossy banks. Given a large planting of various races from various locales, the flowering season extends through April. Occurring with milkmaids and flowering later are buttercups, shooting stars, collinsias, red larkspur, fritillaries, and hound's tongue. Milkmaids are perennials from underground tubers the size of a pearl. They form colonies from these tubers, but the tubers are eaten by gophers and other animals. Plants make two kinds of leaves shortly after the first rains begin. Some bear broad, nearly round leaves close to the ground; others make compound or deeply lobed leaves divided into lance-shaped segments. These gradually become narrower up the flowering stalk. Only the latter bear flowers; the others are taking a rest for the season, but should flower the following year. The racemes bear open, bell-shaped flowers which vary from white to light pink or purple.

Milkmaids must be massed for good effect. They are ideal for a mossy slope on the edge of a shaded spot or near the coast, in full sun along the front of a border. They complement buttercups, shooting stars, and early bulbs. They can also grow in a bluff garden behind coast rockcress and sea thrift. The mountain species should be tried in a meadow. They need summer water with drainage.

The common name milkmaids is most often reserved for the common species, *D. californica*. Two others are worth trying in the garden: *D. pachystigma*, mountain milkmaids, grows in moist, well-drained mountain meadows of the north Coast Ranges and has pinkish flowers and handsome, glaucous foliage. It flowers late spring to early summer as snows melt. *Dentaria gemmata*, Siskiyou

WALLFLOWER—*Erysimum grandiflorum.*

milkmaids, is a choice species from the extreme northwestern corner of the state, where it grows on shaded banks and flowers in June. Flowers are a deep, rich purple.

Erysimum. Wallflower. Mustard family.

HT: 6 to 18 inches　FLW CL: yellow, orange, cream　FLW TM: March to July　PRPG: seeds (fast and easy)　EXP: sun or light shade inland　WT: some summer water

Our native wallflowers are short-lived perennials—most often biennials—capable of blooming their first year when started by early fall. Most grow on sand dunes and ocean bluffs, but a couple wander inland onto steep slopes of foothill woodlands or the granite sands of high-mountain forests. All start life as rosettes with long taproots, but as the flowering stalks emerge, the leaves are carried along. Flowers appear in tight racemes or panicles with a long succession of bloom; stalks often bear buds at the top, flowers in the middle, and seed pods below. Flowers are large and showy, and many are fragrant at close range.

Wallflowers are easy to grow from seed and so can be treated as annuals for the mixed garden border. They thrive on sun, good drainage, and moderate water. Most have completed seeding by late spring and should be cut back then, or started anew the following fall. Young plants are vulnerable to snails, slugs, and the like. They are effective when massed for bright color in the border, although some of the low coastal kinds are also good as single specimens in a rock garden setting with other bluff plants, such as sea thrift, coast rockcress, dudleyas, and eriophyllums. Here is a brief description of some good species:

E. capitatum. Foothill wallflower. Inland foothills from oak woodland to the yellow pine belt. Flower color ranges from yellow to orange; late spring. Nice contrasts with blue-purple lupines and collinsias or yellow composites.

E. concinnum. Bluff wallflower. Closely related to *E. franciscanum*; flowers cream color; plants low; from coastal bluffs and sand dunes. Early to mid spring.

E. franciscanum. Franciscan wallflower. From Bay Area coastal bluffs. Flower color ranges from light to dark yellow, often changing as flowers age. Early spring.

E. menziesii. Menzie's wallflower. From the northern sand dunes. Flowers slightly smaller than Franciscan and bluff wallflowers, and bright yellow. Late spring.

E. perenne. Mountain wallflower. Middle to subalpine zones on forest edges. Flowers are large, bright yellow, closer to the ground than is *E. capitatum*.

Lesquerella. Bladderpod. Mustard family.

HT: a few inches　FLW CL: yellow　FLW TM: May to July　PRPG: seeds (better germination if stratified)　EXP: full sun　WT: some summer water with excellent drainage

Lesquerellas are the tidiest of rock garden plants. A taproot is topped by circles of gray-green leaves which hug the ground; as the plant ages, it sends out new circles around the parent. In early summer, flower stalks emerge from the rosettes to bear short racemes of bright yellow, mustard-like blooms. At their peak on open scree, they look like yellow stepping stones, similar in effect to the coastal footsteps-to-spring. Flowers are followed by small, inflated balloon-like seed pods.

Lesquerellas grow from the subalpine to alpine throughout the dry talus and scree of mountains. The few species look closely similar. They are not for the average garden, and need a combination of sharp drainage with loose gravel around the root crown and winter chill. Coastal gardens are poor places for these charming alpines.

Stanleya. Prince's Plume. Mustard family.

HT: in flower to 5 or 6 feet (or more) FLW CL: yellow FLW TM: spring PRPG: seeds EXP: full sun WT: occasional summer water with excellent drainage

The stanleyas lend elegance and grace by their form. They are desert perennials which grow on stony slopes and sandy soils, the leaves mostly basal on low, branched subwoody crowns, the flowering stalks towering above and carrying racemes of bright yellow flowers reminiscent of cleomes or spider flowers. The leaves vary from being entire and broadly elliptical to pinnately divided: *S. elata* has entire leaves and comes from the high desert mountains around and north of Death Valley; *S. pinnata* is more typical of the western edges of the Mojave and Colorado deserts. Both need excellent drainage in the garden and plenty of heat and sun.

The tall showy racemes of flowers place stanleyas in the back of a dry mixed border, in front of chaparral shrubs, or better yet, in drifts in a desert garden beside cacti, yuccas, or agaves.

Nightshade Family
(Solanaceae)

This mostly subtropical/tropical family is represented in California by a number of desert annuals (*Nicotiana*) and desert shrubs (*Lycium*) in addition to the two genera mentioned here.

Chamaesaracha nana. False Nightshade. Nightshade family.

HT: 6 to 10 inches FLW CL: white with green and yellow center FLW TM: June to July PRPG: seeds (scarify or give acid treatment) EXP: full sun WT: occasional deep summer water

False nightshade is closely related to the true solanums or nightshades and have flowers of similar pattern: five completely fused petals arranged as a wheel with green glands at the base, and central yellow stamens, followed by fleshy berries. The rootstocks, dormant in winter, send out circles of half-sprawling leafy branches, each year the circle growing larger. Leaves are solanum-like, entire and ovate. False nightshade lives at mid-elevations in the openings of coniferous forests in northeastern California where climate is quite arid. In the garden it should have excellent drainage, and occasional water for best appearance.

False nightshade would make an interesting ground cover where foot traffic is not a problem, or sprawled and draped over a rock garden. It performs best with winter chill.

Solanum. Nightshade, Blue Witch. Nightshade family.

HT: 6 inches to 3 feet   FLW CL: blue, purple, or white with yellow center   FLW TM: April to July   PRPG: seeds (acid treatment) and rooted layers   EXP: light shade to full sun   WT: varies

Our solanums fall into several groups: introduced herbaceous weeds, native herbaceous perennials, and perennial subshrubs. It is the perennial subshrubs which put on the best show and have the most ornamental qualities. The several species and many varieties are basically similar in the appearance of their flowers and fruits, but the stature varies. All are woody at the base with green-woody branches, bear simple, elliptical to oval leaves, and in season, a profusion of small umbels of light blue to deep blue-purple flowers. The flowers are open saucer shape, the five petals nearly fused into a single piece, with a lovely pattern of green nectar glands on a white background at their base. These are complemented by a cone of bright yellow stamens in the center. In the garden, some become straggly and pruning is needed to maintain a tight bush shape. One species sprawls close to the ground, and is more effective as a ground cover. All are prone to rotting in wet cold winters, all tend to flower a little most of the year with extra water—although they are quite drought tolerant—and all need full sun.

For garden uses, the two taller subshrubs (to four or more feet) are best for the back of a mixed border or with lower drought-tolerant foundation shrubs—prickly phlox, for example—but the sprawling kinds are fine in the front of a border given the room to spread circular mats. They combine well with the lower growing lupines. Finally, one herbaceous perennial is suitable for shaded woodland gardens of southern California. Here are five species:

S. douglasii. Douglas's nightshade. Closely related to the introduced black nightshade, but this is native to southern coastal oak and riparian woodlands. It is strictly herbaceous, with many branches, bears triangular leaves and nodding, white to purplish, star-like flowers. It is attractive in full flower, naturalized with companions such as canyon sunflower, meadowrue, and Humboldt lily.

S. parishii. Mountain or Parish's nightshade. From the mid-elevations of the northern mountains, this kind sprawls, is hairless, and usually bears light blue flowers of smaller size, but is very floriferous.

S. umbelliferum. Blue witch. The most widespread, especially common in the foothills of central and northern California on chaparral's edge. Leaves are hairy but not glandular, flowers moderately large, mostly blue to blue-purple.

S. wallacei. Island nightshade. From the Channel Islands, with a tendency to sprawl more than *S. umbelliferum* or *S. xantii.* Foliage rather hairy and sticky (many

VIOLET NIGHTSHADE—*Solanum xantii.*

glands), and flowers especially large and showy, of similar color. Cold tender.

S. xantii. Blue witch. Often intergrading with *S. umbelliferum,* and with flowers of similar color, but more typical of the coastal scrub and chaparral of southern California. Leaves hairy, but the hairs forked.

Orchid Family
(Orchidaceae)

Although the orchids are most often thought of as tropical, there are many terrestrial and saprophytic orchids native to North America. Many of California's orchids are small-flowered and not well suited to garden use (for example, many of the habenarias, spiranthes, and listeras). Others have been excluded because of their exacting cultural requirements.

Epipactis gigantea. Brook Orchid, Stream Orchid, Chatter-Box. Orchid family.

HT: 12 to 18 inches   FLW CL: combinations of pink, brown, green, and yellow   FLW TM: May to July   PRPG: divisions   EXP: shade   WT: moist all year

Brook orchid is the single most satisfactory member of the orchid family for garden culture. There are other showier orchids, such as the cypripediums (lady slippers) and fairy slipper (*Calypso bulbosa*), but these are so rare and difficult to grow that they are not recommended.

Brook orchid has a wide range from north to south, even entering desert oases, and occurs over much of the western states. Its habitat is year-round seeps or the edge of permanent water-courses from low to middle elevations. The tough, branched roots seek out crevices between boulders, where they gradually widen the colony each year. In time, a colony may produce dozens of flowering stalks. Winter dormant, the new shoots appear in late spring, the lanceolate leaves closely resembling those of Solomon's plume. By late spring or early summer, each stalk produces a loose raceme of horizontally held, curious orchid flowers with subtle combinations of color, the exact combination varying from population to population. As the common name chatter-box indicates, the lip is hinged, and moves up and down in a breeze.

Brook orchid should be planted where there is good drainage, year-round moisture (but not soggy soil), and dappled shade for part of the day. It naturalizes beautifully around ponds or by streams and can also be incorporated into a woodland garden with, for example, trilliums, lilies, and violets.

Habenaria. Snowy Rein Orchid, Milk Orchid, Bog Orchid. Orchid family.

HT: 1 to 2 feet   FLW CL: white or green   FLW TM: June to August   PRPG: divisions EXP: light shade in hot areas   WT: some all year

STREAM ORCHID—*Epipactis gigantea.*

Of the several species of *Habenaria*, few are suitable to gardens, since their tiny flowers are often greenish, and the leaves on many have dried up before the flowers appear. But *Habenaria dilatata* is showier and easy to grow, so merits consideration. It has vigorous stems to 18 inches clothed with fleshy, lance-ovate leaves, topped by a tight raceme of snowy white flowers, each small flower like a miniature spurred orchid. The snowy rein orchid is fond of permanently wet meadows, and is common along streamlets. Although some populations occur along the north coast, most come from middle to high mountains and are therefore winter dormant and summer flowering. The best strains for the garden are those from low-elevation bogs, such as on Pt. Reyes peninsula. The fleshy rootstocks gradually increase the clump each year in the manner of many liliaceous plants.

Snowy rein orchid needs specific garden conditions: wet soil, room to spread, and inland, protection from the hot summer sun. Its best use is along a pond or stream, combined with brook orchid, lilies, veratrums, larkspurs, and small-to medium-sized ferns. Other mountain meadow companions include monkshood, swamp onion, and ranger's buttons.

Oxalis Family
(*Oxalidaceae*)

The oxalises are represented by a single genus in California, described below.

Oxalis oregana. Redwood Sorrel. Oxalis or sorrel family.

HT: to 6 or 8 inches   FLW CL: white, purple, pink   FLW TM: mostly spring   PRPG: rooted sections   EXP: shade   WT: some summer water

There is only one species of *Oxalis* suitable for the garden. Others are either inconspicuous or are noxious, introduced weeds, such as the creeping *Oxalis corniculata* and the bulbous "Bermuda buttercup," *O. pes-caprae*. Redwood sorrel is a low ground cover in the shadiest of coastal forests where summers remain cool and moist. It is the single most characteristic cover under the giant virgin coast redwoods, and grows with violets, wild ginger, sword fern, and various lily relatives. The plants quickly increase by horizontal, shallow rootstocks, each new bud growing into a short rosette of trifoliate leaves, the leaflets much like clover. Unlike clover, the leaflets fold in sunny weather and have a sour, acidic taste. Leaves are quite handsome—dark green with a pale, whitish splotch at the base and red-violet on the underside. The flowers mostly appear in spring on separate stalks among or slightly above the leaves and vary from white to purple. The vivid purple kinds are the showiest, and go well in the company of violets, trilliums, erythroniums, and star flowers.

Obviously, redwood sorrel is best suited to the foreground or as a ground cover in the woodland garden; it does well with summer water. It has the advantage of attractive foliage all year, as does its frequent companion wild ginger (*Asarum caudatum*), and is easy to control, since the rootstocks are shallow.

Parsley Family

(*Umbelliferae* or *Apiaceae*)

This large, important family consists mostly of perennials, but many of them are poorly known or would be considered unsightly for the garden, either because they are too coarse and weedy or because they lack showy flowers. Nonetheless, the list of genera and species below gives an indication of some of the possibilities from this little-used family.

Angelica. Angelica. Parsley or umbel family.

HT: in flower 3 to 5 feet   FLW CL: white   FLW TM: June to September   PRPG: seeds   EXP: full sun to light shade   WT: some summer water

Angelicas are the truly large plants with stout taproots, pinnately compound leaves often more than a foot long, and sturdy flowering stalks with large umbrellas of white flowers. It is both the distinctive and bold leaf patterns and these showy flowers that make them fine additions to the native garden. All parts have a pleasant smell, which is typical of all members of this genus. Habitats include rocky hillsides, from windswept coastal bluffs to the high, dry eastern slopes of the Sierra. Drainage is thus particularly important, but roots must be placed so they can reach summer moisture.

The boldness of design relegates angelicas to the back of borders, the back edge of meadows, behind ponds, or in planter boxes as specimens. Most species have similar flowers, but leaf detail and habitat varies. Here are four:

A. breweri. Mountain angelica. Especially large leaves with lanceolate, bright green divisions with toothed edges.

A. hendersonii. Bluff angelica. Ideal for the coastal garden. Leaves coarsely and closely divided into dark green, rounded to elliptical segments.

A. lineariloba. Similar in stature to *A. breweri*, but from drier habitats on the east side of the Sierra; leaf lobes very narrow. Perhaps the showiest of all in flower.

A. tomentosa. Foothill angelica. Good for inland gardens. Grows on half-shaded, brushy, rocky slopes. Leaves with more divisions than *A. hendersonii*, the divisions fuzzy to wooly and ovate to lanceolate.

Ligusticum. Wild Celery, Lovage. Parsley or umbel family.

HT: from 6 inches to 3 or more feet   FLW CL: white   FLW TM: June to August   PRPG: seeds   EXP: full sun (near coast) to light shade   WT: some summer water

Another poorly known group with garden potential. All parts of the plant are attractive: the broadly divided, parsley-like leaves with the odor of celery (but do not eat them!), the broad, tight umbels of white flowers, and the prettily winged fruits which sometimes turn rosy when ripe. Ligusticums are typical of coastal bluffs and prairies, or high-mountain meadows. They come from stout

CELERY-LEAVED LOVAGE—*Ligusticum apiifolium.*

taproots, and so are best started from seed. They need excellent drainage and water through their flowering.

Use ligusticums according to species. Here are the two best:

L. apiifolium. Bluff lovage. Commonly found in the rock gardens of coastal bluffs with other bluff plants, and fine for a summer-cool coastal rock garden setting. Attractive fruits.

L. grayi. Mountain lovage. A stouter plant to several feet and often mixed with bright wildflowers such as mountain bluebells, daisies, lilies, and columbines. Ideal for a well-watered mountain meadow.

Lomatium. Indian Biscuit Root, Kouse, Wild Parsley. Parsley or umbel family.

HT: in flower 4 inches to 2 feet   FLW CL: yellow, cream (almost white), greenish, maroon-purple   FLW TM: varies   PRPG: seeds   EXP: full sun to light shade   WT: varies; most need summer rest

Although there are several species, only a few are widely known; many are quite restricted in their range. The most typical lomatiums come from starchy taproots with low rosettes of finely divided, feathery to ferny leaves and showy umbels of flowers carried on relatively short scapes. Fruits on many are quite attractive with two wings around the main body. Although most live in prairies, grasslands, or meadows, a few come from shaded moist banks in interior woodlands. The latter are seldom showy enough for gardens, but the grassland and meadow kinds are attractive in masses. Of the many species, here are four worth detailing:

L. dasycarpum. Rock biscuit root. Partial to barren, rocky slopes or the edge of dry grasslands. Leaves hairy as well as flower umbels. Flowers nearly white fading pinkish and with very attractive fruits. Sunny, inland gardens in a grassland or meadow.

L. mohavense. Desert biscuit root. Very low growing, in sandy to gravelly soils. Excellent drainage. Flowers often a curious maroon-purple color. Fine for hot desert rock gardens.

L. torreyi. Mountain biscuit root. Rather superficially similar to *L. utriculatum*, but from high, moist mountain meadows. Excellent for a mountain meadow garden.

L. utriculatum. Common biscuit root. Perhaps the most widely distributed, from foothill grasslands. Low-growing, light yellow flowers in mid-spring. For the foothill meadow garden.

Osmorhiza. Sweet Cicely. Parsley or umbel family.

HT: 1 to 3 feet   FLW CL: yellow-green or whitish   FLW TM: varies   PRPG: seeds   EXP: light shade   WT: some summer water

These are subtle plants, not used for show but for grace and refinement. Their major attributes are much-divided, compound fern-like leaves which stay green all summer, and a pleasing licorice aroma from crushed fruits. The flowers are so small that they pass unnoticed. In the garden, once established—they may self-sow—give them the shade of a woodland garden, or the edge of a meadow for the high-mountain species.

The two common species are *O. chilensis*, from middle to low elevations in the Coast Ranges and the Sierra (best for woodland gardens), and *O. occidentalis*, from middle to high meadows of the Sierra.

Perideridia. Yampah. Parsley or umbel family.

HT: in flower 1 to 2 feet   FLW CL: white   FLW TM: summer   PRPG: seeds   EXP: full sun   WT: varies

This little-known group of umbels combines the grace of Queen Anne's lace with the late flowering of many composites. They all are winter dormant to either bunches of fibrous roots or small clusters of edible, tuberous roots. In fact the common name, yampah, is from the Indian name for a favorite food plant. When they first come up in spring or early summer, they are scarcely noticed as they bear a few divided leaves, the divisions distant from one another and narrow. But when they send up flowering stalks with delicate umbrellas of white flowers, and these are massed together by the hundreds, a grassland or meadow is transformed. In the garden, they need full sun and water through the flowering period, then a chance to go dry.

Perideridias all add charm to meadow gardens, or in masses in the middle of a border. They combine especially well with yarrow, sneezeweeds, coneflowers, and asters. The foothill species, as always, are best adapted for lowland gardens; look for these in serpentine grasslands. Some of the middle-elevation mountain kinds may also be tried. Forget species identification—it is difficult at best, and horticultural use is similar for all.

Sphenosciadium capitellatum. Ranger's Buttons, Whiteheads, Button Parsley. Parsley family.

HT: 3 to 5 feet   FLW CL: purple in bud; white when open   FLW TM: June to August   PRPG: seeds   EXP: full sun or light shade   WT: summer wet

This parsley relative is recognized at once by the umbellets of flowers, which are so crowded that they look like heads rather than true umbels. In other ways, however, this plant is typical of the family—large, coarsely pinnately compound, aromatic leaves, hollow stalks, and typical flower structure. Button parsley makes its home along rushing streams and wet meadows of the Sierra and northern mountains, reaching full flower in mid to late summer. Plants stand three, four, or five feet tall with several large umbels of flowers, which change from pink-purple in bud to pure white, then fade purplish. It is these changes which lend this plant its special charm.

Ranger's buttons can be used behind a pond or toward the back of a mixed border which receives regular water, where its bold design and late flowering would be appreciated. Since it occurs at relatively high elevations, it is not known how well it would accommodate to garden culture, but I believe it would succeed.

Pea Family

(Leguminosae or Fabaceae)

This large and important family already is richly represented in the garden, and from many parts of the world. California has no lack of natives; however, many have never been tried in such large genera as *Astragalus;* others are strictly annuals or shrubby; still others have limited appeal. Even so, the following genera give a sampling of possibilities.

Astragalus. Locoweed, Rattlepod, Milk Vetch. Pea family.

HT: 2 to 12 inches   FLW CL: white, red-purple, scarlet, purple-pink   FLW TM: varies   PRPG: seeds (stratify)   EXP: full sun   WT: some summer water with excellent drainage

This is an exceedingly large and varied assemblage of plants, and there is a species for every habitat except forests. Although the genus consists mostly of perennials, nonetheless many have a straggly habit or inconspicuous or dully colored flowers. Doubtless, a number still await the discovery of their garden potential. I shall only mention a few, but by and large this is not a highly ornamental group. Also, the species are difficult to identify and one needs fruits as well as flowers. Overall, they are in disrepute because most are quite poisonous, although the roots have nitrogen-fixing nodules which enrich the soil. All can be recognized by their feathery, pinnately compound leaves, racemose flowers, and pods inflated like balloons with seeds rattling around inside. The pods vary in size, shape, markings, and characteristic coverings. Like the lupines, astragaluses must be started from seed; they grow from stout taproots and rootstocks which are easily damaged and prone to rot. Here is a short list for gardens:

A. coccineus. Scarlet locoweed. This is one of the most spectacular of all peas, the low-tufted plants appearing stalkless and the silvery leaves clustered close to the ground. Complementing the foliage are racemes of large scarlet-red flowers (mid to late spring). This rare species grows in the hottest parts of the Mojave around Owens and Death valleys, and must have superb drainage and no summer water. A gem for the desert rock garden, or as a specimen plant.

A. mohavensis. Mojave locoweed. This is a short-lived perennial which sends out circles of semidecumbent, leafy stems ending in bright pink-purple flowers in mid to late spring. It inhabits the low to middle deserts and is summer dormant. This would be a good subject for a desert-type rock garden.

A. pachypus. Low, mounded bush-like clumps of leafy stems arise from a woody rootstock, and the leaves are covered with a close silver tomentum. The racemes have pretty, white pea flowers, although variety *jaegeri* has lemon-yellow flowers. Again, this is a plant for interior and desert rock gardens, and should have a summer rest.

A. purshii. Pursh's or wooly rattlepod. This is an exquisite subalpine to alpine plant of open scree. It sometimes coexists with *A. whitneyi* in the high Sierra. Low stems and leaves are a shaggy white-gray and the flowers vary from off-white to electric pink-purple. The latter color form belongs to the varieties *tinctus* and *longilobus* of the northern mountains. The interesting pods are short and rounded with a small beak, and are covered with shaggy white fur. For the mountain rock garden with excellent drainage.

A. whitneyi. Alpine or speckled rattlepod. This variable species of the high desert and alpine slopes of the Sierra grows on scree. The stems are short and half-decumbent with green leaves and rather unshowy racemes of whitish flowers, sometimes tinged purple. But the seed pods are incredible: little round balloons of bright green, mottled and spotted with red. A collector's item for the mountain rock garden, but difficult of culture; excellent drainage required.

Lathyrus. Wild Sweet Pea. Pea family.

HT: climbers to several feet; others to 8 or 12 inches tall   FLW CL: often bicolor with white and rose, purple, pink, blue, or scarlet   FLW TM: varies   PRPG: seeds (scarify and/or stratify)   EXP: mostly light shade   WT: some summer water

Native vines are seldom mentioned for the garden, yet a genus such as this has many ornamental qualities. The lathyruses have been brought into cultivation in other parts of the world, and have given us hybrid sweet peas. California species are perennials from deep-seated rootstocks which are fall/winter dormant, and the flowers are not fragrant. Like the lupines, they are difficult to transplant, but grow well from seeds. They need special protection from snails and slugs, especially as the tender new shoots emerge in early spring. Most have weak, long stems with pinnately compound leaves, the leaves ending in coiled tendrils by which the plants attach themselves as they climb. A few lack tendrils, and have modified their behavior so that they form clumps close to the forest floor. All produce showy pea-like flowers in white, pink, or purple and are lined with delicate purple veining. In several, the old flowers turn brown and should be trimmed off, although one species has a striking sulfur-orange color that persists. Flowers are followed by pea-like pods. Most wild sweet peas inhabit forest edges, but a few live on the edge of marshes or on beaches. The majority appreciate summer water until the foliage dies back.

Except for the clump-forming species, the wild sweet peas can be used to create a pretty screen up unsightly shrubs or tree trunks—light permitting—or cascading down a steep embankment. The clumped kinds are nice amongst woodland ground covers, flowering in summer when most woodland flowers have already passed. The beach species are excellent for stabilizing sandy soils along with other beach plants: sand verbena, beach bursage, and beach morning glory. Here are some species:

L. japonicus. Beach sweet pea. With such a species name, beach pea obviously has a wide distribution. It grows directly in the sand of beaches of extreme northern California, and although it seldom climbs, it has retained long tendrils. The leaves are bright green, the leaflets wide and quite pea-like. Pretty pea flowers with purple banners and white wings appear in summer.

L. jepsonii. Jepson's sweet pea. This rare species is confined to freshwater marshes around the northern part of San Francisco Bay. Tendril-bearing. The flowers are large, showy, and rose purple.

L. laetiflorus. Southern sweet pea. This looks a lot like *L. vestitus*, but lives on the edge of oak woodland and chaparral in southern California.

L. littoralis. Strand or dune sweet pea. This is the commoner species of sandy areas, particularly dunes from Monterey north. The leaves are densely felted with silvery hairs, and the leaflets short and closely overlapping. No tendrils. The handsome flowers, beautiful in their contrast to the leaves, are purple to red-purple. Must have excellent drainage.

L. nevadensis. Sierra sweet pea. This one is typical of the forest floors of the conifer belt in the Sierra, where it forms foot-high clumps. No tendrils. The pretty flowers are borne in small clusters and are various shades of blue or purple. Good woodland plant.

L. splendens. Pride-of-California; campo pea. This is worthy of any garden. The stems climb high on chaparral bushes in the extreme southern part of the state, and decorate them with red to crimson flowers over one and a half inches long. Choice.

L. sulphureus. Sulfur sweet pea. From the foothill and middle-elevation forests of the Sierra and north Coast Ranges comes this interesting, climbing species with sulfur-orange flowers.

L. torreyi. Redwood sweet pea. Similar habit to *L. nevadensis*, but found in the redwood belt. No tendrils. The few flowers are pale lavender or blue. A whole colony in full flower makes a pretty ground cover.

L. vestitus. Decorated sweet pea. This is the common species on the edge of woodlands in the Coast Ranges. The long racemes of pink to purple flowers turn brown with age, and the banner is delicately lined with a dark tracery of veins. Tendrils for climbing.

Lotus. Lotus, Trefoil, Deerbroom. Pea family.

HT: 4 inches to 2 feet   FLW CL: yellow or bicolored   FLW TM: May to August
PRPG: seeds (stratify)   EXP: full sun (light shade with meadow spp.)   WT: varies

This is a large and varied genus with low, matted annuals, a few weedy species, and a number of herbaceous perennials and subshrubs of varying height and attractiveness. Habitat and even appearance are difficult to generalize; many species inhabit open rocky or sandy banks and flourish after such disturbances as brush fires. A few require constant moisture and seek out wet meadows and seeps. Leaves carry from three to several leaflets. Flowers are borne singly or—a few—in leaf axils or in terminal umbels; color ranges from purplish green to yellow to pale pink, sometimes in striking bicolor patterns. Here are some interesting perennials:

L. formosissimus. Bicolor or coast lotus. This and the closely related *L. oblongifolius* (meadow lotus) grow in wet meadows, coastal seeps, and similar situations. Both are winter dormant from clusters of deep-seated roots and form low, leafy mats in spring before the flowers appear. These are the showiest of lotuses, the former with umbels of pink-purple and yellow flowers, the latter with yellow and white flowers. Both do well in a meadow, in front of ponds, or in the front of a mixed border with summer water.

L. nevadensis. Sierra lotus. Sierra lotus forms low, silvery to gray-green mats on sandy, hot soils at low to middle elevations. It springs from a central taproot. Once established, it should be quite summer drought tolerant. Bright yellow flowers, tinged red, smother the mats in summer. Good in rock gardens or as a ground cover.

L. scoparius. Deerbroom, deerbrush. Technically, this is a subshrub, but its stature and use place it in our perennial category. Plants are low, decumbent, multiply branched, and twiggy with the appearance of small brooms. They abound on the edges of chaparral, especially after fire. In the garden, they drape nicely over rock walls, and in late spring to early summer are covered with spike-like clusters of bright yellow flowers which fade red-orange. Not long lived with summer water, but more attractive that way.

Lupinus. Lupine. Pea family.

HT: in flower 4 inches to 4 or more feet   FLW CL: yellow, cream, blue, purple, pink, red-purple   FLW TM: varies   PRPG: divide some kinds, but better from seed (plant immediately or stratify)   EXP: full sun to light shade   WT: from some summer water to wet all year

California is endowed with so many beautiful species of lupine—there is a lupine for every habitat except for the salt marshes. Horticulturally, lupines fall into three categories; annuals, shrubs, and herbaceous perennials, each with several species. Obviously, it is impossible to generalize about growing conditions or uses in the garden. All lupines should be started from seed, since they transplant poorly (a few might be started from root divisions). All have nitrogen-fixing nodules on their roots to enrich soils. Lupines are identified by their palmately compound leaves and their racemes of pea-like flowers. Flower colors cover the rainbow except for red and orange; hybridization should produce an even wider range, as is the case with the Russell lupines. The seeds are borne in long pea pods which twist open violently to expel the seeds. For purposes of seed collection, paper bags should be tied around the pods before they are ripe. Seed is often infected with insect larvae, and requires careful inspection.

I list here those species with which I am most familiar, but there are many more to try.

L. albicaulis. White-stemmed lupine. This is a tall lupine found in openings of the montane coniferous forest with green leaves and flowering stalks up to three feet tall. The flowers are modest and white to pale purple. Adaptable to woodland gardens, but not showy.

L. albifrons var. *collinus.* Blue bush lupine. Although the regular *L. albifrons* is a shrub this variety is more a prostrate, spreading perennial herb with a woody base. The attractive leaves are gray-green and the wandering branches form large, circular patches on rocky banks from the foothills to middle elevations in the mountains north of San Francisco. In summer, numerous flowering stalks bear blue-purple flowers which complement the leaf color. Excellent for a large rock garden, or the front of a mixed border.

L. breweri. Brewer's lupine, mat lupine. This is yet another low-growing, mat-forming perennial and comes from sandy open flats in conifer forests from middle to alpine elevations. The long, silky hairs on the leaves and the dense flower clusters of blue-purple with yellow and white centers make a pleasing combination for rock gardens. This one is more adaptable to gardens than *L. lyallii.*

L. croceus. Golden lupine. Another upright lupine, with leafy stalks to two feet. It is at once recognized by its bright yellow flowers, not the pale yellows of other species. It comes from open slopes in the yellow pine and red fir forest of the Siskiyou and Klamath mountains. Beautiful in a mixed border with summer water.

L. latifolius. Broadleaf lupine. This widespread species is rather adaptable but may be disappointing since the leafy stems may have dried, brown leaves at flowering time. Flowers vary from purple to blue or pink, and dry brown. Old flowers should be removed. It is variable, and comes from openings and banks in forests up to middle elevations. Superior forms should be selected.

L. lyallii. Lyall's lupine. Another low, prostrate lupine which makes circular mats with silvery silky leaves and short tight racemes of blue-purple flowers. It comes from gravelly flats in the subalpine and alpine Sierra and may not be adaptable to the lowlands.

L. magnificus. Magnificent lupine. Another superb perennial lupine. It lives on sandy, gravelly flats in the high desert with sagebrush and pinyon-juniper woodland in the Panamint Mountains. The wooly leaves give way to four-foot flowering stalks with neat tiers of pink-purple flowers, each with a central yellow spot. Choice but unlikely to succeed in coastal gardens.

L. polyphyllus. Meadow or bog lupine. This is a truly outstanding species and is already parent to the Russell hybrids. In the wild, it grows in bogs, swales, and wet meadows from the north coast to the middle and high mountain meadows.

LUPINE—*Lupinus.*

Leaves are uncommonly broad and robust, and in some clones open a beautiful purple. Flower stalks reach four or more feet with noble spires of blue or purple flowers. For the back of a watered border, or in a meadow garden. Lovely with Jeffrey's shooting star, swamp onion, and California corn lily.

L. sellulus. The best variety is *ursinus*, since it occurs at lower elevations. It is a scree-loving lupine from the high inner north Coast Ranges. It has circular rosettes of low hairy leaves, and a number of central flowering stalks up to 12 inches high; in bud, the symmetry and patterns of leaves are striking; in flower, the color varies from off-white to a delicate purple. Choice for the well-drained rock garden with eriogonums, bladderpod, and phacelias.

L. sericatus. Mayacamas lupine. This restricted endemic deserves recognition. It lives on open banks in mixed-evergreen and ponderosa forests in Lake, Napa, and Sonoma counties. The robust basal leaf cluster sends up a 12-inch flowering stalk with striking red-purple flowers. Choice for the woodland garden.

L. variicolor. Varicolored lupine, bluff lupine. Subwoody, behaves as a creeper, the branches plastered against coastal bluffs. The gray-green leaves contrast well with the blue to purple flowers which decorate the plants in late spring or early summer. This species hybridizes naturally with the yellow bush lupine, resulting in forms and color combinations which might be useful for the garden. Use it as a ground cover or in a coastal rock garden.

Thermopsis macrophylla. False Lupine. Pea family.

HT: in flower to 30 inches   FLW CL: yellow   FLW TM: April to June   PRPG: root divisions   EXP: full sun near coast   WT: occasional summer water

False lupine, true to its common name, has lupine-like flowers. The creeping rootstocks send up leafy stems from 18 inches to 2 feet with spike-like racemes of yellow flowers. After seed has ripened, the stalks gradually go dormant in fall and winter. Each year the colony enlarges but the stems seldom form a dense clump. Rather they wander, leaving space between for other plants. The leaves are divided into three fuzzy light green leaflets with large stipules at their bases. Flowers appear from mid to late spring. False lupine grows in rocky meadows and grasslands which go dry in summer.

Because of the decorative spring leaves and showy flowers, false lupine deserves space in the mixed border as a medium to tall spring flower. It should be trimmed back as the leaves turn brown and grown with other plants which keep their winter leaves.

Trifolium. Clover. Pea family.

HT: 2 to 5 inches   FLW CL: white or purple   FLW TM: varies   PRPG: divisions
EXP: light shade   WT: some summer water

There is a clover for nearly every open habitat from the foothills to the mountain heights. Some are vigorous introduced kinds used for pasturage, others are spring-flowering annuals, still others are native perennials. All trifoliums have leaves divided into three leaflets, and many tiny pea-like flowers crowded into heads. Flower color ranges from white to pink and purple, or is occasionally red or even yellow. The perennial clovers form creeping mats, the stems rooting as they go, and eventually cover large areas. The flower stalks rise a few inches above these mats. Most species grow in wet meadows, or the border of marshes. They need summer moisture and sometimes light shade in the garden, and are often sought by gophers.

Clovers make fine ground covers for areas with light traffic, and have the bonus of late spring or summer flowers. Flowers are bee favorites, and make fine honey. The nitrogen nodules on the roots help enrich soil. Clovers fit nicely into a meadow situation, if grasses and sedges don't overtop them too much. I mention two species here, but others should be tried.

T. monanthum. Mountain clover. This pretty mountain clover occurs above 5,000 feet in wet meadows. Its mat of leaves is very low, and the white flowers are borne in small clusters or singly. Good in a mountain garden or dish garden with tinker's penny and primrose monkeyflower.

T. wormskjoldii. Wormskjold's clover. This is a lowland species from wet prairies, and spreads satisfactorily in a moist situation. Good ground cover. Pretty purple flower heads in early summer.

Peony Family
(Paeoniaceae)

The peonies from the Old World are well established in gardens, but few people are aware that we have native peonies. The family has the single genus *Paeonia* described below.

Paeonia. Wild Peony. Peony family.

HT: 1 to 2 feet   FLW CL: maroon   FLW TM: varies   PRPG: seeds   EXP: full sun to light shade   WT: varies

We have two closely similar native peonies: *P. californica* from the southern California chaparral/sage, and *P. brownii* from the open forests of the northern Sierra. True to the genus, both have attractively dissected leaves of peony design, although the leaves are smaller than in most garden kinds. Both also spring from deep-seated rootstocks and are difficult to transplant; seed is the only practical way. The southern California peony is seldom seen in flower because flowers appear early in the year—often around February. The Sierran peony is similarly early, but early in the mountains means June when snows melt. The Sierran form is a bit more delicate, but either would be an interesting addition to a rock garden, on the edge of a dry meadow, or massed toward the front of a border. Obviously, *P. californica* grows best in hot, lowland gardens, where its early

WILD PEONY—*Paeonia*.

flowers are a distinct asset, and requires a summer dry period; *P. brownii* is best in mountain gardens with at least early summer water.

Phlox Family
(Polemoniaceae)

The phloxes are richly represented in western North America, and occur in a number of difficult-to-separate genera. In addition, many have showy, colorful flowers. The five genera given here only hint at the possibilities, since a large proportion of native species are annuals.

Eriastrum densifolium. Sapphire Flower. Phlox family.

HT: about 1 foot   FLW CL: sapphire blue   FLW TM: May to August   PRPG: cuttings or seeds   EXP: full sun to light shade   WT: summer dry

Sapphire flower is a little-known segregate of the gilias, and all but a single species are ephemeral annuals. This species is a subshrubby erect perennial with many branches, and usually forms compact mounds to about one foot high. The leaves are divided into feathery, spine tipped segments, and the new growth and flower clusters are protected by fluffy, wooly white hairs. The flower heads stand out because of the blue color of the phlox-like flowers. Sapphire flower comes in several varieties with somewhat different habitats: all prefer dry, sandy soils but some grow on coastal sand dunes of south-central California, while others are from middle elevations of the pine belt in southern California, or from the desert edge. The best variety for the garden is the main species from coastal sand dunes.

Because of the flower color, sapphire flower should earn a place for itself in the front or middle of a mixed border, or in front of drought-tolerant shrubs. It should be planted where other foliage can cover its barren look after flowering from midsummer through fall.

Ipomopsis aggregata. Scarlet Gilia, Sky Rocket. Phlox family.

HT: to 3 feet   FLW CL: scarlet, pink, salmon, rose, white   FLW TM: June to August PRPG: seeds   EXP: mostly light shade   WT: some summer water

This is the only *Ipomopsis* for the garden. Many have learned it as gilia, in which genus it used to be included. Scarlet gilia ranges widely through middle and high elevations, on sandy soils in the drier parts of the Cascades and Sierra. It grows on the dry borders of meadows or between openings in low-growing sagebrushes. It is biennial, making a low rosette of feathery, dark green leaves atop a taproot the first year. A flowering stalk appears the second year with an open panicle of flowers, the flowers appearing by midsummer. The flowers are long, trumpet shaped with the petals flared, and usually scarlet-red. The stamens and stigma stand beyond the petals, a sure sign of a hummingbird flower.

PRICKLY PHLOX—*Gilia californica.*

Color variants embrace such colors as pink, salmon, buff, rose, and white. Careful breeding might lead to strains which come true to selected colors. Because scarlet gilia grows where it's hot and dry in summer, it needs excellent drainage. This flower is so showy that it is a worthy subject for mild lowland and coastal gardens.

Scarlet gilia is ideal for the medium to tall part of the mixed border, and the range of flower colors makes it a show all by itself. A good foil for these warm colors is the blues of mountain flax, penstemons, and larkspurs.

Linanthus nuttallii. Perennial Linanthus or Gilia. Phlox family.

HT: 6 to 8 inches FLW CL: white FLW TM: July to September PRPG: seeds (stratify) EXP: full sun WT: occasional summer water

This is the only perennial species in a genus which was once included in the gilias. Linanthuses are separated on the basis of their digitately divided leaves like fingers of a hand, while gilias have pinnately divided or simple leaves. *Linanthus* is a large genus, but is otherwise composed of delicate, ephemeral annuals, of the foothills and deserts. *Linanthus nuttallii* is a low, mat-like perennial of sandy, stony soils of the high desert, and extends on to the east side of the Sierra, where it grows among low sagebrushes in openings of pinyon and Jeffrey pine forests. It is easily confused with mat phlox and prickly mountain phlox, but the former has simple, needle-like leaves while the latter has spinier leaf divisions. All three share similar habitats and bear long-tubed flowers with showy petals. *Linanthus nuttallii* has pure white flowers and its leaves are softer and of a lighter green than the others. In the garden, it should have excellent drainage, plenty of sun, little summer moisture, and (if possible) a winter rest, although it has been successfully grown in coastal botanical gardens. It flowers profusely in mid to late summer, sometimes extending into fall.

The pretty phlox-like flowers and tidy, trim habit recommend perennial linanthus for the rock garden or the front of a mixed border. The profusion of white flowers makes a good edging for other summer flowers. Good companions are the wild buckwheats, penstemons, mat phlox, zauschnerias, and low-growing lupines and asters. Perennial linanthus often reseeds.

Phlox. Phlox. Phlox family.

HT: 4 to 8 inches FLW CL: white, purple, pink, rose FLW TM: varies PRPG: divisions (on nonwoody kinds) or seeds (stratify) EXP: full sun to light shade WT: varies, but good drainage essential

Most true phloxes have ornamental possibilities, and like the penstemons, some have already found their place in the everyday garden. But there is much left to explore in the genus, especially among our own natives. Our phloxes are sometimes subwoody, although some are strictly herbaceous, and they vary from low shrubs and upright herbs to widely sprawling woody mats plastered against rock scree. Most have opposite evergreen narrow leaves, the leaves on several markedly needle-like and even spine-tipped. The true phloxes differ in this detail from the related leptodactylons (prickly phlox), which have leaves divided into narrow segments like the fingers on a hand. Most phloxes grow in gravelly, sandy, or rocky situations, fully exposed to sun, but a few are partial to semishade of brush and woods. Most bloom in late spring or summer and the flowers have long narrow tubes and widely spreading, colorful petals—from rose pink to purple to white. Some mat phloxes put on such a profusion of flower that the leaves are hidden. All need excellent drainage and some summer water.

Because of the variety in shape, garden uses are given below according to species. I have included five of the best:

P. adsurgens. Woodland phlox. This lovely plant prefers open woods at middle elevations of the northern corner of the state. The weak stems may rise to eight inches, but have a tendency to lean over. The leaves are round to narrowly ovate. Flowers vary from pale to bright pink, and continue all summer. A charming flower for summer color in the woodland garden.

P. austromontana. Southern phlox. Here is a low, cushion-forming phlox from barren slopes in the ponderosa zone of the mountains of far southern California. The leaves are needle-like, gray-hairy, and spiny to the touch, and smothered by showy pink to lavender flowers in late spring/early summer. Another rock garden plant needing superb drainage.

P. diffusa. Mat phlox. This is the stunning montane to alpine phlox of the Sierra, appearing at times to grow out of pure granite rock. The low circular woody mats sprawl widely and are densely covered by narrow needle-like but not spiny leaves. In flower, this is one of the best, with showy blossoms from white to lavender to purple to pink. Mat phlox demands a rock garden with superb drainage, and may not adapt well to lowland gardens.

P. speciosa. Showy phlox. This is a foothill to middle-elevation phlox of the northern mountains, and prefers steep slopes on the edge of pine woods or in the protection of montane chaparral. It must have excellent drainage. The plants themselves are low, half-sprawling, and not terribly attractive out of flower. The showy flowers have pink shallowly notched petals and appear from late spring through middle summer. Good for rock gardens or fronts of borders. Grows naturally with other brightly colored flowers such as Indian pink, wooly sunflower, and coyote mint.

P. stansburyi. Desert phlox. This is common on gravelly upland slopes of the eastern desert, beyond the Sierra and in the eastern Mojave mountains. The subwoody stems branch and rebranch to form clumps less than a foot high, which are covered with rose to white flowers in late spring. Gray-green leaves are narrow but not needle-like. Fronts of borders or rock gardens. Give lots of sun and heat.

Polemonium. Jacob's Ladder, Sky Pilot. Phlox family.

HT: in flower 4 to 18 inches   FLW CL: fleshy orange, blue, or purple with yellow centers   FLW TM: summer to early fall   PRPG: divisions or seeds (stratify)   EXP: light shade   WT: summer water

Here is another poorly known native genus of much merit. Polemoniums are winter-dormant plants from rootstocks or thickened rootcrowns which usually live in perennial wet spots, often in light shade. The leaves are pinnately compound, often in the manner of pea leaves, and some have a slight skunky odor when crushed, and either are in basal rosettes or ascend the flowering stalks. Open bell-shaped to bowl-shaped flowers are borne in branched cymes or dense heads and are mostly blue-purple. They appear through the summer.

Polemoniums are best in the front or middle of a mixed border, in full sun along the immediate coast, or in filtered shade elsewhere, except for the alpine species. The last would be beautiful subjects for a rock garden with excellent drainage, but might not adapt fully to the lowland garden. Here are five species:

P. caeruleum. Wet meadow edges of middle and high mountains with basal clusters of leaves and blue flowers. Semishaded gardens. Handsome and adaptable. Often self-sows.

P. californicum. High-mountain meadows in shade of conifers. Flowering stalks leafy with cymes of blue-purple flowers.

P. carneum. Similar to *P. caeruleum,* but flowers vary from purple to pink to buff. From low elevations in the central and northern Coast Ranges. Adaptable to lowland gardens.

P. eximium. Sky pilot. A high alpine flower from scree. Rather sticky leaves whose leaflets are redivided into small segments like a tightly narrow fern frond. Flowers a lovely sky-blue in dense heads. Very choice, but probably not adaptable to lowland gardens.

P. pulcherrimum. Alpine Jacob's ladder. Rocky places near or above timberline. Leaves rather ferny in appearance, the lobes closely overlapping. Small blue flowers. Fine for a rock garden.

Pink Family
(Caryophyllaceae)

Aside from our native silenes, there are few showy native species in the pink family; many have tiny nondescript flowers or are weedy. Three genera are included here.

Arenaria. Sandwort. Pink family.
HT: in flower to 6 or 8 inches   FLW CL: white   FLW TM: June to August   PRPG: crown divisions or seeds   EXP: full sun   WT: some summer water with excellent drainage

The sandworts include delicate, ephemeral annuals but are best known for the perennial, cushion-forming species of high-mountain rock outcroppings, where they join other cushion plants such as buckwheats, penstemons, and sedums. Although the degree to which the mats are compact or open varies with the species, most grow from a multibranched, subwoody crown covered liberally with narrow needle-like to grass-like leaves. It is the form of these leaf cushions which are its main attribute; in summer, delicate, branched stems produce a number of tiny, white, star-like flowers. In the garden, arenarias must have perfect drainage, and if possible, a winter rest.

Arenarias are best used as subjects for close-up inspection in a mountain rock garden planted between chinks of rock. Their mats contrast well with other textures such as the gray-green eriogonums or fleshy sedums. Although there are several species, the overall appearance and horticultural use is quite similar for all.

Cerastium arvense. Bluff Chickweed, Mouse-Eared Chickweed, Field Chickweed. Pink family.

HT: to 6 inches   FLW CL: white   FLW TM: March to April   PRPG: root divisions or seed   EXP: light shade inland   WT: some summer water

Bluff chickweed is named inappropriately. Although it does occur along wind- and fog-swept coastal bluffs in central and northern California, it is only distantly related to the pesky garden chickweed from Europe. There are also native species of the true chickweed (*Stellaria*) which are charming, diminutive, overlooked plants of mountain meadows and forests. Perhaps they would adapt to a cool coastal rock or meadow garden, but their horticultural uses seem limited due to lack of showy flowers and difficulty of establishment in lowland gardens.

C. arvense forms sprawling mats which do justice to a rock garden or between flagstones of a path or in front of a border. The mats are smothered in white flowers with notched petals from late March through April, but after seeding look ragged and should be trimmed back. Plant bluff chickweed with other evergreen bluff plants such as sea thrift, coast buckwheat, or coast rockcress. Its appearance stays neater with some summer water, but drainage must be good.

Silene. Indian Pink, Wild Pink. Pink family.

HT: 4 to 18 inches   FLW CL: white, pink, rose-purple, scarlet   FLW TM: May to August   PRPG: seeds, root sections, cuttings   EXP: mostly light shade   WT: most, occasional summer water

Silenes grow from deep taproots or clusters of fleshy roots, forming compact to widely straggling bunches of herbaceous stems carrying pairs of rather narrow, sometimes slashed leaves. The overall appearance hints at untidiness, so interplant them with plants whose leaves lend grace and neatness (for example, ferns and sedums). In flower, many are showstoppers with their brightly colored blossoms of graceful form which most closely approach true pinks (*Dianthus*) from the Old World. Most silenes need a rest immediately after flowering, at which time the old foliage can be severely cut back to encourage new growth later. Foothill species flower in late spring to early summer, then rest; mountain species flower through the summer, taking a rest in late autumn or during winter and early spring.

INDIAN PINK—*Silene californica.*

Silenes are plants of rocky slopes, where they gain a strong foothold by deeply searching roots and rhizomes. There they have little competition. Silenes also grow through low brush for protection from deer browsing. Thus, they may be interplanted with other low-growing plants, given excellent drainage and filtered sun or light shade. Many are drought tolerant once established. Most species work well in a rock garden setting; the brighter colored ones are excellent near the front of a mixed border. The species given here include only those with which I am most familiar, minus several that have too-small flowers or are weedy.

S. californica. Indian pink. Perhaps the showiest of all, with flowers up to an inch across of brilliant scarlet-red, the petals notched or slashed like those of a pink, and a hummingbird favorite. It grows well in light shade at the border of a woodland garden, planted with low ferns and flowers from late spring through middle summer. Plants get straggly with age and stems grow close to the ground.

S. campanulata and varieties. Bell pink. From the far northwestern mountains, has nodding flowers with bell-shaped sepal tubes and showy, slashed white petals. The white and green color pattern and the form of the flowers is intriguing for a lowland rock garden. Stems to one or more feet.

S. hookeri. Hooker's or ground pink. Equally as spectacular as the Indian pink, with very large flowers on creeping to decumbent stems, petals deeply slashed, and colors ranging from near white to deep rose. Again, colors should be carefully selected for best effect. Suitable only to very well drained soils, as in lightly shaded lowland rock gardens—does best with summer heat, but generous winter rains.

S. laciniata. Southern Indian pink. Much like *S. californica,* but flowers are slightly smaller, petals more deeply slashed, and plants stand upright. The form of the plant is really prettier than *S. californica,* and desirable for a foothill rock garden but is used in a different manner, being more appropriate to the middle section rather than the front.

S. nuda. Naked-stemmed pink. A charming pink from dry, slightly alkaline mountain meadows of the east Sierra. The low leaf mats later produce flowering stalks to over a foot with several horizontally held pink to rose flowers. Dry meadow or mountain rock garden.

S. occidentalis. Western pink. From middle elevations of northern mountains comes this pretty pink, with stalks to a foot tall, carrying modest white to deep pink flowers, the petals prettily divided or slashed. Color forms should be carefully chosen; some pink forms are pretty with such companions as scarlet gilia and penstemons. Light shade.

S. scouleri. Seaside or bluff pink. Grows in the natural rock gardens of bluffside coastal promontories, flowering in late spring to early summer. The low sticky leaves are inconspicuous until the flowering stalks appear. These carry pink-purple, fringed flowers in orderly succession. Nice with other coastal rock plants such as dudleyas, armerias, eriophyllums, and paintbrushes.

Plumbage Family

(Plumbaginaceae)

We have but two genera, each with a single species. Although there is a native in the second genus, *Limonium californicum* or marsh rosemary, that might have limited use in salty soils, I have ignored it here. Its close relative, the garden statices of the same genus, have much greater cultural worth but are not native.

Armeria maritima. Sea Thrift, Sea Pink. Plumbage family.

HT: in flower to 12 inches   FLW CL: pink-purple   FLW TM: May to July   PRPG: divisions or seeds   EXP: full sun   WT: some summer water

The common sea thrift is already under cultivation, having been selected from forms originating in the Old World. A number of different cultivars are already in use under that name, since this species has wide distribution. Our own form has merits, too. It is found on old sand dunes and wind-blown bluffs from central California north. The strong taproot anchors the plant between rocks and bears a close-cropped tuft of long, narrow, grass-like evergreen leaves. From this a naked flower scape rises no more than a foot with ball-shaped heads of pretty pink purple onion like flowers. The whole is surrounded at the base by brown, papery, turned-down bracts. The attractive pompons of flowers and the neat foliage make this a fine garden plant. It grows best with year-round moisture, but should have good drainage to avoid overly soggy soils.

Sea thrift can be used effectively in a coastal rock garden as companion to many other plants from its natural habitat: California phacelia, coast rockcress, wallflower, and dudleya, for example. Or it is good in the front of a mixed border, where the attractive foliage stays green after the flowers have faded.

Polypody Family

(Polypodiaceae)

The polypodies are ferns which are prominent in the tropics, but are represented by a single genus here in California. All are unusual in that they grow epiphytically on rocks or trees.

Polypodium. Polypody, Licorice Fern, Leather Fern. Polypody family.

HT: 4 to 8 inches   PRPG: rhizome sections or spores   EXP: light near coast to full shade   WT: some summer dry; one not

This large genus is represented in California by only three species, all of which are small epiphytic ferns; that is, ferns which attach themselves to tree bark (or rocks) for support and light, but not for food. The rhizome is covered with

SEATHRIFT—*Armeria maritima.*

scaly brown hairs and bears alternate fronds. The fronds are once pinnately deeply divided with circular naked spore bodies (sori) on their backs. Polypodies will grow in garden soil with excellent drainage, but are best draped over a mossy rock wall or on top of an old stump. They need shade, and at least occasional summer water, although two species are summer dormant and put out their new fronds after the first winter rains. The third is evergreen with tough fronds. Here is a brief description:

P. californica. California polypody. This species ranges from the foothills of southern California through the Coast Ranges to a little north of San Francisco, where it overlaps with *P. glycyrrhiza*. Summer dormant; fronds shorter than the others; light green. Easily naturalized.

P. glycyrrhiza. Licorice fern. Licorice fern continues where California polypody leaves off, being common in coastal forests of central and northern California. Its fronds are longer, the segments sharply pointed. Summer dormant.

P. scouleri. Leather fern. This is the best for the garden because the handsome dark green fronds stay on all year. Found in coastal forests of central and northern California; grows into large clumps with time. Striking in a basket or over an old tree stump.

Poppy Family
(Papaveraceae)

The poppies that grow in western North America are among the showiest, and many merit serious consideration for the garden. While three genera are included here, many species are not because they are annual (most of the Eschscholzias); and one is a large showy shrub (*Dendromecon rigida*, or bush poppy).

Argemone munita. Prickly Poppy. Poppy family.

HT: to 4 or more feet   FLW CL: white with yellow center   FLW TM: June to September   PRPG: seeds   EXP: full sun   WT: occasional summer water

This short-lived perennial or biennial is often mistaken for the gorgeous Matilija poppy, so similar are its huge, white flowers. But this plant is heavily armed with spines on the slashed, gray-green leaves, the much branched stems, and even the sepals. Prickly poppy may reach four or more feet under ideal conditions. A long show of buds, flowers, and seed pods occurs in summer, the individual flowers of shallow saucer shape, several inches across, the petals of crepe paper consistency, the center filled with numerous yellow stamens. This is a pollen plant, and a favorite, therefore, of bees. Prickly poppy lives in some of the most inhospitable environments: steep road banks, scree, and the edge of sagebrush-covered flats, but wherever it occurs, it seeks out excellent drainage for the taproot, full sun and hot summers, and a spot that lacks competition. Plants with similar needs include showy milkweed and blazing star, and these could be included with it in a planting.

Prickly poppy is a must for any large garden with plenty of sun, and is a showstopper in the back of a mixed border. It should accept some summer water if the drainage is sharp, and can be used wherever tall plants with showy summer flowers are needed.

Eschscholzia californica. California Poppy. Poppy family.

HT: to 12 or more inches   FLW CL: orange or yellow   FLW TM: March to August   PRPG: seeds (self-sow)   EXP: full sun   WT: some water through the growing season

The famous California poppy probably needs no description, but a few points need be made. There are several other species, but they are annual. Only the true California poppy is a short-lived perennial, but it is often treated in the garden as an annual. There are many races in the wilds, from coastal dunes to the interior grasslands, but all have stout, orange taproots and basal clusters of finely divided, glaucous ferny leaves, and bear cup- to tulip-shaped orange or yellow flowers. Size of flower and coloration changes even on the same plant between early and late spring. The most distinct race is that from the immediate coast: leaves lie nearly flat against the soil and are a beautiful silvery color, and the large bicolored flowers are carried well above.

California poppies have long been cultivated, and there are garden forms which are seldom seen in nature: doubles, reds, creams, and pinks. All readily hybridize, so that seed may not come true. Once established, unwanted seedlings have to be removed, since they spread so effectively by exploding seed pods. Older plants become leggy and should be severely trimmed back, or new plants started. The long blooming season guarantees a succession of color from spring through summer with a minimum of care. Poppies are especially good in a natural grassland setting, or in the middle zone of the mixed border. Good companions include lupines, buttercups, and various bulbs.

Romneya coulteri. Matilija Poppy. Poppy family.

HT: to 6 or 7 feet   FLW CL: white with yellow center   FLW TM: May to September   PRPG: root divisions, cuttings, seeds (fire pretreatment)   EXP: full sun   WT: summer dry

Matilija poppy is neither strictly a shrub nor an herbaceous perennial, but somewhere in between. It inhabits hot flats in the coastal scrub and chaparral of southern California, and is particularly common in the mountains of Ventura County. Its underground roots and rootstocks spread widely and invasively, soon forming colonies several yards in extent. Winter dormant, the old branches should be severely pruned to near their bases to encourage healthy new growth in spring. The tall branches are somewhat top heavy in flower and often lean over; staking is helpful. By summer these stems reach four, five, six

CALIFORNIA POPPY—*Eschschoizia californica.*

or more feet and carry a long succession of flower buds. The enormous flowers (the largest of any native) are wide open, with six crumpled white petals and myriad bright golden stamens. Like the prickly poppy, this is strictly a bee pollen plant and offers no nectar.

Matilija poppy is not recommended for a small garden because it spreads rapidly, unless it is containerized. On the other hand, when given the space, it puts on a show unequaled in summer and is wonderful behind a mixed border, or next to drought-tolerant chaparral shrubs. It can be combined with fremontias, ceanothuses, and manzanitas and does not need summer water.

Portulaca Family

(*Portulacaceae*)

This is a modest native family, and although three genera are included here, some species are excluded because they are annual. The genus *Claytonia* has not been included because of its specialized habitat and relatively unshowy flowers.

Calyptridium umbellatum. Pussy Paws. Portulaca family.

HT: in flower 4 to 6 inches   FLW CL: pale purple to deep rose-purple   FLW TM: June to August   PRPG: seeds   EXP: full sun   WT: some summer water with good drainage

Pussy paws is a familiar mountain flower, from mid-elevations to near timberline on sandy flats along the dry edge of meadows or openings in coniferous forests. People often mistake them for some sort of purple buckwheat because of the flower arrangement—flowers are tightly clumped into fuzzy-looking rounded pompons. The plant starts life from a taproot as a neat circle of dark green leaves with handsome veins. These lie absolutely flat against the soil. From the center, several reddish stems bear the characteristic flowers. Color ranges from very pale purple to a vibrant rose-purple. The latter color shows to greater advantage in gardens; the paler forms tend to blend into the background soil color.

Massed, pussy paws are spectacular between stepping stones, or in the front of rock gardens. They are not long lived, but come easily from shiny black seeds which are produced in abundance. Other species of *Calyptridium* are found in California, but most are either rare or undecorative.

Lewisia. Lewisia, Bitter-Root. Portulaca family.

HT: in flower 2 inches to 2 feet   FLW CL: white, purple, pink, rose   FLW TM: varies   PRPG: in some, divisions; seeds for all   EXP: full sun to light shade   WT: varies

Lewisias were named in honor of Capt. Meriwether Lewis and are renowned as rock garden plants. They are also noted for their difficulty, since most species demand excellent drainage and need a definite dry rest after flowering. The several species vary considerably in particulars, although all live on rocky promon-

PUSSY PAWS—*Calyptridium umbellatum.*

tories or the edge of wet meadows. All produce neat rosettes of fleshy leaves close to the ground—some with tubular long leaves, others with spoon-shaped or ovate leaves. From these, flowering stalks of varying heights arise: some carry single large flowers; others make tall, open panicles of much smaller flowers. Flowers are different from the family standard—sepals are frequently more than two and petals more than five, and stamens may also occur in greater numbers. Flower color ranges through the pinks and purples with some approaching an orange or yellow-red; a few are pure white. Many cultivars have been selected from the more popular species. Lewisias demand perfect drainage in the garden since their corm or taproot is easily rotted at the top—a dressing of pea gravel should be placed around the leaf crown. A few species like moist soils while flowering, but many need only occasional water, and a definite dry dormancy after seeding.

Lewisias are easiest as specimen plants in containers, but are lovely in a rock garden with appropriate plant companions—these could include small buckwheats, wooly sunflower, and alpine daisies, for example. Here are the best species:

L. cantelowii. From a corm-like root. Leaves in basal rosettes, oblanceolate and clearly toothed; flowers in delicate, open panicles, small, light pink to white. Wet, mossy cliffs along the Feather River. Rare.

L. congdonii. From a taproot with leaves mostly basal and oblanceolate; flowers scattered in a tall panicle, and rose colored. Middle elevations of the south-central Sierra.

L. cotyledon. Broadleaf lewisia. From a taproot and fleshy underground stem. Leaves in handsome basal rosettes, spoon-shaped to obovate, sometimes finely toothed. Flowers quite large and showy, in short panicles; variable in color—mostly white or pink striped, but selected named cultivars in rose, apricot, and cerise. One of the very best and easiest for garden culture. Light shade on rocky embankments. Fine with rock ferns. From the Siskiyous.

L. leana. From a fleshy underground stalk. Leaves linear and nearly cylindrical; flowers in tall open panicles, red-purple or white with red-purple veins. Siskiyou Mountains. Choice.

L. nevadensis. Sierra lewisia. From a fleshy taproot. Low basal rosettes of linear to narrowly oblanceolate leaves and short flowering stalks bearing single modest pure white flowers. Good for the well-drained meadow garden in the forefront.

L. pygmaea. Pygmy lewisia. Similar in habit and habitat to *L. nevadensis*, but the flowers somewhat smaller in size. A gem for a moist meadow.

L. rediviva. Bitter-root. The state flower of Montana, and with wide distribution throughout the northwest. The stout taproot penetrates the cracks of rocks—granite, lava, serpentine, and others—with low rosettes of cylindrical, dull green leaves which shrivel by or just after flowering. Flowers borne on single low stalks, the largest of the genus (to two inches across), with white to rose petals.

Extremely handsome in flower; barely noticeable out of flower. Difficult to grow, but choice for rock gardens.

Montia. Miner's Lettuce, Spring Beauty. Portulaca family.

HT: 4 to 12 inches　FLW CL: white or striped rose　FLW TM: mainly late spring to early summer　PRPG: divisions (some species) or seeds (may self-sow) EXP: shade　WT: some summer water

The familiar native food plant miner's lettuce (*M. perfoliata*) is the best-known member of the genus, but it and several others are spring annuals. There are two less familiar species which are low-growing herbaceous perennials. Both occur in cool, shaded situations. One is evergreen and nearly ever-flowering in the garden, the other decidedly summer/fall dormant. Both bear fleshy rosettes of narrowly spoon-shaped leaves and central flowering stalks only inches high with delicate, open, notched-petaled flowers. Flowers are borne in long succession, and plants frequently reseed themselves.

The first species, Siberian miner's lettuce or candy-stripe (*Montia sibirica*), seeks moist stream banks and seeps in cool coastal forests or middle elevations of mixed conifer forests. Its evergreen leaves are dark green and the flowers white-striped pink or red-purple. The forms with darkest striping and largest flowers are most desirable, and in cool woodland gardens, flower almost without stop through the year when watered. Although individual plants are short lived, they replant themselves by seed, but are easily controlled because the fibrous roots are easily pulled out. The second species, moss spring beauty or small-leaf montia (*M. parvifolium*), grows in the crevices of moss-covered rocks from low to middle elevations in partial shade of the nearby forest canopy. It goes dormant because the roots grow on steep banks where soils dry in summer. The growing season may be extended by additional water, and the plants are tolerant of summer water as long as they have good drainage. Plants send out stolons to colonize adjacent areas. These create an attractive ground cover on mossy rocks of a woodland garden. They combine well with small saxifrages, mist maidens, and sedums of similar habitat.

Primrose Family

(*Primulaceae*)

Our native primroses and their relatives number rather few, but there are at least three garden-worthy genera. Habitats vary widely in the wild, and consequently so does garden use for each.

Dodecatheon. Shooting Stars. Primrose family.

HT: in flower from 8 inches to 2 feet　FLW CL: pink or purple (occasionally white)　FLW TM: varies　PRPG: divisions or seeds　EXP: full sun on the coast; light shade elsewhere　WT: varies

SHOOTING STARS—*Dodecatheon.*

Our several dodecatheons are all herbaceous perennials which look like miniature cyclamens with beak-like stamens. Some are summer/fall dormant and
spring flowering, while others are winter dormant and summer flowering.
The former inhabit woodlands and coastal prairies of the foothills; the latter
mid- to high-mountain meadows. All gradually increase the size of their colonies, either by creeping rootstocks or by stolons, and all produce basal rosettes
of broad, rounded leaves. Naked flowering scapes rise from a few inches to a
foot or more to bear umbels of pink, red-purple, rose, or white flowers.
Although buds are at first upright, their stalks gradually bend down so that the
flowers hang. Later they right themselves as the seed capsules ripen. The flowers
are unique and always captivating. The four or five showy petals are swept back-
ward, and the beak-like dark stamens and stigma shoot forward and downward.
Cultural conditions vary according to habitat for shooting stars: summer-
dormant kinds need a rest with little water, and ample winter/spring moisture.
They thrive in full sun near the coast and filtered light inland. Winter-dormant
kinds should have a winter rest, and require ample water from late spring
through summer. Some may not be amenable to lowland gardens, but at least
the middle-elevation *D. jeffreyi* accommodates itself well. Mass summer-dormant
species in the front of a mixed border with spring bulbs, or grow them in containers with spring annuals, then store them away when dormant. The winter-
dormant kinds are fine in a meadow garden, or edging a pond. Here are some
common species:

D. clevelandii. Cleveland's shooting stars. This is a more robust species than *D. hendersonii*, from southern California, and its flowers are paler and larger. Some forms
bear white flowers. The variety *insularis* from the Channel Islands is especially
large and vigorous, with flowering stalks to over a foot. Choice. Summer dormant.

D. hendersonii. Henderson's shooting stars. The most common species of the central and northern foothills: summer dormant. Flowers vary from purple to pink,
and some races have four while others have five petals. Easy in containers.

D. jeffreyi. Jeffrey's shooting stars. The giant of shooting stars, from middle to high
mountain meadows. Its roots need moisture all growing season. The leaves turn
upright and may be six inches or more long. Tall flowering stalks bear lovely red-
purple flowers. The best of the mountain shooting stars for the garden.

D. subalpinum and *alpinum.* Alpine shooting stars. These are closely similar species
of high-mountain meadows, needing constant moisture. They are mountain versions of *D. hendersonii* in size and flower shape, the flowers mostly pink-purple
and showy. These may not adapt well to lowland gardens, but are worth trying
for their fine summer floral display.

Primula suffrutescens. Sierra Primrose. Primrose family.

HT: 4 to 6 inches   FLW CL: rose-pink   FLW TM: July to August   PRPG: rooted sections or seeds (stratify)   EXP: full sun   WT: some summer water with excellent
drainage

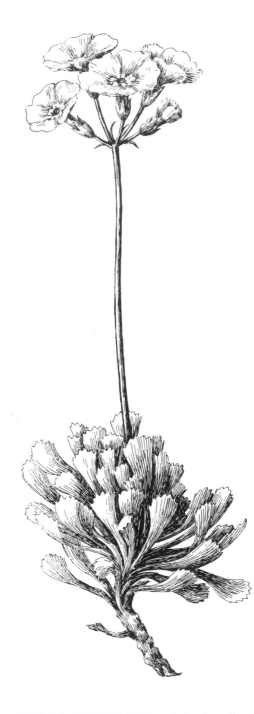

SIERRA PRIMROSE—*Primula suffrutescens.*

It's fitting in a book about perennials to talk about our only native *Primula*. Although it is woody, it is scarcely shrubby, being rather a subwoody creeper with widely searching branches whose long, deep roots anchor it periodically as it crawls over rock scree at timberline. Its habitat suggests a marriage between perfect drainage and abundant moisture from receding snowbanks. The stems are heavily clothed with bright green, narrowly elliptical toothed leaves; shortly after growth has resumed, these are partly hidden by the numerous, short-stalked clusters of gaudy, electric rose-pink or rose-purple flowers with yellow throats. The color of Sierra primrose nearly matches that of several other high-mountain gems: mountain pride penstemon, rockfringe, and red heather.

In the garden, Sierra primrose would be the perfect choice for a mountain rockery where it could run between gravelly stones and drape down a bank. Unfortunately, it is unlikely that it ever will do well in lowland gardens. The only possibility of success lies with acclimating seedlings from field-collected seed.

Trientalis latifolia. Star Flower. Primrose family.

HT: 4 to 6 inches   FLW CL: white to pink   FLW TM: April to June   PRPG: offsets or divisions   EXP: shade   WT: some summer water

Star flower is a delicate fall/winter-dormant herb from a small deep-seated tuber. In spring, the delicate new light green leaves unfold a bit later than trilliums. The resemblance to the latter includes the broad whorled leaves, but flowering-size plants bear four, five, or six leaves as compared to the three for trilliums. Star flower is delicate, with a thread-like stalk; grows only inches high; and bears graceful white to pale pink flowers, each a perfect five- to seven-pointed star. Star flowers are best appreciated at close range; plant them in colonies for best effect. They live in cool, shaded coast redwood forests or moist slopes of mixed conifer forests in the mountains. They combine well with redwood sorrel, trilliums, modesty, violets, and Solomon's plumes.

Star flower is suitable only for cool woodland gardens. The colony increases through underground vegetative reproduction, but is never invasive. Other companions include the smaller ferns.

Rockrose Family
(Cistaceae)

The rockroses from the Mediterranean countries are prominent in California gardens, but little is known of our own natives in their single genus. Because they are less showy, they will never fulfill the role held for the Mediterranean kinds, but they are charming in their own right.

Helianthemum. Sunrose, Rush Rose. Rockrose family.

HT: 6 to 9 inches   FLW CL: yellow   FLW TM: March to July   PRPG: half-woody cuttings or seeds (burn treatment)   EXP: full sun   WT: little summer water

California has three sunroses, all small subshrubs slightly woody at the base with numerous, green, rush-like branches. They suggest miniature brooms, growing no more than a foot tall and dwelling on dry, sometimes compacted soils on the edge of chaparral. They are particularly abundant after fire when they have little competition with more aggressive, taller shrubs. For success, they require full light.

Sunroses are seldom cultivated; the same genus has several showy garden-worthy species from the Mediterranean region. Still, our sunroses lend an interesting note to a rock garden where their green branches contrast with the ferny foliage of horkelias, the wooly white leaves of dune sage, or the gray-green spoon-shaped leaves of eriogonums. In summer, they bear perky, star-like flowers. There are three species: the common one, *H. scoparium*, ranges through the foothills and has small flowers; the two others are narrow endemics—*H. suffrutescens* from the Ione area (too rare to consider) and *H. greenei* from the Channel Islands. The latter has the showiest flowers but is not readily available.

Rose Family
(Rosaceae)

The roses are among our most diverse and important families, and are legendary for their garden uses. Well over half of our native genera belong, however, to woody genera: *Rosa, Rubus, Spiraea, Holodiscus, Heteromeles, Prunus, Osmaronia, Amelanchier, Malus, Crataegus, Adenostoma*, the list goes on and on. Still, the following entries attest to a number of fine perennials.

Acaena californica. Acaena, False Burnet. Rose family.

HT: in flower to 12 inches   FLW CL: green   FLW TM: April to May   PRPG: rhizome sections   EXP: full sun on coast   WT: some summer water

Acaena has basal clusters of pinnately divided and slashed leaves, rather like a narrow fern frond with parallel sides, and is similar to the true burnet of Europe. These develop from branched, subwoody rhizomes which travel through rocky soils atop coastal bluffs. The interesting and attractive leaves give *Acaena* garden merit—the flowers are more curious than showy, rising on stalks a few inches high with tight clusters of starry green petalless flowers with red-purple stamens. Because it comes from a mild winter and summer foggy climate, false burnet is probably not cold hardy, and would benefit from summer water. It is evergreen, keeping its leaves for long periods.

False burnet lends interesting texture to the front of a mixed border, or as a component of a coastal rock garden with rockcress, sea thrift, wallflower, creeping lupine, and others.

Aruncus vulgaris. Goatsbeard. Rose family.

HT: in flower to 3 or 4 feet   FLW CL: white   FLW TM: May to July   PRPG: root divisions   EXP: light shade   WT: summer water

Goatsbeard belongs to one of those groups which is horticulturally difficult to define. While it is winter dormant, it grows large with a base that becomes woody, yet it is really not a shrub. Found in the moist northwest corner of the state, along river banks and streams, goatsbeard springs from widely wandering roots each year. The leaves may reach three feet in length, and are much divided, the segments ovate with sawtooth edges, and the flowering panicles top these, attaining four or five feet, with hundreds of tiny white flowers in feathery plumes.

Goatsbeard is a superb plant for the back of a mixed border as long as it is given space, good drainage, and summer water. The old flowering stalks should be removed by mid to late summer as they turn brown. The rose-colored spiraeas and the shrubby ocean-spray with creamy flowers (*Holodiscus discolor*) might complement goatsbeard with similar flowers and flowering time, or plant it with large, feathery ferns.

Fragaria. Wild Strawberry. Rose family.

HT: 4 to 6 inches   FLW CL: white   FLW TM: varies   PRPG: rooted stolons   EXP: light to full shade (sun near coast)   WT: some summer water

Our three wild strawberries are almost irrepressible in the garden. They start as single low rosettes, the leaves divided in the fashion typical for strawberries into three broad, conspicuously veined leaflets with saw-teeth along the edge. Soon the mother rosette sends out stolons to anchor new rosettes, and these in turn send out their own stolons. Thus, strawberries are great colonizers and stabilizers. One species grows on coastal sand dunes and bluffs; another frequents coastal and yellow pine forests, and the third climbs into subalpine forests along the edges of wet meadows. All three bear a succession of short-stalked single flowers with showy white petals and numerous yellow stamens, and are followed by tasty red berries. Once established, the strawberries can carry on with little summer water, but they look better when watered.

Because of their invasive qualities, the wild stawberries are not often used with timid plants. They make a fine ground cover, the coastal kind in full sun, the forest kinds in shade, but will tolerate only modest amounts of foot traffic (this is one way to keep them in bounds). They are also controlled by pulling out the new stolons, and digging out the rooted plantlets. Obviously, they are excellent for quickly establishing a ground cover on bare earth. Here are the three species:

F. californica. Woodland strawberry. From woods of low to middle elevations. Dull green leaves with conspicuous veins. Small but tasty fruits if given plenty of water.

F. chiloensis. Coast strawberry. Quite drought tolerant; bears shiny, dark green leaves. Flowers are uncommonly large, but plants are dioecious, and only the female bear fruits, which are uncommonly large.

F. virginiana (platypetala). Mountain strawberry. From middle to subalpine zones; otherwise much like *F. californica*, but the leaves are bluish green. Not as vigorous in the lowland garden.

Geum. Geum, Avens. Rose family.

HT: in flower 6 inches to 2 feet   FLW CL: yellow or cream and pale pink   FLW TM: June to August   PRPG: divisions or seeds (stratify)   EXP: full sun   WT: some summer water

Geums superficially look much like potentillas, but differ in fruit: geums retain their styles as part of the dispersal mechanism. Our few species don't have the showy flowers found in cultivated kinds from other lands, but there are three species which add a note of interest and charm to gardens.

G. ciliatum/canescens. Alpine geum, pink plumes, or nodding avens. This species pair is much different from *G. macrophyllum*. Pink plumes has low rosettes of felted leaves which are divided (and in the second-named species, redivided) into narrow pinnate segments. Low flowering stalks bear nodding, bell-shaped flowers of pale pink-purple and cream—charming although not individually showy—and are followed by puffs of plume-like fruits. They grow in sandy soils on the edge of dry meadows, and may bloom sporadically in lowland gardens. Plant them with whorled penstemons and potentillas.

G. macrophyllum. Large-leaf geum. This common mid- to high-mountain species grows in moist meadows. The leaves look very much like those of the garden geums; pinnately compound with the terminal leaflet much larger than the lateral ones. Unfortunately, the tall flowering stems bear disappointing small yellow flowers. The seed heads, however, add interest; they look like pink pincushions.

Horkelia. Horkelia. Rose family.

HT: 4 to 8 inches   FLW CL: white   FLW TM: May to August   PRPG: divisions   EXP: full sun   WT: summer dry

This little-known genus has no well-established common name, but is closely allied to the potentillas. It differs by having smaller flowers and by the strong, sage-like odor of the foliage. Short rootstocks gradually increase the size of local clumps, each a dense basal rosette of pinnately divided leaves, the divisions often toothed or slashed and the overall pattern fern-like. From these, naked flower stalks inches high bear dense clusters of small white flowers. The various horkelias are difficult to distinguish and for horticultural purposes this is unimportant. They grow in coastal prairies, sandy or rocky soils on the edge of brush and woodlands, and often, as with the lone horkelia, on nutrient-poor soils. In addition they thrive on little summer water and hot summers, although moderate water will enhance the appearance of the leaves. Stressed plants may lose most of their leaves until the rainy season.

Horkelias are best used where the attractive, aromatic foliage is a plus—especially in rock gardens, or the front of a dry mixed border. The flowers themselves are insignificant.

Ivesia. Rock Potentilla, Mouse-tails. Rose family.

HT: in flower 4 to 12 inches   FLW CL: yellow, light purple, white   FLW TM: June to August   PRPG: some divisions or seeds (stratify)   EXP: full sun   WT: some summer water with excellent drainage

Ivesias are close relatives to horkelias and potentillas; they bear finely pinnately dissected leaves (mostly in basal rosettes), and open cymes or panicles of small white, pink, or yellow flowers. Leaves are not aromatic as they are in horkelias, and flowers are individually smaller than those of potentillas. Ivesias are to be sought in high granite crevices and rocky borders of subalpine and alpine meadows. They have charming leaves and delicate, graceful flowers and make fine additions to rock gardens; the majority thrive only in mountain gardens. Here is a sampling of species:

I. lycopodioides. Yellow mouse-tail. Leaves are not quite so finely divided as in *I. santolinoides* but still give the impression of a green tail, and the flowers are bright yellow. Grows on the edge of alpine meadows.

I. muirii. From subalpine rock scree. Coarsely divided leaves and dense clusters of yellow flowers. Very nice for a rock garden.

I. santolinoides. White mouse-tail. The leaves of this species are so finely dissected, and the segments overlap so tightly, that the overall effect is like a real gray-green mouse tail. Open panicles bear small white flowers.

I. unguiculata. This is the *Ivesia* most likely to grow in lowland gardens, since it lives as low as 6,000 feet on the borders of dry meadows. Leaves are coarsely divided, and the cymes of flowers are pink-purple.

Potentilla. Cinquefoil, Potentilla. Rose family.

HT: 4 inches to 2 feet   FLW CL: white, cream, yellow, purple   FLW TM: varies   PRPG: divisions or seeds (stratify) or rooted stolons   EXP: full sun to light shade   WT: some summer or full summer water

Potentillas are a varied group whose strawberry- or buttercup-like flowers are usually white or yellow. The leaves are most often pinnately compound, but some have only three leaflets, and one kind has palmately compound leaves. The common name cinquefoil, old French for five leaves, applies because of the divisions. Most species have rootstocks or short rhizomes, but a few creep and root or send out strawberry-like runners with new plantlets. One species is a low shrub. Potentillas range from coastal marshes and bluffs across foothills and

CINQUEFOIL—*Potentilla.*

mountains to the alpine. The most common habitat is mountain meadows. Most are either evergreen or winter dormant, and require year-round moisture and full light in the garden. A few require soggy soil for healthy growth. The best use for most is in a natural meadow or around a pond, but the woody species is nice at the back of a mixed border. Here are some worthy species:

P. drummondii/breweri. Mountain cinquefoils. Closely related species from high mountain meadows, often in sandy soils. The leaves are pinnately compound, gray-green to silvery (the latter), and with showy yellow flowers. Trim and neat habits, but not proven adaptable to lowland gardens.

P. egedii/anserina. Silverweed, creeping cinquefoil. The former grows along coastal marshes, the latter in wet mountain meadows. Both are tolerant of slightly alkaline soils, and they spread by red runners. Leaves are pinnately compound, bright green above and silvery-white beneath. Flowers are showy, bright yellow, much like buttercups. Easy to grow, but invasive.

P. fruticosa. Shrubby cinquefoil. Circumboreal species from the scree of high mountains. Several cultivars are available for lowland gardens. The small leaves are deeply toothed and lobed, and the flowers bright yellow.

P. glandulosa. Sticky cinquefoil. This is the most widely distributed, having varieties from seashore to timberline. The leaves are reminiscent of strawberry, but have more leaflets, and the rather small flowers vary from cream color to yellow. The upper stems have glandular hairs, hence the name. Easy to grow, but only the high-mountain races are attractive.

P. palustris. Marsh cinquefoil. Has creeping stems and lives in shallow water of coastal marshes and mountain bogs with acid soils. The pinnately compound leaves are gray-green, and the curious flowers are deep red-purple. Pretty for a marsh or pond.

St. Johnswort Family

(Hypericaceae)

Our single genus, *Hypericum*, is modest but already familiar to gardeners from the several species in cultivation from other parts of the world. California has three worthy of attention.

Hypericum. St. Johnswort, Tinker's Penny, Goldwire. St. Johnswort family.

HT: 2 to 18 inches   FLW CL: yellow, salmon-yellow   FLW TM: June to September
PRPG: root divisions or seed   EXP: full sun to light shade   WT: varies

The familiar ground cover *H. calycinum* and the noxious weed *H. perforatum* are species not discussed here. The native hypericums vary from tiny, sprawling meadow plants to clump-forming wiry-stemmed perennials which grow on the edge of chaparral. All bear opposite, close-set leaves, dotted with dark glands

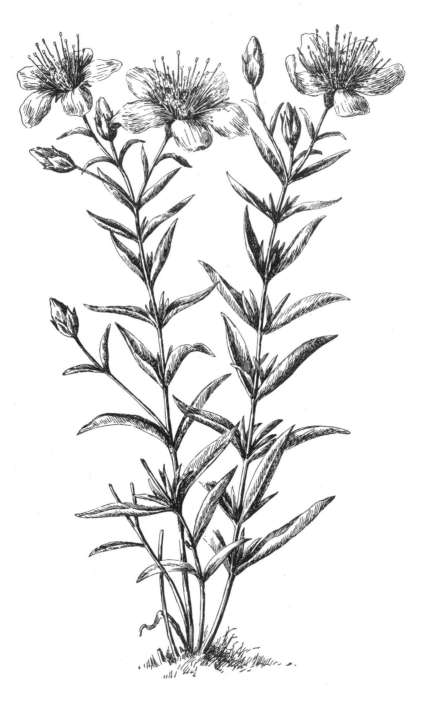

ST. JOHNSWORT—*Hypericum.*

along the edge, and all bear pretty, open yellow pimpernel-like flowers with numerous yellow stamens arranged in bunches. All flower in summer.

H. anagalloides. Tinker's penny. An inch-high, trailing plant with stems along the surface of wet soil of open meadows where there is little competition for light. The pale green, rounded leaves are complemented by miniature salmon-yellow flowers similar in appearance to the scarlet pimpernel. Tinker's penny adapts well to gardens, but is limited because of its requirement for little competition and constant moisture. It is delightful along the front edge of a pond, or in a planter with such other miniatures as mountain white violet, primrose monkeyflower, and mountain clover.

H. concinnum. Goldwire. Drought tolerant. The low clumps form a nice ground cover in front of chaparral shrubs or in front of a dry mixed border. The blue-green leaves are narrow and curl on hot days. Clusters of the bright yellow St. Johnswort flowers appear in early summer. Good with sunrose and little-leaf ceanothus (*C. foliosus*).

H. formosum scouleri. Meadow St. Johnswort. Resembles Klamath weed, but is not aggressive. It has upright leafy stems to almost two feet, is winter dormant, and covered with bright yellow flowers in early summer. A nice plant for the middle of a watered mixed border or meadow garden.

Saxifrage Family
(Saxifragaceae)

Like the roses, the saxifrages are a large and varied clan with many species already well known to gardeners everywhere. The several shrub genera, particularly *Carpinteria*, *Philadelphus*, and *Ribes*, are fine subjects for the garden, but don't belong in a book on perennials. Most of our herbaceous saxifrages are of easy culture and fit beautifully onto rocky, mossy, semishaded banks.

Boykinia. Brook Saxifrage, Rock Saxifrage. Saxifrage family.
HT: in flower to 12 or 15 inches   FLW CL: white   FLW TM: summer   PRPG: divisions   EXP: shade   WT: some summer water

Our two species are closely similar—one from the northern mountains, and one from the forests of the coast and foothills. Their habitat is quite specific: roots embedded in mosses of rocks along permanent streams. Here they find home next to liverworts, horsetails, brook orchids, and sedges, the rhizomes never far from the spray of cascading water. The broad, nearly round leaves have margins with coarse, pointed to scalloped teeth, and the flowering stalks arise from the rosette centers to branch into graceful, airy panicles of small, white, star-like flowers. In the garden, they should receive good drainage and year-round moisture in light shade. Snails and slugs are particularly fond of the foliage.

   The brook saxifrages add delicacy and charm to the woodland garden and are pretty by a waterfall, stream, or pond edge. The two species differ in size: *B. elata* is the common lowland kind with small flowers; *B. major*, the mountain species with more robust leaves and flowers twice the size.

Heuchera. Alumroot, Coral-Bells. Saxifrage family.

HT: in flower 6 to 30 inches   FLW CL: white to pink   FLW TM: May to August
PRPG: divisions or seeds   EXP: light to full shade   WT: some summer water

The alumroots all grow from sturdy rootstocks on rocky slopes in partial shade, or in the high mountains, fully exposed to the subalpine sun. The leaves are not only prettily scalloped, but in the sun develop beautiful mottling, the veins turning deep purple. Thus, the leaves provide a show by themselves. In late spring to summer airy panicles of flowers are carried up to 12 inches above the leaves, according to species. The numerous tiny flowers are bell shaped, white to pink, and hang prettily from the ends of thread-like stalks. Of all the woodland saxifrages, this genus is the easiest to grow and most satisfactory in flower. Although plants are quite drought tolerant once established, they look fresh longer with some summer water.

The use of alumroots depends upon the species: the lowland kinds are lovely in woodland settings, perhaps mixed with some of their close relatives and various small ferns. The high-mountain kinds are better subjects for the rock garden owing to the scale of the flowering stalks and their need for full sun. There are several cultivars now available from hybrids between our native heucheras and the New Mexican coral-bells (*H. sanguinea*). The result is long-flowering with lovely bell-shaped pink flowers. Here are some of the best species:

H. maxima. Island alumroot. Closely related to the *H. micrantha* but with even larger leaves and taller panicles. Easy in the woodland garden and attractive all year with water. Somewhat tender in cold climates. Flowers larger.

H. micrantha. Common alumroot. Grows readily in the garden, and comes from lowland forests. Its decorative leaves and graceful, tall plumes of flowers are good in woodland settings. Flowers dainty and small in white or pink.

H. pilosissima. Shaggy alumroot. Grows on rocky bluffs near the coast in northern California. The panicles are shorter and stockier, the individual flowers larger, and the whole covered with attractive, shaggy, white hairs. Woodland gardens or shaded rock gardens.

H. rubescens. Mountain or alpine alumroot. The best kind for the rock garden. It is much like a very scaled-down *H. micrantha*, the leaf rosettes low and neat, and the panicles nicely in balance. Choice. Flowers white to pink.

Jepsonia Parryi. Jepsonia. Saxifrage family.

HT: in flower to 6 or 8 inches   FLW CL: white to pinkish   FLW TM: September and October   PRPG: seeds, offsets   EXP: full sun   WT: some summer water with drainage

This is a surprising, little-known member of the saxifrage clan. It is winter dormant to a corm-like underground stem, sends up rosettes of round, lobed leaves in spring, and as these gradually wither away, a short cyme of white or white-striped pink flowers appear by fall. Not only is such a life cycle unusual, but the flowers appear when most other plants have long since set seed. In nature, Jepsonia is uncommon, finding refuge amongst lava and other rocks in foothill situations away from the competition of the surrounding chaparral or scrub. Since the plants vary considerably, different varieties—even separate species—have been named, but horticulturally all can be treated alike.

Jepsonia is not a showy plant and would be lost in a border. Rather, its best use is as a potted specimen where it receives the excellent drainage it requires, or in a lowland rock garden setting with other saxifragaceous plants. It does well with small rock ferns which could hide the faded, browned leaves and naked flowering stalks.

Lithophragma. Woodland Star. Saxifrage family.

HT: in flower 8 to 18 inches   FLW CL: white or occasionally pink   FLW TM: mostly April to May   PRPG: divisions or offsets   EXP: shade   WT: summer dormant (dry)

The delicate woodland stars are common on shaded rocky moss-covered banks in woodlands throughout the foothills. A couple wander up to middle or subalpine heights, but most stay to the low country. All come from bulb-bearing rootstocks and are mostly summer/fall dormant. The leaves, forming small rosettes, usually don't exceed an inch in length and are rounded and palmately lobed. In some they become intensely reddish or purple. From these unassuming leaves, racemes arise with white (rarely pink) flowers whose five petals look like snowflakes or stars. Other wildflowers sharing this habitat include clarkias, shooting stars, fairy lanterns, and collinsias, all of which make fitting garden companions.

In the garden, woodland stars can be massed on the edge of a woodland on a mossy bank with small ferns and some of the flowers mentioned above. They need to be planted this way in order to be noticed and also protected from snails and slugs, which easily decimate the flowers. They are tolerant of summer water, and must have filtered light to flower properly. I will not list the species since they are difficult to identify and have similar cultural requirements.

Mitella. Mitrewort, Bishop's Cap. Saxifrage family.

HT: to 6 inches   FLW CL: green   FLW TM: variable   PRPG: rooted stolons   EXP: shade   WT: summer moist

The few species of mitrewort wander from low coastal forests to the subalpine forests of the Sierra, always staying in shaded, damp situations. It is no understatement that mosquito and mitrewort habitats go hand in hand. The leaves are a light green, generally smaller than those of the other look-alikes, and rosettes send out stolons to start more rosettes in strawberry fashion. The flowering

WOODLAND STAR—*Lithophragma.*

stalks are the shortest of the group, no more than a few inches tall, but provide great beauty of form at close range or under magnification. The delicate green flowers reveal their full beauty with rounded sepals and slender, feathery, almost snowflake-like petals. Plant these where they can form a ground cover in the woodland garden, in front of a pond, or running over a rocky seep with small ferns. Two stand out for gardens: *M. ovalifolia* from northern forests is vigorous, almost invasive, and stands deep shade; *M. pentandra* from high mountains prefers a bit more sun, has larger leaves, and is less exuberant.

Parnassia. Grass-of-Parnassus. Saxifrage family.

HT: in flower to 8 inches   FLW CL: cream   FLW TM: July to September   PRPG: divisions or seeds (stratify)   EXP: light shade   WT: wet all year

The two or three parnassias are quite similar; all live in bogs or wet meadows and have basal clumps of simple, rounded, bright green leaves from perennial roots and are winter dormant. The six-inch flowering stalks bear showy flowers with cream-colored petals and curious stamens, some sets transformed into gland-bearing sterile staminodia. The difference between species lies in details of these staminodia and in whether petals are fringed or not: *P. fimbriata* has fringed petals; *P. palustris* has entire petals. The elevations for *P. palustris* span 500 feet to timberline, but *P. fimbriata* comes only from middle to high elevations.

   Since they are lovers of moisture, parnassias must be planted where it is constantly wet; in front of a pond (with tinker's penny, primrose monkeyflower) or in the front of a meadow garden.

Peltiphyllum peltatum. Umbrella Plant, Indian Rhubarb. Saxifrage family.

HT: in flower to 3 1/2 feet   FLW CL: white to pink   FLW TM: May to July   PRPG: rhizome sections   EXP: light shade   WT: summer wet

This is the granddaddy of all saxifrages and has among the largest of any leaves of a California native. The plants are late fall/winter dormant, the husky rhizomes showing no signs of life until middle to late spring, when suddenly they send up naked flowering stalks to three or four feet. These branch into attractive panicles of white or pale pink flowers, which are followed by decorative reddish follicle-type seed pods. Just after the flowers, the leaves gradually unfold, the unfolding process itself interesting. Fully expanded, the leaves stand two or more feet on sturdy petioles, the blades peltate like an umbrella with nearly circular outline and spreading to three feet across. With some fall chill, leaves turn various shades of russet before being lost to the winter cold. Umbrella plants line permanent streams and rushing mountain rivers in the middle elevations of the Sierra and northern mountains, where their rhizomes find room to root between boulders on the edge of rushing torrents of a spring thaw. They are often accompanied by wild grape, sedge tufts, lilies, and stream orchids.

In the garden, the size and boldness of this plant make it highly ornamental, and it may stand alone as a specimen, or as a dramatic backdrop to a pond or beside a waterfall. The roots must have year-round moisture. Fitting companions with leaves on a similar scale include chain fern, aralia, and skunk cabbage.

Saxifraga. Saxifrage. Saxifrage family.

HT: in flower 4 inches to 20 inches   FLW CL: mostly white   FLW TM: varies   PRPG: rooted sections or seeds   EXP: mostly light shade   WT: varies

This genus gives the family its name, and it is well distributed through rocky areas of the mountains of the northern hemisphere, with many ornamentals already grown from mountains of the Old World. Our natives are poorly known, but they have all of the charm of other saxifrages. They seek out mossy spots on rocky walls or along rushing mountain brooks and damp meadows. Never showy, they make up for this by grace and form. Flowers are small but borne in airy panicles or dense racemes, and are white or pinkish. Leaves are borne in basal rosettes but vary considerably in shape. All go dormant, but the lowland kinds are summer/fall dormant while the mountain ones are winter dormant. Saxifrages are best suited to shaded rock gardens or the edge of woodland gardens, and many blend well with close relatives such as alumroot, fringe cups, and brook saxifrage. Here are four species for the garden:

S. californica. California saxifrage. Here is another summer-dormant plant from moss-covered rocks of foothills, where it grows with shooting stars, red larkspur, and woodland star. The low rosettes are fuzzy and the leaves broadly tongue shaped but with few small teeth. The small white flowers are in dense cymes and are complemented by the red-pink sepals. Vulnerable to snails and slugs.

S. mertensiana. Merten's or foothill cliff saxifrage. This is one of our dramatic summer-dormant denizens of moss-covered rock walls and cliffs in the foothills of the Coast Ranges. As soon as winter rains start the new leaves emerge, and when spring rains cease, the flowering stalks have already dried up. Leaves are broad and round with an even row of jagged teeth; flowers are borne in open panicles.

S. oregana. Meadow saxifrage. This, despite its species name, is a common species of high wet Sierran meadows. The leaves are reminiscent of *S. californica*, but longer and rather pale green, and the stout flowering stalks rise a foot or more with tight spike-like racemes of white and pink flowers. Ideal around a pond.

S. punctata. Dotted saxifrage. This is a close relative to *S. mertensiana*, but grows along high-mountain streams. Leaves are of similar shape, but darker green and not hairy, and the delicate white flowers have petals with a yellow dot at their base.

Tellima grandiflora. Fringe Cups. Saxifrage family.

HT: in flower to 18 inches or more   FLW CL: green, white, or pink   FLW TM: April to June   PRPG: divisions or seeds (may self-sow)   EXP: shade   WT: some summer water

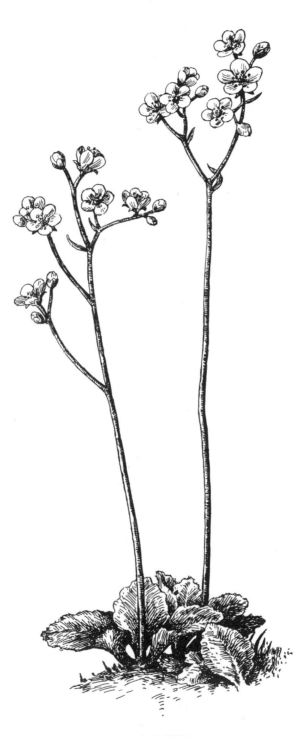

CALIFORNIA SAXIFRAGE—*Saxifraga californica.*

Fringe cups is often confused out of flower with alumroot. The leaves of the two are of similar shape and about the same size, but the underside of fringe cups leaves is a bit more boldly veined, and they seldom develop the mottling or purple coloration that alumroot leaves do in sun. The clumps increase slowly, but seeds start new plants with great enthusiasm. The flowering stalks are up to a foot high, bearing a long succession of cup-shaped flowers crowned by their white, green, or pink fringed petals. The variation in color means that some selection beforehand will result in a prettier show of flowers. Fringe cups, being taller and with more robust leaves, can be used with or even behind some of the smaller ground covers, or along mossy banks with various small- to medium-sized ferns.

Tiarella unifoliata. Sugar Scoops, Western Foam Flower. Saxifrage family.

HT: to 6 or 8 inches   FLW CL: white   FLW TM: May to July   PRPG: divisions   EXP: shade   WT: some summer water

There are several herbaceous saxifrage relatives from wooded situations, all of which have similar requirements and vegetative appearance; these include sugar scoops, mitreworts, alumroots, piggyback plant, and fringe cups. They are hard to separate by their leaves. I will discuss them here in some detail. All come from rootstocks which gradually increase the colonies, and all form short rosettes of broad, rounded leaves whose edges are variously scalloped, lobed, and toothed. Leaves all have interesting, intricate net-like patterns of veins, and all send up central, nearly leafless racemes or panicles of small flowers. Flower detail best identifies the various kinds.

Sugar scoops has rather dark green leaves whose lobes are more pointed than with the others, and the flower stalks, usually a few inches tall, carry horizontal to nodding shallow, bell-shaped white flowers followed by curious fruits which look like old-fashioned sugar scoops. These plants are seldom as common in nature as their other relatives, but are found in dark, damp coastal forests of the northwestern corner of the state. They are easy to establish, but really require summer water. Leaves remain evergreen through the year, but are a bit tired looking by winter.

All of these saxifrage relatives do well along stream banks, on mossy rocks, and in the foreground of a woodland garden, where they make nice texture contrasts with redwood sorrel, wild ginger, western bleedingheart, and redwood violet.

Tolmiea menziesii. Piggyback Plant. Saxifrage family.

HT: in flower to 15 inches   FLW CL: maroon-brown   FLW TM: May to June   PRPG: plantlets on leaves, division   EXP: shade   WT: water all year

This familiar houseplant is generally grown inside in hanging baskets but is really a native of the northwest coast, where it seeks the damp draws in deep shade of redwoods and Douglas fir. Few people are familiar with the flowers, but know the side shoots which form new rosettes and the vivaparous leaves (hence the name piggyback) which bear young plantlets at the junction of stalk and blade. Planted outdoors in cool, coastal gardens, they increase rapidly and flower every spring. The flowering stalks, up to a foot high, bear tiny, dark purple flowers, and petals thread-like and curling back like the legs of a spider. Obviously, piggyback will never win attention by its flowers but is another pleasing foliage plant, which is well adapted to the shade with summer water and cool temperatures. It is at home in the garden in much the same way as sugar scoops, except that it is inclined to increase its home territory more rapidly.

Whipplea modesta. Modesty, Yerba De Selva. Saxifrage family.

HT: 6 to 12 inches   FLW CL: white   FLW TM: May to July   PRPG: layering or rooted stems   EXP: shade   WT: some summer water

Here is a change from the usual saxifrage theme: the leaves are not in rosettes nor is the plant wholly herbaceous; instead we have a creeping half-woody, much-branched ground cover, often cascading over the edge of steep, rocky banks where it helps stabilize the soil. As such, modesty is useful in its native home and in the garden, and can be used as an evergreen creeper for difficult-to-contain slopes in a woodland setting. In this sense, it is much like the unrelated but similar appearing yerba buena, but the latter has aromatic leaves and is not fuzzy, as modesty is. In flower, modesty bears tight panicles of numerous tiny white, saxifrage-like flowers which are the reason for the common name. Modesty grows throughout the forests of the Coast Ranges, including some of the drier interior mountain mixed forests, and so is relatively drought tolerant when established.

Shield Fern Family
(*Aspidiaceae*)

The shield ferns embrace some of the most typical of our woodland ferns, many with rather lacy fronds. They are mostly medium-sized ferns which lend great beauty to woodland gardens.

Athyrium. Lady Fern. Shield fern family.

HT: up to 3 1/2 feet   PRPG: divisions or from spores   EXP: shade   WT: moist all year

Lady ferns are the epitome of delicate, lacy ferns. They provide an airy effect in a forest setting, and are especially nice around the back of a pond or in the background. Although the fronds are arranged in clumps, the rhizome eventually divides into several branches on old plants. Fronds are large, on the same order as those of the common sword fern. Since the common lady fern lives near streams or in forests from sea level to middle elevations, it should receive summer water in the garden.

Lady ferns are winter dormant, and their worst feature is the ragged, tattered fronds in fall before they die away entirely. These should be trimmed off. But the flush of new spring fronds is especially attractive. There are two kinds of lady fern, but only *A. filix-femina* is commonly cultivated. The alpine lady fern, *A. alpestre*, grows amongst granite boulders by rushing mountain streams, and is a smaller fern with tighter frond segments. It would be interesting to try it in lowland gardens, but it may well prove difficult and in need of a winter cold spell.

Dryopteris. Wood Fern. Shield fern family.

HT: 1 to 2 1/2 feet   PRPG: spores   EXP: shade   WT: moist all year

The wood ferns are medium-sized evergreen ferns of woodland situations. Altogether they are tough but with attractive, lacy fronds and are rather drought tolerant when established. They are also evergreen, although they pass through a winter period when the fronds look old and worn. Nonetheless, the fall and winter fronds do not all turn brown, nor are they particularly tattered as with the lady fern, giving them an advantage in filling a niche suitable to either. In the garden, wood ferns work well with common sword fern and lady fern in the shade. Both wood fern species should be used in front of or beside the slightly taller sword and lady ferns. Coast wood fern (*Dryopteris arguta*) is the tougher of the two, and quite drought tolerant when established. It can get by with light shade near the coast. The slightly taller spiny wood fern (*Dryopteris dilatata*) has broader, more delicate fronds which look surprisingly similar to those of lady fern and contrast well with the moisture-loving five-finger fern. It requires summer water and tolerates deeper shade. As with common sword fern, the wood ferns should periodically have their dead fronds removed.

Polystichum. Sword Fern. Shield fern family.

HT: 8 inches to 4 feet   PRPG: spores   EXP: shade   WT: some summer water

This genus has some of the most attractive and adaptable ferns for the garden. All are evergreen, but for proper appearance, the old brown fronds need to be periodically removed. Polystichums commonly live on dark forest floors and canyons, but some inhabit talus and scree in full sun at middle elevations. Although the latter appear highly drought tolerant, their fibrous roots reach deeply for hidden moisture; such kinds must be fully established in the garden before summer water is withheld. In time, polystichums establish roots capable of tapping hidden moisture, and even the common sword fern is quite summer drought tolerant when roots are fully established.

Polystichums vary from clumps six inches high for the scree-growing kinds to plumes three or four feet tall for the common sword fern (*P. munitum*). The lat-

SPREADING WOOD FERN—*Dryopteris dilatata.*

ter is most reliable and is always attractive in woodland gardens, especially with lacy ferns, and in the company of such shrubs as western azalea, spicebush, flowering currant, or mock orange. The smaller and rare *P. dudleyi* and *P. californicum* (Dudley and California sword ferns) have fronds partly to wholly twice divided. These establish themselves slowly, but are quite attractive in midspring with their flush of new fronds.

The remaining polystichums—holly fern (*P. lonchitis*), Shasta fern (*P. lemmonii*), and rock sword fern (*P. imbricans*)—are closely tufted, tough-fronded small rock ferns whose establishment is difficult, but they are attractive in a watered rock garden, or as potted plants.

Thelypteris. Water Fern. Shield fern family.
HT: 12 to 18 inches   PRPG: spores or divisions   EXP: shade   WT: all year

Our two native thelypterises have been passed from genus to genus, now classed as a *Dryopteris*, now as a *Lastrea*, but belong to the present genus according to current usage. Both are medium-sized, lacy ferns in the manner of lady and wood ferns, but are rare and difficult to obtain. This is a shame, for these are among the most beautiful of all lacy ferns even with their winter dormancy; the patterning of the new spring fronds and the graceful carriage of the fronds as they spill over a rock wall or cascade down a bank is a fine sight. Both live in protected, shaded canyons where running water is always present, and may be accompanied by such beautiful companions as Venus-hair fern, lady fern, twisted stalk (*Streptopus*), and fairy and Humboldt lilies. They should do well if they are carefully watched to prevent drying out, and are given supplemental summer water.

The best use is for the woodland garden, edging a pond, stream, or moist bank and planted, as suggested above, with some of their companions. Other partners could include wild ginger, snowy rein orchid, canyon sunflower, meadowrue, and red columbine. The two species come from different parts of the state: *T. nevadensis* from the northern Sierra at middle elevations; *T. pubescens* from coastal canyons of southern California. The former should be winter hardy in mountain retreats, while the latter is rather tender and best for coastal gardens.

Sunflower Family
(Compositae or Asteraceae)

This is our largest family, and has so many genera that it boggles the mind of the beginner. Unfortunately, the composites have been underrated as ornamentals both for fear of misidentification and because of their commonness; nonetheless, there are many dependable and colorful perennials deserving of garden space. Many provide color late in the year: summer and fall when other natives are dormant.

Achillea. Yarrow. Mayweed tribe, sunflower family.

HT: in flower to 2 feet   FLW CL: white (rare pink forms, also)   FLW TM: May to August   PRPG: divisions   EXP: full sun   WT: summer dry when established

The yarrows are well known in gardens, and the usual varieties come from the Old World. Our own native yarrows are scarcely different from some of these, although normally they have white flowers only, unlike the selected pinks and yellows so common in gardens (there is a pink form from the Channel Islands). All are vigorous, even invasive plants from creeping rootstocks with large clumps of much dissected, aromatic, feathery, fern-like narrow leaves. Yarrow has been used medicinally throughout the northern hemisphere for the oils in the leaves; fresh, they smell like strong, bitter sage. Leaves remain green all year with summer water; without, they turn brown and die back in summer. The flowers are borne in heads, each tiny head complete with ray and disc flowers; the heads are in turn borne in flat-topped cymes, so that they produce a showy effect in garden borders. Cut flowers last a long time, and may be dried for fall arrangements. Flowers appear mainly in late spring to early summer, although our yarrows have such wide range in elevation that subalpine and alpine forms flower late into summer. Plants vary from robust in the foothills to only a few inches high at timberline. Two species and a few varieties are recognized and encompass nearly every open habitat, including serpentine soils. The varieties are, however, difficult to distinguish, and for the gardener are rather meaningless. Yarrows are one of the least demanding natives, but one must remember that under good conditions they may get out of bounds.

Anaphalis margaritacea. Pearly Everlasting. Everlasting tribe, sunflower family.

HT: to 2 feet   FLW CL: white and yellow   FLW TM: July to September   PRPG: root divisions   EXP: sun or light shade inland   WT: occasional summer water

Members of the sunflower family are best understood by the tribe they belong to. The everlastings all have wooly stems and leaves and flower heads which keep their color and form when dried early. Some everlastings are weedy, especially in the genus *Gnaphalium*. Pearly everlasting is a satisfyingly easy garden plant which grows as a colonizer along coastal bluffs, stabilized sand dunes, and at middle elevations on rocky meadow margins. Coastal forms adapt best to most gardens. The plants spread by rootstocks, so give them plenty of room to wander. In spring, new shoots carry narrow wool-covered leaves, attractive in themselves. By summer, the leafy stems have grown into flat-topped clusters of flower heads, from one to two feet tall. Each head is surrounded by several rows of pearly white bracts with tiny yellow flowers in the center. The massed effect is quite showy. Flowering stalks die back in fall and should be trimmed to the ground.

Pearly everlasting is great in a mixed border in the middle section, planted with perennials which don't die back in winter. Flowers are particularly good to use in dried arrangements. The plants are relatively drought tolerant, but look better with occasional summer water.

Antennaria. Pussytoes. Everlasting tribe, sunflower family.

HT: a few inches   FLW CL: rose to off white   FLW TM: June to August   PRPG: rooted divisions, seeds (stratify)   EXP: sun or light shade inland   WT: some summer water with good drainage

Pussytoes is the other everlasting with horticultural merit. Don't confuse it with pussy paws (*Calyptridium*) in the portulaca family or pussy ears (*Calochortus tolmiei*) of the lily family. Antennarias are like scaled-down pearly everlastings, but the rootstocks creep at soil level and are completely covered with a mat of low, soft, wool-covered leaves. Small clusters of white to pink flower heads are carried only inches above the leaves. Antennarias are mountain dwellers of open, sandy soils, dry edges of meadows, or amongst rocks.

Pussytoes have seldom been tried in home gardens. Their growth habits at low elevations may become ranker with the longer growing season; some may languish for want of cold winters. The several species are hard to differentiate without technical aid; it is more important to select them on the basis of tidiness and from the lowest elevations so that growth cycles more closely match those of lowland gardens. Pussytoes are a charming addition to rock gardens, or between stepping stones as a ground cover with low foot traffic.

Arnica. Arnica. Senecio tribe, sunflower family.

HT: in flower 1 to 2 feet   FLW CL: golden yellow   FLW TM: May to August   PRPG: root divisions or seeds   EXP: mostly light shade   WT: some summer water

The arnicas are close cousins to the senecios, but not nearly so variable. Although California boasts a couple of dozen species, some are unsuitable horticulturally because the heads only have small disc flowers. Still, many have showy heads with both ray and disc flowers, and are found from middle to subalpine zones of mountains throughout the state. Most prefer shaded meadow edges or openings in coniferous forests, and look best with some summer water. Arnicas make small clusters of upright leafy branches, the leaves opposite and varying from lance-shaped to broadly heart-shaped. The showy yellow flower heads are carried above the leaves.

Use arnicas for the edge of a woodland garden, or in mountain meadows, or massed in the middle of borders. The several species will not be enumerated here, as they differ on rather inconsequential particulars; they should be chosen on the basis of their habitat.

Aster and Erigeron. Aster, Fleabane, Wild Daisy. Aster tribe, sunflower family.

HT: from 2 inches to 4 feet   FLW CL: white, pink, purple, or blue with yellow centers

FLW TM: variable   PRPG: divisions or cuttings and seeds   EXP: full sun to light shade   WT: some summer water

These two genera are closely related, and to all but the experts, difficult to tell apart with reliance. For garden purposes they are both rather similar, which is to say that they vary according to habitat, but most have similar looking flowers: heads with several to numerous white, pink, purple, or blue rays around many tiny yellow disc flowers. Some are invasive, spreading by creeping root-stocks; others are tiny alpine gems with close cushions of fuzzy leaves with a taproot. Each kind needs to be considered on its own merits for the garden. Some high-mountain species will not adapt readily to lowland gardens, but as always, experimentation is needed: some mountain meadow species should grow happily at low altitudes.

Of the several aster species, there are few with a reliable enough reputation to recommend for the garden. *Aster subspicatus* is one such, which, while vigorous, provides a late summer and autumn show with minimal care. Flowering stalks to two feet bear several pretty heads reminiscent of Michaelmas daisies (developed from eastern U.S. asters). Others are either too invasive or have straggly stems and poor flower show (the rays looking half missing or ragged). For example, *A. chilensis* is a coastal species which invades everything in sight.

Rather than detail asters, therefore, I mention here several erigerons with which I am familiar. Many more should be tried.

E. cernuus. Siskiyou daisy. Grows on rock outcroppings at moderate elevations in the far northwestern Siskiyous. Its low, tidy clumps of narrow bright green leaves produce short stalks of pretty blue and yellow daisies in early summer. With deep watering, the plants become larger, but still retain attractive proportions; with little extra water, the plants remain cushiony, and are perfect for the lowland rock garden.

E. compositus. Alpine daisy. The finest of all rock garden daisies with tight mounds of wooly, pinnately divided leaves and miniature white and yellow daisies borne on stalks an inch high. It must have granite gravel and good drainage, and is a real star in a mountain rock garden.

E. glaucus. Seaside daisy. One of the most reliable species, occurring on bluffs and dunes along the central and north coast. Multiply branched stems form compact leafy tufts with broad, pale green to blue-green leaves which remain in good condition all year with summer water. Large daisy heads decorate stems through the summer, with a longer season next to the immediate coast. Rays are typically blue-purple, but forms with white rays are known.

E. inornatus. Rayless aster. Varies in size according to elevation, but consistently bears several upright branches with narrow, almost linear leaves, and bunches of bright yellow flowers at the top. The flowers are exclusively disc flowers without the familiar rays. Some larger forms flower in late summer at middle elevations and would put on a good show in the middle of a mixed border.

BEACH ASTER—*Erigeron.*

E. peregrinus/coulteri. Mountain daisies. These two showy species are commonly encounterd in the middle and subalpine parts of the mountains, mostly in meadows. They flower freely in summer, have undistinguished clumps of leafy stems, and once established gradually increase their numbers.

E. philadelphicus. Common daisy. Occurs sporadically throughout the foothills in microhabitats of grassy places which stay moist late. Under favorable circumstances plants grow to 18 inches tall, from basal clusters of leaves, and produce a succession of attractive daisy flowers with numerous narrow rays. Color varies from nearly white to deep pink-purple, and color selections should be made accordingly. Under garden conditions, common daisy may act like an annual, but readily reseeds itself. It should be cut back after flowering. It does best with summer water.

E. pygmaeus. Pygmy aster. Although not so scaled down as *E. compositus,* pygmy aster also is a low plant from near timberline. It sends up a few short stalks with narrow leaves and a few large heads of flowers with intensely red-purple or blue-purple rays and yellow discs. It would be more amenable to the ordinary garden than alpine daisy, although it grows best in a mountain rock garden with winter chill.

Balsamorhiza. Balsamroot. Sunflower tribe, sunflower family.
HT: in flower 2 to 3 feet   FLW CL: bright yellow   FLW TM: varies   PRPG: divisions or seeds   EXP: full sun   WT: varies

In most respects the balsamroots are just like the mule's ears (*Wyethia*). In the high Sierra, the two genera often grow intermixed, and in such cases, the amateur has great trouble distinguishing them. In all, the large handsome leaves come from branched rootstocks which form large colonies; large showy flower heads are carried above with golden yellow ray and disc flowers. Balsamroot leaves come in two forms: wooly gray leaves with a triangular outline, or gray to green leaves which are deeply slashed or pinnatifid.

Balsamroots, because of size and space, need a large-scale meadow garden, a large area of a border, or the back part of a mountain rock garden. Although several come from the drier mountains of the Siskiyous and eastern Sierra, at least one species—*B. macrolepis*—is found near San Francisco Bay and should be quite amenable to garden conditions in the foothills. It and a companion species from further north—*B. hookeri*—are the ones with deeply slashed leaves.

Chrysopsis villosa. Golden Aster. Aster tribe, sunflower family.
HT: 8 to 12 inches   FLW CL: yellow   FLW TM: June to August   PRPG: divisions or seeds   EXP: full sun   WT: occasional summer water

This is the only species worthy of consideration in this small genus. It has a wide geographic range and lives in exposed rocky places, often on sandy soil—coastal bluffs, the edge of chaparral, or exposed mountain slopes. The rootstocks creep between rocks to establish broad mats of basal leaves, the leaves covered with pretty white adpressed hairs. Branched flowering stalks a few inches high are produced from summer to early fall and bear several bright yellow heads of aster-like flowers. In seed, the hairy pappus makes conspicuous puffs which some find unattractive: the stalks should be cut off at this stage. Golden aster always keeps some leaves and so may be useful around winter-deciduous plants. The roots should be summer drought tolerant, except in the most sandy soils.

According to size and habit, golden aster shows to best advantage in a rock garden, either with other coastal plants—sea thrift, coast rockcress, golden yarrow—or with higher mountain flowers—mat phlox, sulfur buckwheat, pussy paws, spear pod.

Cirsium. Native Thistles. Thistle tribe, sunflower family.

HT: from 8 inches to 6 or more feet   FLW CL: white, pink, rose, purple, red   FLW TM: late spring to summer   PRPG: mostly seeds   EXP: full sun to very light shade   WT: varies

You may be familiar with the nonnative thistles as terrible pests; they are signs of poor land management. Yet, our own native thistles never behave this way; they keep to undisturbed places from coastal bluffs up to timberline, mostly favoring sandy or rocky soils, often where there is little competition with other plants. A few are narrow endemics, and a few live around permanent springs. The majority live in full sun, although coastal species should have light shade inland, and a few mountain species inhabit forest margins. One of the best features of native thistles is their attractive foliage, typically displayed in a basal rosette atop a strong taproot, the flowering stalks arising from the center. The life cycle is often biennial, the first year spent in the rosette stage, the second in producing flowers. Thistle leaves are coarsely toothed to shallowly pinnately lobed, the lobes ending in protective spines, and the leaves often covered with beautiful white to gray wool. Flowering stalks may top six feet, although in some coastal and subalpine species they nestle within the leaf rosette to avoid strong winds. Flower heads are quite large (sometimes more than two inches high), protected by wicked spiny bracts, the individual flowers long and tubular, and in many species, brightly colored. Flower structure favors nature's most colorful pollinators: butterflies and hummingbirds.

Thistles thrive in sandy well-drained soils, and cannot be expected to live long in the garden. They are favorite gopher food, so may need to be containerized. Their bold leaf patterns set them apart; they should be planted to take advantage of this. Low-growing species could go in the fore of a rock garden, tall-flowered kinds toward the back of a border. Here are some of the showiest species:

C. andersonii. Sierra thistle. A forest edge species growing up to about three feet with very showy heads of red-purple flowers.

C. breweri/vaseyi. Seep thistles. Grow in wet places with tall flowering stalks to six or more feet, mostly with red-purple flowers. Back of pond.

C. drummondii. Alpine thistle. Forms low clumps with very spiny green leaves and central white to purple flowers. Edge of a meadow garden or mountain rock garden.

C. eatonii. Eaton's thistle. Very decorative ruffled, gray foliage and striking heads of rose-red flowers to two feet. High mountains.

C. occidentale/coulteri/californicum. Cobweb thistles. A series of closely related species, mostly with cobwebby wooly hairs on leaves and bracts, and with showy heads of flowers which range from purple to rose-red; flowering stalks to six feet. Dry borders.

C. quercetorum. Oakleaf thistle. Forms low mounds on bluffs overlooking the ocean, with tight central clusters of white to purple flowers. Coast rock garden.

Coreopsis. Coreopsis, Sea Dahlia. Sunflower tribe, sunflower family.

HT: 2 to 6 feet   FLW CL: yellow   FLW TM: April to June   PRPG: stem cuttings (well-healed) or seeds   EXP: full sun or light shade inland   WT: summer dry

Most native coreopsises are spring annuals of deserts and dry foothills, but two are perennial. They are large, showy plants with bold design, and come from coastal areas of southern California. Both start life as plants with large rosettes of bright green, fern like leaves which give rise to circles of large, bright yellow flower heads of great beauty. Individual heads are surrounded by deep green bracts, showy, coarsely toothed ray flowers, and numerous central disc flowers. Flowers appear in profusion from mid to late spring. Plants look untidy later as flower heads go to seed—these should be cut off—and leaves get ragged and turn brown when plants are not watered. Perennial coreopsises need a summer/fall rest, but look better with moderate summer water. They do poorly with hot, dry summers.

The sea dahlia, *C. maritima*, keeps its leaves longer but is rather short lived. In flower it may attain three feet and is handsome toward the back of a mixed border, or as a specimen plant in a large container which can be moved when the flower show is finished. It is cold tender and will not survive in areas of hard frosts. The tree coreopsis, *C. gigantea*, produces its leaves on a stem which grows into a trunk up to six, seven, or eight feet. It is prone to rot in cold, wet winters and is frost tender. Its worst feature is the loss of all leaves in dry summers, so that the stems look like so many dead green sticks. If it is to be treated as summer drought tolerant, it should be planted in a desert garden setting with cacti and summer-dormant desert shrubs such as ocotillo, mesquite, and palo verde. Otherwise, it can be grown in the back of a mixed border where lower plants hide the barren stems. The show of flowers and the delicate ferny leaves merit the effort.

Corethrogyne californica. Dune or Bluff Aster. Aster tribe, sunflower family.

HT: 2 to 4 inches   FLW CL: lavender with yellow center   FLW TM: June to October   PRPG: rooted sections or seeds   EXP: full sun   WT: some summer water

The corethrogynes were once classified as asters and are very closely related, differing principally in the gray-wooly leaves and the tawny pappuses. They are plants of sandy areas, along coastal bluffs and dunes; other species grow inland in openings of scrub, chaparral, and pine forest. These upright kinds are not included here—our one species being the sprawling coastal plant whose habit is best suited to garden situations. Widely scrambling stems root as they go, and are clothed with pretty spoon-shaped leaves covered with a close felt of silvery hairs. In summer, the stems produce a long succession of showy flower heads with pink-purple rays and yellow centers, which contrast pleasingly with the foliage. Dune aster will tolerate some summer water, especially inland, and grows well in coastal rock gardens with yellow grindelia, seaside daisy, and sea thrift.

Encelia californica. California Brittle-Bush or Incienso. Sunflower tribe, sunflower family.

HT: 1 to 4 feet   FLW CL: yellow rays and purple disc flowers   FLW TM: late winter through spring   PRPG: softwood cuttings or seeds   EXP: full sun (near coast)   WT: occasional summer water with good drainage

Most of the encelias are woody shrubs, but California brittle-bush qualifies more as a bushy perennial, being woody just at the base. The sturdy roots send out circular bunches of rather brittle green-woody branches; on one variety these lie close to the ground, while otherwise they radiate outwards and upwards. Leaves are harsh, pale green, and ovate, and when watered stay on the plant all year. Large daisy heads are produced over a long period near the coast; rays are bright yellow, and central disc flowers dark purple. Brittle-bush needs perfect drainage or sandy soils, where it grows with other coastal sage plants, and is intolerant of hard frosts.

The bushy form gives brittle-bush a place toward the back of borders or in coastal rock gardens.

Enceliopsis argophylla. Panamint Daisy. Sunflower tribe, sunflower family.

HT: in flower to 18 or 24 inches   FLW CL: yellow   FLW TM: April to June   PRPG: seeds or softwood cuttings   EXP: full sun   WT: summer dry or very occasional water with perfect drainage

This handsome perennial is the emblem of the California Native Plant Society. It is a rather rare plant, confined to steep ravines in the desert mountains near Death Valley, particularly the Panamints. There it lives on very small amounts of highly seasonal rainfall in rocky soils which drain rapidly—it must have perfect drainage in the garden with gravel around the crown and lots of heat and sun. It repays the effort of growing it with large circles of oval silvery leaves atop a stout woody taproot and flowering stalks carrying large yellow daisies to 18 inches or more. Curiously, the seeds are very easy to germinate, but damp off readily and rapidly lose their viability.

Use Panamint daisy in a desert garden, the back of a rock garden, or as a specimen by itself in a large container. Choice.

Eriophyllum. Wooly Sunflower, Oregon Sunshine, Golden Yarrow, Lizardtail. Sneezeweed tribe, sunflower family.

HT: 4 to 18 or more inches   FLW CL: golden yellow   FLW TM: May to August   PRPG: cuttings and seeds   EXP: full sun to very light shade   WT: many, summer dry

Technically, the eriophyllums are either subshrubs or annuals, but their uses dictate mention here. The perennial species have multiple, spreading, half-decumbent branches, the ends of which are fully herbaceous. Leaves vary from short and deeply toothed to pinnately dissected and are covered with wool underneath, but are usually green on top. Wool also clothes the stems and bracts around the flower heads. The latter are borne in open cymes from late spring through summer, each head with bright yellow ray and disc flowers. The massed effect is showy wherever found. The three species cited range from coastal bluffs to timberline in the Sierra, but all live on rocky or sandy banks, usually with full sun or light shade. They are highly drought tolerant and ever-green, and are short-lived in the garden, especially with summer water (although this promotes better looking foliage and longer flowering).

None grows more than a foot to 18 inches tall and all grow as open cushions or mounds. With some tip pruning to shape them, the coastal species make tidy rounded clumps which look neat in the coastal rock garden; the others are also amenable to a rock garden provided they're given plenty of space. Otherwise, they're good in the front of a mixed border where the mass of summer bloom is welcome. Here are three species:

E. confertiflorum. Golden yarrow. Generally occurs inland in the chaparral and scrub of central and southern California. It is a stiffer plant with upright branches and very finely divided gray-green leaves. Flower heads are individually small, yellow, in flat-topped cymes. Easy in gardens but may rot in wet winters.

E. lanatum. Wooly'sunflower or Oregon sunshine. This is our most variable species, and ranges from open woodlands at low elevations through the central and northern foothills across the mountains to timberline. It is very drought tolerant, and also short lived, but puts on the most impressive display and has the largest flower heads. There are many varieties, some with tighter leaf mats and exceptionally large flowers; these live on high-mountain scree, and may not be fully garden adaptable.

E. stachaedifolium (var. *artemisaefolium*). Lizardtail. A coastal species which is salt and wind tolerant, and welcomes occasional summer water. It can form large mats which spread widely with leaves dark green above and silvery below. The flower heads are individually small, but borne in large numbers in flat-topped cymes. Easy to grow. The typical variety given here has pinnately lobed leaves.

Eupatorium occidentalis. Eupatorium or Western Thoroughwort. Eupatorium tribe, sunflower family.

HT: to 2 feet   FLW CL: pale purple to red-purple   FLW TM: July to September
PRPG: divisions or seeds (stratify)   EXP: full sun   WT: some summer water

Here is a low subshrub which loves bright, sunny places between granite rocks along the east slope of the Sierra from middle to high elevations. It seldom grows more than two feet tall and is covered with short, broad, pointed bright green aromatic leaves topped by masses of red-purple flower heads. These appear from late summer to early fall, when many other plants have gone dormant. It needs good drainage, some summer water, and a winter-cold dormancy. Because of its showy, late flowers, it is worth a try in lowland gardens.

Use western eupatorium against bold rocks in the rock garden, or in the middle zone of a mixed border. Place it so that its late flowers show to advantage when others have given up. Other late-bloomers to grow with it include goldenrods, asters, and hummingbird fuchsia.

Franseria chamissonis. Beach or Dune Bursage. Ragweed tribe, sunflower family.

HT: in flower to 12 inches   FLW CL: green   FLW TM: March to September   PRPG: divisions   EXP: full sun (coast)   WT: none in summer once established

Few of the franserias would seem to have garden merit; some are even weeds. But the beach bursage has ornamental possibilities. The flowers, atypical of the family, are not showy, but rather in small green wind-pollinated heads. In fact, it is this trait that gives the ragweed tribe its reputation for causing hayfever. The bursages have separate male and female heads: the female, lower on the stalk, grow into sharp-spined burs which are liabilities to bare feet on the beach. The widely creeping rootstocks help stabilize sand dunes and send up close mats of green to silvery ferny, pinnately dissected leaves. In some forms, the leaves are merely cleft, but in others they're redivided. Thus, bursage is a foliage plant for contrast of texture and color. Grow it in front of a border or in front of drought-tolerant shrubs. Once established, the plants need little summer water to spread, but the roots must have excellent drainage. Don't attempt it where wet and cold rule in winter. Beach bursage is particularly useful for beachfront property or slopes close to the coast. It is wind and salt tolerant.

Grindelia. Gumweed. Aster tribe, sunflower family.

HT: to 4 inches   FLW CL: yellow   FLW TM: June to September   PRPG: layers or rooted sections   EXP: full sun   WT: some summer water

GUMWEED—*Grindelia.*

Gumweeds are characterized by spoon-shaped to elliptical dark green leaves of firm texture, and showy bright yellow heads of numerous ray and disc flowers. The heads are covered by a sticky white gum in bud, hence the common name. Gumweeds occur in interesting habitats, often on the upper edge of coastal salt marshes, bluff tops, and sand dunes as well as openings in chaparral and woodlands, and along roadsides in hard-packed soils. Thus, they are candidates for soils with poor aeration, salts, and in windy spots. Not all gumweeds have attractive enough habit to warrant their use. The upright subshrubby kinds are difficult to identify, and tend to look coarse and weedy, but two species have sprawling, decumbent branches and merit serious consideration as ground covers: *G. stricta* and *G. latifolia* (dune or bluff gumweeds). These two grow on wind-swept bluffs and sand dunes, and flourish in a garden setting. Give them some summer water and a well-drained soil.

Use the prostrate grindelias as a tough ground cover, to stabilize steep banks and slopes (they root as they travel), or in the front of a mixed border, but be sure to allow room for rambling. The attractive leaves are succulent and evergreen, but old growth and flower heads need to be removed by fall.

Helenium. Sneezeweed. Sneezeweed tribe, sunflower family.

HT: in flower 1 to 3 feet   FLW CL: yellow, with center dark (or in some, also yellow)   FLW TM: June to September   PRPG: division, seeds   EXP: full sun (light shade inland)   WT: all summer

The sneezeweeds are lovers of wet meadows, springs, and seeps throughout the foothills and mountains. They are recognized by the decurrent leaf blades (blades run down the stem), the yellow flower heads with the rays turned down (rather than sticking straight out as they do for most composites), and disc flowers attached to a rounded receptacle. In flower, they attract a variety of insects, including bees and butterflies, and color meadows late in summer, along with coneflowers, asters, goldenrods, and other composites. In the garden, they must have summer water to succeed; after flowering the stalks should be cut back.

The two sneezeweeds with greatest ornamental merit are *H. hoopesii* (from high Sierran meadows) and the common *H. bigelovii* (from meadows and seeps at many elevations in Coast Ranges and the Sierra). The latter is more adaptable to lowland gardens. Use them massed toward the back of the border (stalks reach two and a half to three feet high), or toward the back of a pond or meadow.

Helianthella californica. Chaparral Sunflower, Little California Sunflower. Sunflower tribe, sunflower family.

HT: to 18 inches   FLW CL: yellow   FLW TM: May to September   PRPG: seeds (fire pretreatment)   EXP: full sun   WT: summer dry

The helianthellas are subbushy, low-growing sunflowers of dry, summer-hot habitats on the edge of woodland and chaparral. They occur in great abundance after brush fires, but are crowded out later by the taller reinvading shrubs. They are not long lived. They burn out in the garden with additional water, but look better for the occasional summer moisture. The multiple branches are covered with evergreen, lance-ovate leaves. From late spring through summer, showy yellow sunflower heads are borne singly on stalks above the foliage.

The helianthellas make a good addition to the middle zone of the mixed border or in front of a planting of chaparral shrubs with similar requirements: ceanothuses, romneyas, fremontias, manzanitas, and others. The only species with wide distribution is *H. californica*.

Helianthus californicus. California or Wild Sunflower. Sunflower tribe, sunflower family.

HT. 6 to 8 feet   FLW CL: yellow   FLW TM: July to September   PRPG: root divisions   EXP: full sun   WT: some summer water

Most everyone has seen the ruderal, weedy nonnative sunflowers along valley roadsides. They flourish in great numbers beside cultivated fields and orchards and are tall, short-lived annuals with yellow rays and dark-central-disc flowers. Everyone is also familiar with the giant cultivated sunflowers whose tall stalks bear single heads of flowers. Neither of the latter is native, whereas California sunflower, described below, is a true native perennial. It is winter dormant, has gradually spreading, shallow fleshy rhizomes, and lives along stream banks in well lighted places of the inner foothills, often between summer-dry chaparral shrubs and riparian willows. Because of its special niche, it requires occasional summer water or a place where its roots can delve deep to find water. Given full sun, it grows rapidly in the garden. In spring, the rhizomes send up leafy shoots which start slowly, then grow ever more quickly toward the sky. Each shoot supports many narrowly ovate, bright green leaves. By late spring, the top branches multiply into flower-bearing stalks, the flowers opening by early summer. The floral display peaks by late summer and lasts until early fall. Each flower head is small for a sunflower, measuring a couple of inches across, with bright yellow ray and disc flowers. Because the heads are borne in profusion, the plant is spectacular at its peak. By fall, leaves have become unsightly, flower heads have gone to seed, and the stems need to be cut back to the ground. Because the stems are so tall, they also need staking to prevent them from flopping over.

California sunflower can be used as a specimen plant or next to large shrubs such as ceanothuses and manzanitas (those species that are tolerant of occasional water) to provide summer color when the latter have ceased to bloom, or it can be used as a very tall backdrop for a mixed border. Be sure to allow the rhizomes plenty of room to travel.

Lasthenia macrantha. Coast or Bluff Goldfields. Sneezeweed tribe, sunflower family.

HT: 4 to 6 inches   FLW CL: yellow   FLW TM: April to May   PRPG: divisions or seeds   EXP: light shade inland   WT: some summer water

All other lasthenias are annuals, and among the best-known spring wildflowers of our foothills. *L. macrantha* is a short-lived perennial or biennial from wind-swept coastal bluffs. There its taproot searches out space between rocks and the stems branch close to the ground to form succulent mats of dark green leaves. Showy golden flower heads cover the mats in middle spring. Since the wild plants receive fog in summer, they should be given supplemental summer water in the garden, but with good drainage. This is not a plant for hot, inland gardens.

Coast goldfields is ideal for the coast rock garden and complements sea thrift, dudleya, coast rockcress, lizardtail, and wallflower.

Machaeranthera. Desert Aster. Aster tribe, sunflower family.

HT: 1 to 3 1/2 feet   FLW CL: pink or blue rays and yellow disc flowers   FLW TM: var-ies   PRPG: seeds   EXP: full sun   WT: varies

The machaeranthera are close aster relatives separated on the basis of their tap-root (asters have fibrous roots) and the small spine at the tip of the leaves. They range from short-lived perennials to small shrubs; showiness and flower size also vary. Only two of the species have showy-enough flowers for the garden—these come from dry, gravelly slopes with lots of summer heat. Flower heads start at about an inch across, the rays violet, pale blue, or purple and the disc flowers bright yellow.

Desert asters are best in inland gardens with hot summers where they can be incorporated into mixed borders, or as specimens in a desert-style garden. Here are the two species:

M. shastensis. This strictly herbaceous species forms low mounds of leafy stems, the narrowly spoon-shaped leaves covered with fine white hairs. Flower heads are mostly borne in open flat-topped clusters, and average about an inch across. Several plants should be massed together for best effect. Summer flowering.

M. tortifolia. Mojave aster. A low subshrub to about two feet high with rounded form. Leaves narrow with spine-tipped teeth. Flower heads borne over a long period in spring, individually large and showy—several inches across. Choice with other desert shrubs and subshrubs: apricot mallow, incienso, desert senna (*Cassia armata*).

Petasites palmatus. Western Coltsfoot. Senecio tribe, sunflower family.

HT: in flower to 30 inches or more   FLW CL: white to pinkish   FLW TM: March to May   PRPG: rhizome divisions   EXP: shade   WT: summer water

Western coltsfoot is a curious streamside ground cover of moist low-elevation forests. The growth cycle is such that in a dry year the leaves are shaggy and dead by fall. In any case, the plant goes dormant to widely creeping rhizomes by winter. In early spring, new leaves appear in tightly curled form, strung out along the underground rhizomes. At about the same time, or a bit before, the rhizomes send up one- to two-foot-high scaly flowering stalks. The flowers are borne in rather flat-topped clusters, each head of flowers with minute rays and showy star-like white to pink disc flowers. The showiness of these early flowers coupled with the curious leaves, which later become broadly palmate, maple-like affairs, make western coltsfoot unique for a woodland garden. Seed heads become ragged and should be removed.

Rudbeckia. California Coneflower, Black-Eyed Susan. Sunflower tribe, sunflower family.

HT: in flower to 5 or 6 feet   FLW CL: golden with dark center   FLW TM: July to September   PRPG: divisions or seeds   EXP: full sun to light shade   WT: summer wet

Rudbeckias are favorite summer and fall flowers throughout the prairies of North America. In California, *R. californica* is found in mid-elevation montane meadows. The leafy flowering stalks rise to four or five feet and do not appear until the early meadow flowers (for example, camass, shooting stars, rein orchids, and swamp onion) have browned. Coneflowers are typical of meadow borders, where they receive some protection from the hot summer sun by the late afternoon shade of the adjacent forest. The flower heads are large even for composites, with showy horizontal to slightly reflexed yellow rays and distinctive long central cones which bear myriad purplish disc flowers. One of the charms of coneflowers is their attractiveness to such beautiful pollinators as butterflies.

Races from low elevations should adapt well to gardens with summer water, and provide welcome color at the end of fall. They're attractive at the back of a watered border or meadow. Variety *glaucum* occurs in bogs and seeps of northwestern mountains; its leaves are an attractive blue-green color.

Senecio. Ragweed, Groundsel, Butterwort, and Others. Senecio tribe, sunflower family.

HT: from about 4 inches to 4 feet   FLW CL: yellow   FLW TM: June to September   PRPG: divisions (for some) and seeds   EXP: mostly full sun   WT: varies

Senecio is one of the largest genera of flowering plants on earth, with hundreds of species from all sorts of habitats and on most continents. Even in California, it is difficult to generalize about such a diverse group. Some exotic species are already well established in gardens: the popular cinerarias, the curious succulent "kleinias," and the spreading vine Germany ivy are common examples. Our own senecios range from introduced weeds to alpine cushion plants, with a number of forms which are neither showy nor worthy of garden space. Many have rather small flower heads, and several lack showy rays. I have selected some that are likely to look good in garden settings. Few have yet been tried. Several offer a riot of bright golden flowers during the summer, and are of relatively easy culture.

S. blochmanae. Blochman's or dune senecio. This is also a half-shrub. It occurs on coastal dunes in south-central California, where the shrubs are pruned by wind into compact plants with rather symmetrical leaves and, again, showy heads of ray and disc flowers. Well adapted to the coastal garden, but short lived in cultivation.

S. douglasii. Douglas's senecio or shrubby senecio. This half-shrub is included here because it can be treated as a perennial. It is a much-branched plant, woody at the base and short lived with extra water and fertilizer. The narrow green branches create a rush-like effect to 18 inches or 2 feet, with numerous, bright golden flower heads and with both ray and disc flowers through summer. It rots easily in wet winters, and needs severe pruning to remain shapely.

S. pauciflorus. Burnt orange butterwort. Although this plant is not especially distinguished out of flower—it bears leafy foot-high stalks in high mountain meadows—the flower color is arresting. Each flower head bears several disc flowers of intense burnt orange color. It is a showstopper when combined with such other yellow and blue composites as common butterwort, rayless aster, and meadow daisy.

S. triangularis. Common butterwort. One of the most prolific wildflowers of wet, half-shaded Sierran meadows, where it grows in pure stands, or blends with lilies, shooting stars, swamp onion, monkshood, and larkspur. It needs constant moisture for its three- to four-foot-high stalks, decorated with bright green triangular leaves and topped by open sprays of bright golden flower heads with a long succession of bloom. Cut back by late summer.

S. werneraefolius. Werner's senecio, alpine butterwort. A compact cushion-like plant from exposed granite of high mountains, with gray wooly leaves and low, bright golden yellow flower heads. Good for a mountain rock garden.

Solidago. Goldenrod. Aster tribe, sunflower family.

HT: 8 inches to 3 1/2 feet   FLW CL: golden yellow   FLW TM: July to September
PRPG: divisions or seeds   EXP: full sun   WT: some summer water

Easterners are well acquainted with the goldenrods which come in myriad forms and dominate roadsides from late summer through fall. Few seem to know California's goldenrods, which share the same propensity for open areas and late flowering. Some are so showy they should not be overlooked for the garden border. They flower when many plants have already gone dormant, and so add welcome color. Goldenrods are vigorous perennials from creeping rootstocks, and may become invasive in the garden. They should be given plenty of room for a good show, and can easily be controlled. They establish easily, in full sun to slightly shaded places, and are drought tolerant, but not harmed by summer water. The biggest job is to pick off the old flowering stalks before they become "unsightly" and spill their fuzzy fruits everywhere.

Most species should accommodate well to the garden, but some are better than others:

S. californica. California goldenrod. One of the showiest and easiest, from throughout the foothill country. Give full sun, a little extra summer water, and watch it flower from midsummer to fall. Even in bud, the tall wand-like flowering stalks are colorful. Use them with purple daisies and hummingbird fuchsia.

S. canadensis. Canada or mountain goldenrod. Looks similar to *S. californica*, with tall leafy stalks and big open wands of golden flowers, but the leaves are toothed, while California goldenrod has entire leaves. It will accommodate to most gardens, but is most appropriate for the mountain garden.

S. multiradiata. Alpine goldenrod. Seeks out rocky meadow edges in the Sierra high country. Makes creeping clumps with flowering stems mostly less than a foot high, the flower heads not as numerous as on the bigger kinds, but individually larger with many golden-yellow ray flowers. Nice for mountain rock gardens.

S. spathulata. Bluff goldenrod. A diminutive kind which creeps along rocky promontories and sand dunes of the central and north coast. The leaves are dark green, rather spoon-shaped and attached to widely creeping stems; the flower wands are only a few inches high. It combines with other summer coast flowers such as dudleyas, grindelias, buckwheats, and seaside daisy.

S. spectabilis. Oasis goldenrod. Another vigorous species, this is adapted to seeps and springs along the eastern side of the Sierra and in desert mountains. It needs constant moisture, will take plenty of heat, and repays by lavish late-summer floral displays. Not for coastal gardens.

Stephanomeria cichoriacea. Bluff Lettuce, Wandflower. Chicory tribe, sunflower family.

HT: in flower to 18 inches or 2 feet   FLW CL: pink   FLW TM: summer   PRPG: well-healed divisions or seeds   EXP: full sun (light shade inland)   WT: summer dry

Most of the stephanomerias are slender annuals or biennials with nearly leafless stems and rather unshowy pink or white chicory-like flowers. Bluff lettuce makes handsome rosettes of silver-gray leaves, the leaves narrowly ovate and with coarse teeth. From these decorative bases, the wand-like flower branches arise to make many attractive pink flower heads. The pink and gray colors complement each other. Bluff lettuce lives on steep, coastal cliffs and bluffs from Monterey south. In the garden, it needs plenty of light, excellent drainage, and mild winters. It is drought tolerant once established.

Obviously, bluff lettuce belongs in rock gardens with other natural companions: dudleyas and Indian pink (*Silene laciniata*) and various buckwheats. It could also be the front border for drought-tolerant chaparral shrubs.

Tanacetum. Tansy. Mayweed tribe, sunflower family.

HT: in flower to 16 inches   FLW CL: yellow   FLW TM: May to September   PRPG: divisions   EXP: full sun   WT: occasional summer water

The tansies like the yarrows come from the Old and New Worlds, and one often sees the European kind, *T. vulgare*, naturalized. All have attractive, dissected, bright green to gray-green fern-like leaves with much the same strong sage aroma as the yarrows. Not only is the evergreen foliage attractive most of the year (although old leaves need to be removed), but the flat-topped cymes of flower heads are showy. Flower heads are somewhat larger than those of yarrow—about the size of a nickel—and bright yellow, with a broad pincushion of disc flowers, and barely perceptible ray flowers.

Tansies live in sandy soils in full sun; our two best-known species come from coastal sand dunes in central and northern California. In addition, there are two rather rare kinds from the high Sierra and the high desert to the east, but I have no idea how these would fare in gardens. The coastal tansies spread rapidly by stolons, and like yarrow become invasive when watered liberally. They will take summer drought, but look better with occasional watering. They are ideal for the front of a mixed border, for a very coarse ground cover, or to bind sand in a coastal situation. The two coastal species are closely similar: *T. dougalsii* from the north coast with rather green leaves and *T. camphoratum* from the San Francisco region with whitish-green, rather wooly leaves. The latter is rare and endangered in its native habitat, since most of that habitat has been developed, while the former occupies areas less developed.

Venegasia carpesioides. Canyon Sunflower. Sunflower tribe, sunflower family.

HT: to 4 or 5 feet   FLW CL: yellow   FLW TM: February to September   PRPG: root divisions or seeds   EXP: light shade   WT: some summer water

Canyon sunflower lives in wooded canyons of south-central and southern California, where it associates with coast live oak, canyon gooseberry, Humboldt lily, snowberry, and various ferns. Creeping rootstocks send up tall leafy stems crowned by pleasant bright yellow flower heads. Leaves are broadly ovate and light green, and the overall effect brightens stream sides where color is needed. As soon as flowers have faded stalks should be cut back close to the ground, since they become ragged looking otherwise. Canyon sunflower needs a rest from late summer through winter, but still should receive occasional thorough watering.

Canyon sunflower is ideal in the garden in the back of a partly shaded border, next to lilies and larkspurs. It can also be incorporated into the back of an informal woodland garden, or behind a pond.

Wyethia. Mule's Ear. Sunflower tribe, sunflower family.

HT: 1 to 2 feet   FLW CL: yellow   FLW TM: varies   PRPG: seeds (soak or scarify)
EXP: full sun to light shade   WT: occasional summer water

It is a pity that the wyethias have not been tried more often in gardens. Although they are late summer/fall dormant (except for the high-mountain kinds), they have attractive basal clumps of large bright green leaves and large, showy sunflower-like flower heads. All come from thick, creeping aromatic rhizomes which increase the size of the colony each year, and all bear bright yellow flowers. As a bonus, the uncommonly large seeds are edible in the manner of sunflower seeds. There are several species, many of which look quite similar, that range through open woodlands and grasslands of the foothills, but a couple are characteristic of sandy flats in the high mountains. The latter would be poor candidates for ordinary gardens.

The mule's ears are appropriate for the front or middle of a mixed border, some growing more than a foot tall, and should be planted where they have room to expand. The old dead flower heads need to be trimmed off before they turn brown unless seed is wanted. The various kinds differ in leaf shape and hairiness: *W. glabra* has broad shiny bright green leaves; *W. helenioides* has broad leaves, fuzzy when young; and *W. angustifolia* has narrow, tongue-shaped leaves. *W. mollis* (mountain mule's ears) has broad gray leaves and is best for mountain gardens.

Valerian Family
(Valerianaceae)

The valerians are a small family in California; only the genus *Valeriana* is perennial; the native plectritises are all annuals.

Valeriana. Valerian. Valerian family.

HT: in flower 1 to 2 feet   FLW CL: mostly white   FLW TM: varies   PRPG: division of clumps or seeds   EXP: full sun to light shade   WT: summer water

The wild valerians are shy, modest plants, not so gaudy as the weedy Jupiter's beard or red valerian so often naturalized near the coast. They form small clumps with leaves mostly in basal rosettes, the others smaller up the flowering stalk. Leaves are pinnately divided in a fashion typical of the group but difficult to describe in words, and are opposite. The flowering stalks bear open flat-topped cymes of small white or pale pink flowers with minute nectar sacs in back. Massed with other meadow flowers, these add an interesting note of form and leaf texture. They are also pleasing in fruit when the rolled up sepals unfurl into feathery pappus-like appendages atop each fruit.

Valerians are ideal for a mountain meadow garden and go well with erigerons, columbine, horsemint, larkspurs, and meadowrue. The two species for consideration are *V. capitata* (mountain valerian), from mid to high Sierran meadows and open woods, and *V. sitchensis* var. *scouleri* (northern valerian), from rocky walls in open coniferous woods. The latter is more adaptable to lowland gardens, occurring at less than 1,000 feet along the Smith River in northwestern California, and could be used in a rock garden with summer water.

Violet Family
(*Violaceae*)

Although we have but a single genus, *Viola*, there is great diversification of species in a wide variety of habitats. Violets are among some of the most satisfactory flowers for the garden, and there are many to choose from.

Viola. Wild Violet, Johnny-Jump-Up, Wild Pansy. Violet family.

HT: 3 inches to 12 inches   FLW CL: white, blue, yellow   FLW TM: varies   PRPG: rooted stolons and divisions (some species) or seeds (may self-sow)   EXP: full sun to full shade   WT: varies

There are violas for nearly every habitat in California, excepting the hot deserts, salt marshes, and beaches. The majority are woodland and forest dwellers, but several grow on scree in the mountains, or atop coastal bluffs, in grasslands, or in wet meadows. Although all are low-growing with rosettes of leaves, the root systems differ, as do dormancy requirements, flowering period, method of vegetative increase, flower color, leaf shape. Many bear the typical heart-shaped violet leaf, but quite a number have highly lobed, pinnatifid, or even compound leaves. Flower colors range from blues and purples to white and bright yellow. Many yellow kinds have the backs of the upper two petals colored brown or purple, and most have pretty dark lines on the lower petals leading to the nectary or spur. All violets have attractive showy flowers followed by self-fertile flowers produced near the ground which never open. Some species are notoriously difficult to obtain and establish—those, especially with deeply seated clusters of fleshy roots (these are summer dormant) are susceptible to rot. On the other hand, those with shallow roots which are mostly winter dormant are easy in gardens.

Here is a list of some of the many:

V. adunca. Dog or blue violet. This is a species with spring flowers on coastal bluffs or summer flowers in high mountain meadows. Choose your source according to your winter temperatures. All form creeping mats, the flowers borne only inches high, and color ranges from light blue to deep blue-violet. Good, for example, for a ground cover or in front of ponds. Reseeds freely. Some summer water.

V. douglasii. Douglas's violet. Much like *V. pedunculata* in habitat, the flowers almost as large, but the leaves finely slashed or divided. Summer dormant.

CALIFORNIA GOLDEN VIOLET—*Viola pendunculata.*

V. glabella. Smooth yellow violet. Ranges from cool, moist redwood forests to the subalpine meadows of northern California where it often grows under thickets of alder or willow. Roots need moisture all year. Large, bright green leaves and pretty yellow flowers just above. Easy to establish in woodland gardens. May reseed.

V. hallii. Hall's violet. One of the most charming but rare violets. Leaf clumps are grayish-green, grow in scree, and need excellent drainage. Flowers are like johnny-jump-ups, two toned, light yellow and blue. Difficult to grow. Needs late dormancy. Recommended for mountain rock gardens with free drainage.

V. lobata. Lobed violet. Open forests, mostly mixed-evergreen or in the ponderosa pine belt. Leaves vary from simple and undivided to deeply lobed into coarse segments. Yellow flowers with purple backs in mid to late spring. Dormant late summer to deep roots.

V. macloskeyi. White mountain or meadow violet. This is a charming creeping violet, of much the same stature as *V. adunca* or even shorter. The summer flowers are white marked purple, and have an unusual arrangement of petals. They come from middle- to high-mountain meadows, but adapt to lower elevations. Summer moist.

V. ocellata. Western heartsease. Discrete clumps with narrow, pointed, heart-shaped leaves and delicate white flowers, marked on the back and lower lip with purple. Deep-seated fleshy roots. From coastal forests. Late summer rest.

V. pedunculata. Johnny-jump-up or wild pansy. Summer dormant to very deep fleshy roots. Low leaves appear after rains begin in foothill grasslands. Unusually large, butter-yellow flowers with beautiful brown-purple nectar guides on lower petals. Plant it in front of a border with little summer water and excellent drainage.

V. purpurea. Pine violet. One of the most variable violets, typically in the yellow pine zone of mountain forests. Tight clumps of gray-green leaves from deep roots form mats among pine needles or on high gravelly scree slopes of forest edges. Perky, bright yellow flowers are borne in circles, the upper petals purple behind. Good for mountain rock gardens.

V. sempervirens. Redwood violet. A low trailing violet, rooting as it extends the stems, and a fine ground cover along the edge of the woodland garden or over a shaded bank. Leaves are small, almost round, and deep dull green. Bright yellow flowers rise an inch or two above the leaves, peaking in spring but appearing almost year-round near the coast. May reseed.

V. sheltonii. Shelton's violet. Forests from the ponderosa pine zone to subalpine in northern mountains. Leaves slashed deeply into finger-like lobes, dull or dark green. Flowers yellow much like *V. lobata.* Late dormant to deep-seated fleshy roots. Pretty with columbines, western bleedingheart, and waterleaf. Flowers early.

Waterleaf Family
(Hydrophyllaceae)

The waterleaf family, like the phloxes, is amply represented in the western states. The several genera are often difficult to identify, and in at least one genus—*Phacelia*—there is difficulty in keying to the dozens of species. Several genera are not included here, because they are entirely annual, like *Nemophila* (baby-blue-eyes) and *Pholistoma*, for example; their demands are difficult to meet, like *Nama*; or because they are shrubs, like *Eriodictyon* (yerba santa).

Hydrophyllum. Waterleaf. Waterleaf family.

HT: to 15 inches   FLW CL: pale purple, off white   FLW TM: April to July   PRPG: root sections   EXP: shade   WT: some summer water

Like the perennial phacelias, the waterleafs' best feature is the attractive foliage rather than the flowers. Both species live in moist forests and increase by underground stolons forming broad, low-growing colonies, with time. Both have coarsely pinnately divided, fuzzy leaves with interesting outlines. The mountain species also has curious pale green spots at the base of the leaf divisions. In flower, the coils open to reveal pale purple, phacelia-like, open bell-shaped flowers.

Waterleafs naturalize well in a woodland setting, complementing other ground covers such as vancouverias, wild gingers, and redwood sorrel. The coastal forest species, *H. tenuipes*, creeps rapidly and may become invasive. It does best with summer water, and is winter dormant. The mountain species, *H. occidentale*, forms discrete clumps and travels less widely. Some populations grow as low as 2,000 feet in the Feather River country, and should adapt well to lowland gardens.

Phacelia. Phacelia, Caterpillar Flower. Waterleaf family.

HT: 8 inches to 2 feet   FLW CL: white, purple, blue-purple   FLW TM: variable   PRPG: seeds   EXP: full sun to shade   WT: some summer water

Most phacelias are annuals of foothills and deserts. Several species are herbaceous perennials which live in a variety of habitats. Some are of interest for their foliage but few have truly ornamental flowers. As a group, they are not horticulturally outstanding, but three perennials deserve mention here.

P. bolanderi. Bolander's or woodland phacelia. One of the few which lives on the borders of coastal forests, and is useful in the woodland garden where summer color is rare. It bears a few semierect stems from a perennial root, and has broad, coarsely toothed leaves. Each stem ends in coiled flower buds, as do all phacelias. The saucer-shaped flowers are an attractive pale blue-purple. This phacelia goes nicely with small ferns. Often reseeds. Short lived.

PACIFIC WATERLEAF—*Hydrophyllum tenuipes.*

P. californica. California or bluff phacelia. There are a number of close relatives, the several species difficult to differentiate. All grow from a closely branched sub-woody root crown which is closedly covered with rosettes of simple to coarsely pinnately divided leaves. The leaves are covered with silky hairs and have attractive patterns of "indented" parallel veins. Habitats of the group range from coastal bluffs to rock scree at timberline. Most are good rock garden subjects, but with varying success in the lowland garden. *P. californica* is a low-elevation species which grows easily and is attractive with other coastal bluff plants, such as rockcress, sea thrift, and wallflowers. It also has the most attractive flowers of the lot—purple fiddleheads appear in abundance from middle to late spring. Selection for deeper and clearer color would improve the appearance. The other species have white to off-white flowers, more curious than attractive.

P. ramosissima. A wide ranging short-lived perennial, growing on rocky banks in the foothills or on sand dunes along the central and southern coast. The weak, decumbent stems bear attractive, pinnately divided leaves rather like coarse, hairy ferns, the divisions with rounded scallops. The flowers are small and off white to pale purple. Color selection would improve the ornamental value. Easy from seed or cuttings.

Romanzoffia. Mist Maidens. Waterleaf family.

HT: 3 to 6 inches   FLW CL: white   FLW TM: April to May   PRPG: offsets   EXP: shade   WT: summer dry

The romanzoffias are delightful creeping herbs from fleshy tuberous roots. They cover mossy rocks with their saxifrage-like leaves in winter and spring, then go dormant to the roots in summer and fall. The broad, scalloped or toothed leaves set off the dainty clusters of white, cup-shaped flowers in mid-spring.

Because their season is limited, romanzoffias should be planted in a special part of the woodland garden reserved for other plants of similar life cycle, and be given their own space, since they compete poorly. Companions could include the summer-dormant polypody ferns, the red larkspur, *Saxifraga bolanderi, Boykinia, Heuchera micrantha,* and *Montia parvifolia.*

Water-Lily Family
(Nymphaeaceae)

The highly specialized aquatics called water-lilies belong to a family all by themselves. We only have two genera, with one species each, but the second genus, *Brasenia schreberi* (water shield), is rare and not entirely ornamental—the flowers are inconspicuous.

Nuphar polysepalum. Yellow Pond-Lily. Water-lily family.

HT: flowering stalks up to about a foot above water   FLW CL: golden yellow   FLW

YELLOW POND-LILY—*Nuphar polysepalum.*

TM: summer   PRPG: pieces of rhizome   EXP: full sun or light shade   WT: saturated soil to standing water at all times

Yellow pond-lily is a natural companion to arrowhead, and is even more widespread in our state, ranging from coastal ponds and marshes to subalpine lakes and bogs in the Sierra. Almost any "lily" lake in California is named for this water-lily relative, since the true water-lilies (*Nymphaea*) are missing here. Large stands often occur in water about knee deep. The large starchy rhizomes branch and rebranch, effectively anchoring the plants. Leaf petioles and flowering stalks rise through the water, the rounded, nearly peltate leaf blades carried slightly above the water, and very reminiscent of true water-lily pads. The flowering stalks rise a bit higher, carrying very showy, single golden yellow flowers whose petals look like they've been carved out of wax. Inside are numerous, curious flattened yellow stamens and a stout central pistil with multiple dark stigmatic "bands" on top. Like arrowhead this plant, unless containerized, is for relatively large ponds with plenty of room to spread. Other companions could include cotton-grass, arrowhead, and a rare gentian relative, the buckbean or bogbean, *Menyanthes trifoliata*.

Water Plantain Family

(*Alismaceae*)

All of the water plantains live in aquatic environments—the edge of bogs, ponds, marshes, or vernal pools. The majority are rather unshowy, as is the genus *Alisma* itself, or are annuals. Only the sagittarias seem sufficiently showy to include here.

Sagittaria. Arrowhead, Wapato, Indian Potato. Water plantain family.

HT: 12 to 18 inches above water   FLW CL: white with yellow center   FLW TM: July to August   PRPG: offsets or seeds   EXP: full sun   WT: covered with water or saturated soils at all times

Arrowhead is one of a handful of truly aquatic plants with ornamental possibilities. The tuberous rhizomes are anchored in mud; the leaf petioles and flowering stalks must rise through several inches of water (usually quiet ponds and acid bogs) to reach the surface where the arrowhead-shaped leaves are borne. In summer, the separate flowering stalk carries racemes of attractive white, three-petaled flowers with numerous yellow stamens in the center. Arrowhead has a broad range, from near sea level in the north to middle elevations.

Arrowhead is easily grown in a water garden such as a shallow pond. Like so many aquatic plants, its roots spread readily, and some dividing of old clumps will be necessary. It is an attractive addition to a moderately large pond and is pretty grown with yellow pond-lily. In addition, the roots are edible. The only reasonably common species in California is *S. latifolia*.

INDIAN POTATO—*Sagittaria latifolia.*

part three

References and Resources for the Native Gardener

APPENDIX 1.
Species Pairs and Triplets for the Garden

Species pairs and triplets are provided as a means of identifying some small groupings of natives useful for the garden. Each pair or triplet constitutes a unit with similar cultural requirements and flowers and/or leaves which complement each other. In many cases flower colors are in the same range or complementary. Each unit also represents species with overlapping blooming times. Many of the species in the units grow naturally together in the wild.

For the reader's convenience, each pair or triplet has been placed under the appropriate garden heading (mixed border, woodland garden, water garden, meadow garden, and rock garden). Under each heading, units are listed alphabetically by the first species of the pair or triplet.

Mixed Border (full sun)

Apricot mallow and brittle-bush (shrub)
Apricot mallow and prince's plume
Apricot mallow, desert aster, and Panamint daisy
Apricot mallow, blue bush lupine, and Douglas's senecio
Beach ryegrass and California goldenrod
Bistort and whorled penstemon
Bistort and erigerons
Blazing star and prickly poppy
Blazing star and scarlet bugler
Blue-eyed grass, coast rockcress, and mouse-eared chickweed
Blue flax and scarlet gilia
Blue flax and *Potentilla gracilis*
Blue flax and mountain paintbrush
Bluff goldenrod, seaside daisy, and coastal buckwheat

Bluff gumweed and seaside daisy
Bridge's penstemon and azure penstemon
Bridge's penstemon and flattop buckwheat
Bridge's penstemon and coyote mint
Broadleaf lupine and Indian paintbrush
Broadleaf lupine, scarlet gilia, and mountain coyote mint
Bush monkeyflower and blue witch or island nightshade
California coneflower, yarrow, and sneezeweed
California phacelia, varicolored lupine, and lizardtail
California poppy and seaside daisy
California poppy, cream cups, and baby-blue-eyes (annuals)
California poppy, tidytips (annual), and lupines
California poppy and goldfields (annual)
California poppy and golden eardrops
Cardinal larkspur, blue bedder penstemon, and yarrow
Catalina mariposa, blue dicks, and blue-eyed grass
Checkerbloom and blue-eyed grass
Chinese houses and clarkia (annuals)
Clarkia (annual) and western larkspur
Coast buckwheat and coyote mint
Coast buckwheat, coyote mint, and paintbrush
Coyote mint and pearly everlasting
Coyote mint and golden yarrow
Davis's knotweed, rabbitbrush, and sagebrush (shrubs)
Deerbroom and bush monkeyflower
Deerbroom and blue bush lupine
Deerbroom and coast buckwheat
Douglas iris and checkerbloom
Dune sage, bluff gumweed, and seaside daisy
Explorer's gentian, lupine, and Indian paintbrush
Explorer's gentian and mountain coyote mint
Explorer's gentian and erigerons
False lupine and Douglas iris
False lupine, yarrow, and blue-eyed grass
Fireweed and giant larkspur
Flattop buckwheat, Oregon sunshine, and erigerons
Flattop buckwheat, Oregon sunshine, and hummingbird fuchsia
Flattop buckwheat and purple sage (shrub)
Golden eardrops and blue witch
Golden eardrops and prickly poppy
Golden eardrops and penstemons
Golden stars and southern Indian pink
Golden stars and blue bedder penstemon
Golden stars and bush monkeyflower
Golden stars and cardinal larkspur
Golden stars and Ithuriel's spear
Golden stars and larkspurs

Goldenrod, yarrow, and erigerons
Hooker's evening primrose and cardinal lobelia
Horsemint, yampah (or lovage), and giant larkspur
Hummingbird fuchsia and California goldenrod
Little California sunflower and coyote mint
Lizardtail and seaside daisy
Matilija poppy and California goldenrod
Matilija poppy and golden eardrops
Matilija poppy and prince's plume
Matilija poppy and bush poppy (shrub)
Meadow daisy, mountain coyote mint, and paintbrush
Mountain bluebells, horsemint, and common butterwort
Mountain checkerbloom, lupine, and mountain valerian
Mountain coyote mint, paintbrush, and Oregon sunshine
Mountain coyote mint, lupine, and common butterwort
Mountain coyote mint, lupine, and Indian paintbrush
Mountain hollyhock, yampah (or lovage), and *Potentilla gracilis*
Mountain hummingbird fuchsia and sulfur buckwheat
Mountain hummingbird fuchsia and goldenrod
Ookow or wild hyacinth and white mariposa
Oregon sunshine, bush monkeyflower, and blue bedder penstemon
Rayless aster and blue erigerons
Sea dahlia and dune sage
Sea dahlia and our lord's candle (yucca)
Showy phlox, mule's ear, and Indian pink
Sneezeweed, yampah, and erigerons
Southern Indian pink, St. Catherine's lace, and dudleya
Western larkspur, wild hyacinth, and golden mariposa
Western wallflower and Oregon sunshine
Western wallflower and blue bush lupine
Western wallflower, clarkia (annual), and larkspur
Wild pansy and California poppy
Wild pansy and larkspurs
Yellow bush lupine (shrub) and varicolored lupine
Yellow bush lupine (shrub) and California poppy
Yellow bush lupine (shrub) and blue witch
Yellow bush lupine (shrub) and bush monkeyflower
Yellow bush lupine (shrub) and blue bedder penstemon
Yellow bush lupine (shrub) and hybrids and common woodmint

Woodland Garden

Brook orchid and brook saxifrage
Brook orchid, five-finger fern, and blue lobelia
California fawn lily, golden fairy lantern, and Ithuriel's spear
Chinese houses (annual) and clarkia (annual)
Common stonecrop, alumroot, and Merten's saxifrage
Common stonecrop and little-leaf montia

Common stonecrop and skullcap
Common stonecrop and Indian pink
Golden fairy lantern and red ribbons clarkia (annual)
Golden monkeyflower and pink monkeyflower
Golden monkeyflower and scarlet monkeyflower
Ground iris, golden fairy lantern, and Fremont star-lily
Ground iris and Indian warrior
Hound's tongue, woodland star, and Henderson's shooting stars
Indian pink, Oregon sunshine, and golden fairy lantern
Indian rhubarb and chain fern
Indian rhubarb and brook orchid
Indian warrior, iris, and hound's tongue
Purple pussy ears and lobed violet
Red columbine, larkspur, and common butterwort
Red larkspur, woodland star, and alumroot
Red ribbons clarkia (annual) and Chinese houses (annual)
Waterleaf and Indian pink
Western wallflower and Oregon sunshine
Western wallflower and golden fairy lantern
Western wallflower, clarkia (annual), and larkspur

Water Garden

Brook orchid and brook saxifrage
Brook orchid, five-finger fern, and blue lobelia
Coast woodmint and meadow lupine
Coast woodmint and oasis goldenrod
Common butterwort, fairy lily, and whiteheads
Common butterwort, fairy lily, and monkshood
Common butterwort, fairy lily, and common corn lily
Explorer's gentian and red heather (shrub)
False lupine and wooly woodmint
Fireweed and giant larkspur
Fireweed, monkshood, and whiteheads
Golden fairy lantern and red ribbons clarkia (annual)
Golden monkeyflower, downingia, and meadowfoam (annuals)
Golden monkeyflower and pink monkeyflower
Golden monkeyflower and scarlet monkeyflower
Golden monkeyflower and Wormskjold's clover
Hooker's evening primrose and cardinal lobelia
Indian rhubarb and chain fern
Indian rhubarb and brook orchid
Jacob's ladder, shooting stars, and golden monkeyflower
Jeffrey's shooting stars, broadleaf lupine, and swamp onion
Jeffrey's shooting stars and camass
King's gentian and oasis goldenrod
King's gentian, snowy rein orchid, and meadow lupine
Leopard lily, California coneflower, and camass

Leopard lily, yarrow, and sneezeweed
Long-rayed brodiaea and leopard lily
Long-rayed brodiaea and sneezeweed
Long-rayed brodiaea and California coneflower
Lotus formosissimus and silverweed
Lotus formosissimus and snowy rein orchid
Lotus formosissimus and ground brodiaea
Mountain clover and miniature epilobiums
Mountain clover and primrose monkeyflower
Mountain clover and tinker's penny
Sierra gentian (annual) and epilobiums
Sierra gentian (annual), snowy rein orchid, and sneezeweed
Swamp onion, monkshood, and common butterwort
Tinker's penny and musk monkeyflower or primrose monkeyflower
Tinker's penny and miniature epilobiums
Tinker's penny and alpine speedwell

Meadow Garden

Beach ryegrass and California goldenrod
Bistort and whorled penstemon
Bistort and erigerons
Bistort, larkspur, and shooting stars
Blue flax and mountain paintbrush
Broadleaf lupine and Indian paintbrush
Broadleaf lupine and mountain valerian
Broadleaf lupine, scarlet gilia, and mountain coyote mint
California poppy, cream cups, and baby-blue-eyes (annuals)
California poppy, tidytips (annual), and lupines
California poppy and goldfields (annual)
Catalina mariposa, blue dicks, and blue-eyed grass
Checkerbloom and blue-eyed grass
Clarkia and western larkspur
Cleveland's shooting stars and wild pansy
Common butterwort, fairy lily, and whiteheads
Common butterwort, fairy lily, and monkshood
Common butterwort, fairy lily, and common corn lily
Coneflower, yarrow, and sneezeweed
Douglas iris and checkerbloom
Explorer's gentian, lupine, and Indian paintbrush
Explorer's gentian and red heather (shrub)
Explorer's gentian and erigerons
Explorer's gentian and coyote mint
False lupine and Douglas iris
False lupine and wooly woodmint
False lupine, yarrow, and blue-eyed grass
Fireweed and giant larkspur
Fireweed, monkshood, and whiteheads

Golden monkeyflower, downingia (annual), and meadowfoam (annual)
Golden monkeyflower and pink monkeyflower
Golden monkeyflower and scarlet monkeyflower
Golden monkeyflower and Wormskjold's clover
Golden stars and Ithuriel's spear
Golden stars and larkspurs
Goldenrod, yarrow, and erigerons
Henderson's shooting stars, milkmaids, and California buttercup
Henderson's shooting stars, woodland star, and blue dicks
Horsemint, yampah (or lovage), and giant larkspur
Jacob's ladder, shooting stars, and golden monkeyflower
Jeffrey's shooting stars, broadleaf lupine, and swamp onion
Jeffrey's shooting stars and camass
King's gentian and goldenrod
King's gentian, snowy rein orchid, and meadow lupine
Long-rayed brodiaea and sneezeweed
Long-rayed brodiaea and coneflower
Meadow daisy, mountain coyote mint, and paintbrush
Meadow star tulip, shooting stars, and suncups
Mountain bluebells, horsemint, and common butterwort
Mountain checkerbloom, lupines, and mountain valerian
Mountain clover and miniature epilobiums
Mountain clover and primrose monkeyflower
Mountain coyote mint, lupine, and Indian paintbrush
Mountain hollyhock, Jeffrey's shooting stars, and meadow lupine
Mountain hollyhock, yampah (or lovage), and *Potentilla gracilis*
Mountain mule's ears and balsamroot
Mountain mule's ears, balsamroot, and mountain coyote mint
Ookow or wild hyacinth and white mariposa
Rayless aster and blue erigerons
Rayless aster and red columbine
Rayless aster and monkshood
Red columbine, larkspur, and common butterwort
Red columbine, meadow paintbrush, and erigerons
Red columbine, mountain bluebells, and lovage
Sierra gentian (annual) and epilobiums
Sierra gentian (annual), snowy rein orchid, and sneezeweed
Sneezeweed, yampah, and erigerons
Suncups and blue-eyed grass
Suncups and California poppy
Swamp onion, monkshood, and common butterwort
Western larkspur, wild hyacinth, and golden mariposa
White fritillary, shooting stars, and blue-eyed grass
White fritillary, checkerbloom, and blue-eyed grass
Wild pansy and California poppy
Wild pansy and larkspurs

Rock Garden

Blue flax and scarlet gilia
Bluff goldenrod, seaside daisy, and coastal buckwheat
Bluff goldfields and baby-blue-eyes (annual)
Bluff goldfields, blue-eyed grass, and Douglas iris
Bluff gumweed and seaside daisy
Bluff paintbrush, dudleya, and California phacelia
Bridge's penstemon and azure penstemon
Bridge's penstemon and flattop buckwheat
Bridge's penstemon and coyote mint
Bush monkeyflower and blue witch or island nightshade
California phacelia, varicolored lupine, and lizardtail
Checkerbloom and varicolored lupine
Coast rockcress, mouse-eared chickweed, and varicolored lupine
Coastal buckwheat and coyote mint
Coastal buckwheat, coyote mint, and paintbrush
Coastal wallflower and coast rockcress
Common stonecrop, alumroot, and Merten's saxifrage
Common stonecrop and little-leaf montia
Common stonecrop and skullcap
Coyote mint and pearly everlasting
Coyote mint and golden yarrow
Deerbroom and blue bedder penstemon
Deerbroom and bush monkeyflower
Deerbroom and blue bush lupine
Deerbroom and coastal buckwheat
Dudleya, *Stephanomeria cichoriacea*, and island buckwheat
Dune evening primrose and Conejo buckwheat
Dune evening primrose and pink sand verbena
Dune evening primrose and foothill wallflower
Dune sage, bluff gumweed, and seaside daisy
Golden stars and blue bedder penstemon
Ground brodiaea and sea thrift
Ground iris, golden fairy lantern, and Fremont star-lily
Little California sunflower and coyote mint
Lizardtail and seaside daisy
Mountain coyote mint, paintbrush, and Oregon sunshine
Mountain hummingbird fuchsia and sulfur buckwheat
Mountain paintbrush, mat phlox, and sulfur buckwheat
Mountain pride penstemon and azure penstemon
Oregon sunshine, bush monkeyflower, and blue bedder penstemon
Oregon sunshine and showy penstemon
Oregon sunshine and *Solanum parishii*
Pink sand verbena and bluff gumweed
Pink sand verbena and dune evening primrose
Purple pussy ears and coast or sickle-leaf onion

Purple pussy ears and ground brodiaea
Purple pussy ears and lobed violet
Pussytoes and Brewer's or Lyall's lupine
Pussytoes and sulfur buckwheat
Pussytoes and erigerons
Sapphire flower and Oregon sunshine
Sea dahlia and *Dudleya pulverulenta*
Sea dahlia and dune sage
Seaside daisy, sea thrift, and dudleya
Showy phlox, mule's ear, and Indian pink
Sierra mariposa and showy penstemon
Sierra mariposa and Oregon sunshine
Sierra mariposa, Sierra onion, and alpine larkspur
Sierra mariposa, mountain paintbrush, and mountain coyote mint
Siskiyou daisy and pearly everlasting
Siskiyou daisy and pussytoes
Siskiyou daisy used in place of seaside daisy
Siskiyou daisy and Oregon sunshine
Sunrose and blue bedder penstemon
Tree coreopsis, *Stephanomeria cichoriacea*, and *Dudleya pulverulenta*

APPENDIX 2.
Societies and Gardens with Special Plant Sales

Strybing Arboretum Society
9th Ave. & Lincoln Way
San Francisco, CA 94122

California Native Plant Society
909 12th St., Suite 116
Sacramento, CA 95814

(Each chapter has its own special
time; after you have joined,
inquire of your local chapter.)

**University of California
Botanical Garden**
Strawberry Canyon,
U.C. campus
Berkeley, CA 94720

**Regional Parks Botanical
Garden**
Tilden Regional Park
Berkeley, CA 94708

Santa Barbara Botanic Garden
1212 Mission Canyon Rd.
Santa Barbara, CA 93105

**Rancho Santa Ana
Botanic Garden**
1500 N. College Ave.
Claremont, CA 91711

APPENDIX 3.
Commercial Sources of Natives

Plant Sources

Beecher's Nursery; 1218 N. Beecher Rd., Stockton, CA 95205

Blue Oak Nursery; 2731 Mountain Oak Lane, Rescue, CA 95672

Bordier's Nursery; 7231 Irvine Blvd., Irvine, CA 92714

C. H. Baccus; 900 Boynton Ave., San Jose, CA 95117

Calaveras Nursery; 1622 Highway 12, Valley Springs, CA 95252

California Flora Nursery; P.O. Box 3, Fulton, CA 95439

The Clark Nursery Co.; 3581 Coffey Lane, Santa Rosa, CA 95401

Darling's Nursery; 7000 Petaluma Hill Rd., P.O. Box 570, Penngrove, CA 94951

Endangered Species; 12571 Red Hill, Tustin, CA 92680

Hortica Gardens; P.O. Box 308, Placerville, CA 95667

Las Pilitas Nursery; Star Route Box 23, Santa Margarita, CA 93453

Lawson Valley Nursery; 3616 Rudnick Dr., Jamul, CA 92035

Leonard Coates Nurseries, Inc.; 400 Casserly Rd., Watsonville, CA 95076

Mayacama Botanicals; 2600 Eastside Rd./P.O. Box 689, Ukiah, CA 95482

Mendo-Natives Nursery; P.O. Box 351, Gualala, CA 95445

The Native Nursery; P.O. Box 1684, Big Bear City, CA 92314

Native Sons Wholesale Nursery; 379 West El Campo Rd., Arroyo Grande, CA 93420

Pecoff Bros. Nursery & Seed, Inc.; Rt. 5, Box 215, Escondido, CA 92025

Redwood Nursery; 2800 El Rancho Dr., Santa Cruz, CA 95060

Robinett Bulb Farm; P.O. Box 1306, Sebastopol, CA 95473-1306

San Marcos Growers; 125 S. San Marcos Rd., P.O. Box 6827, Santa Barbara, CA 93111

San Simeon Nursery; Star Route, Villa Creek Rd., Cayucos, CA 93430

Saratoga Horticultural Foundation; 20605 Verde Vista Lane, P.O. Box 308, Saratoga, CA 95071

Shooting Star Propagation; 9950 O'Connell Rd., Sebastopol, CA 95472

The Shop in the Sierra; Box 1, Midpines, CA 95345

Siskiyou Rare Plant Nursery; 2825 Cummings Rd., Medford, OR 97501

Skylark Wholesale Nursery; 6735 Sonoma Hwy., Santa Rosa, CA 95405

The Theodore Payne Foundation; 10459 Tuxford St., Sun Valley, CA 91352

U.C. Santa Cruz Arboretum; Crown College, UCSC, Santa Cruz, CA 95064

Villager Nursery, P.O. Box 1273 Truckee, CA 95734

Wapume Native Plant Nursery Co.; 8305 Cedar Crest Way, Sacramento, CA 95826

Wildwood Farm; 10300 Sonoma Hwy., Kenwood, CA 95452

Yerba Buena Nursery; 19500 Skyline Blvd., Woodside, CA 94062

Seed Sources

Abundant Life Seed Foundation; P.O. Box 772, Port Townsend, WA 98368

Carter Seeds; 475 Mar Vista Dr., Vista, CA 92083

Clyde Robin Seed Co., Inc.; P.O. Box 2855, Castro Valley, CA 94546

Earthside Nature Center; c/o Mrs. John Connelly, 138 El Dorado St., Arcadia, CA 91006

Larner Seeds; P.O. Box 11143, Palo Alto, CA 94306

Las Pilitas Nursery; Star Route Box 23, Santa Margarita, CA 93453

Mistletoe Sales; 910 Alphonse, Santa Barbara, CA 93103

Moon Mountain; P.O. Box 34, Morro Bay, CA 93442

Redwood City Seed Co.; Craig Dremann, P.O. Box 361, Redwood City, CA 94064

Regional Parks Botanic Garden; Tilden Regional Park, Berkeley, CA 94708

S & S Seeds; 910 Alphonse, Santa Barbara, CA 93103

Santa Barbara Botanic Garden; 1212 Mission Canyon Rd., Santa Barbara, CA 93105

Southwestern Native Seeds; Box 50503, Tucson, Arizona 85703

Stover Seed Co.; P.O. Box 21488, Los Angeles, CA 90021

The Theodore Payne Foundation; 10459 Tuxford St., Sun Valley, CA 91352

Twin Peaks Seeds; 12721 Ave. de Espuela, Poway, CA 92064

A World Seed Service; L. Hudson, Seedsman, P.O. Box 1058, Redwood City, CA 94064

APPENDIX 4.

Suggested Reference Books for Identification of Natives

Collins, Barbara J. *Key to Wildflowers of the Deserts of Southern California.* 1979. California Lutheran College, Thousand Oaks, CA.

A rather complete guide with easier than average keys, and some rather sketchy line drawings.

Crampton, Beecher. *Grasses in California.* 1974. University of California Press, Berkeley.

Includes the more common genera and species with line drawings and some color photos. Keys are difficult to use (microscope needed) and illustrations are not all of high quality.

Ferlatte, William J. *A Flora of the Trinity Alps of Northern California.* 1974. University of California Press, Berkeley.

Fairly complete, with technical keys and descriptions. Several line drawings of good quality.

Ferris, Roxanne. *Flowers of Pt. Reyes National Seashore.* 1970. University of California Press, Berkeley.

Includes the common species with line drawings. No keys; flowers are listed by color. Good for the amateur but incomplete.

Howell, John Thomas. *Marin Flora.* 1949. University of California Press, Berkeley.

A complete, technical flora of natives in Marin County. No drawings or photos in the main text. Technical keys.

Jepson, Willis L. *A Manual of the Flora of California.* 1909 to 1943. University of California Press, Berkeley.

A large technical manual which was complete for its time, but is now superceded by Munz (see below). Several fine illustrations; some people prefer the keys here. A number of names have been changed in newer works.

Keator, Glenn. *The Sierra Flower Finder.* 1980. Nature Study Guild, Berkeley.

A pocket-sized guide to the most common Sierra flowers above 4,000 feet; most species illustrated with line drawings. Designed for the beginner; incomplete.

Keator, Glenn, and Ruth Heady. *The Pacific Coast Fern Finder.* 1981. Nature Study Guild, Berkeley.

A pocket-sized guide to the most typical ferns of the area with line drawings of most. Designed for the beginner; rare ferns omitted.

Mason, Herbert. *Flora of the Marshes of California.* 1957. University of California Press, Berkeley.

> A complete, technical book covering plants associated with wet ecosystems. Superb line drawings.

Munz, Philip. *California Desert Wildflowers.* 1962.
           California Spring Wildflowers. 1961.
           California Mountain Wildflowers. 1963.
           California Seashore Wildflowers. 1964.

All University of California Press, Berkeley.

> Field guides for the amateur with good line drawings and some good to poor color photos. No keys. Arranged by flower color. Incomplete in each of the categories.

Munz, Philip and David Keck. *A California Flora.* 1959 (with Supplement, 1968). University of California Press, Berkeley.

> The most complete technical work for the whole state. Few illustrations. Technical keys. Recommended for the advanced student only.

Niehaus, Theodore. *A Field Guide to Pacific States Wildflowers.* 1976. Houghton and Mifflin Co., Boston.

> No keys. Short descriptions and color illustrations of most species. Incomplete, but the majority of common species are included. Flowers arranged by color (sometimes inaccurately).

Smith, Clifton. *A Flora of the Santa Barbara Region, California.* 1976. Santa Barbara Museum of Natural History, Santa Barbara.

> A complete book for Santa Barbara County; no keys. Technical descriptions and some line drawings.

Thomas, John Hunter. *Flora of the Santa Cruz Mountains of California.* 1961. Stanford University Press, Stanford.

> Complete, technical flora of the Santa Cruz Mountains. Some line drawings. Technical keys.

Watts. Phoebe. *Redwood Region Flower Finder.* 1979. Nature Study Guild, Berkeley.

> A pocket-sized guide to the most common flowers of the redwood forest region; most species illustrated with line drawings. Designed for the beginner; incomplete.

Weeden, Norman. *Survival Handbook to Sierra Flora.* 1975. Distributed by Wilderness Press, Berkeley.

> Pocket-sized guide. Complete but with technical keys and rather poor line drawings. Useful for the experienced person.

glossary

achene. A one-seeded fruit in which the seed is dispersed contained inside the walls of the fruit (e.g., unshelled sunflower "seeds").

acid. A measure of soil pH where the value is less than 7 (neutral). Acid soils are typical of cool wet climates and are particularly common in coniferous forests.

adpressed. Pressed against, as for example, when hairs are pressed against a leaf or stem.

aeration. The flow of air (oxygen) through water or soil. Particularly important for maintaining health in most roots.

alkaline. A measure of soil pH where the value is above 7 (neutral). Alkaline soils are typical of dry, desert climates.

alpine. Plants which live above the natural timberline in the mountains. Alpine conditions are very harsh with short, intense growing seasons.

alternate. Describes the arrangement of leaves where there is a single leaf attached at any one place (node) on the stem.

axil (axillary). The angle between the leaf and the stem where it's attached. Axillary flowers are borne in the axil of the leaves.

banner. The uppermost back petal of a typical pea-like flower, or the upright sepals of an iris flower.

biennial. A plant which lives two years—typically, forming a rosette of leaves the first year and blooming the second.

bisexual. Both sexes are present in the same flower (stamens and pistil).

bract. Any modified leaf associated with flowers. Some bracts are merely small versions of ordinary leaves; others are highly colored or modified in various ways.

bulb. An underground storage organ which consists of enlarged, modified leaf bases enclosing a bud. When cut across, a bulb consists of various layers, indicating the various leaf bases (e.g., an onion).

bunchgrass. Perennial grasses typical of California's original grasslands, where the leaf clusters and underground stems are densely bunched or grouped together.

capsule. A seed pod which has two or more compartments inside, *and* opens to shed its seeds.

cauline. Of or about stems. Cauline leaves are leaves borne up a stem (not at the base of the stem).

chaparral. A kind of vegetation occurring on hot, rocky slopes consisting of dense evergreen shrubs. Such vegetation is typical of the Mediterranean climate.

circumboreal. Describes a distribution around the northern hemisphere. A number of plants are circumboreal, occurring in North America, northern Europe, and northern Asia.

clone. A vegetative section of a plant and thus identical genetically to the original plant from which it came.

coastal prairie. The proper name for grasslands which occur along or near the coast.

coastal sage (scrub). A plant community of coastal southern California which is an open form of chaparral with soft-leaved shrubs, often with heavy sage odor. By contrast, "hard" chaparral is dense, with stiff-textured leaves.

compound. A leaf which consists of two or more discrete, separate leaflets (rather than a single blade). A compound leaf may be distinguished by the fact that the axillary bud is at the base of the whole leaf, and, when stipules are present, they too are at the base of the whole leaf (not the leaflets).

conifer (coniferous). Plants, usually trees, bearing cones rather than flowers. Coniferous forests are dominated by such trees (including pines, firs, and spruces).

corm. A bulb-like storage organ which is really an underground modified stem, and thus is solid when sliced across (e.g., a gladiolus corm).

corona. A crown-like outgrowth from the center of the petals (common in forget-me-nots and daffodils).

cultivar. An abbreviated word for cultivated variety. Cultivars are propagated vegetatively so that their peculiar genetic traits do not change. Most cultivars are mutants or odd variants which crop up occasionally in a population of more ordinary plants and, if the mutant is considered superior, are then named and propagated as a special cultivar.

cyme. Often applied rather indiscriminately to flat-topped clusters of flowers.

damping off. A fungal disease which attacks new seedlings as they first emerge from the soil. The condition is indicated by the top of the seedling suddenly wilting or leaning over.

deciduous. Describes a plant which loses all of its leaves at one time, typically in the fall.

decumbent. A plant which tends to grow near the ground, the ends of the branches only gradually turning up.

digitate. Said of leaves which are divided into finger-like segments.

disc flower. The small central flowers found in most members of the sunflower or composite family. Under magnification, the individual disc flowers have five star-like petals.

dissected. Deeply divided—in the case of leaves, lobes divided almost deeply enough to separate them into different leaflets.

dormant. Describes a plant or seed in a resting state. During dormancy, plants grow little, or may die back to specialized buds or underground parts.

ecosystem. An entire unit of living organisms within a given framework. Technically, ecosystems include not only all of the organisms but their complex interactions.

endemic. Restricted to a specific area. In California, many species are endemic to highly specialized environments, such as serpentine soils.

entire. A leaf or petal with no lobes or teeth.

epiphyte. A plant which lives on another for the purpose only of occupying a space; not parasitic in any way.

evergreen. A plant which does not lose all its leaves at one time. This does not mean, however, that evergreens keep their leaves permanently; they simply retain some leaves throughout the year, but also shed older leaves throughout the year.

family. A typically large grouping of species (although some families are so small they have a single species) which are linked together by common traits (usually based on flower and fruit characteristics). When attempting to identify a new flower, the first step is to find its family. Family names usually end in -aceae. Thus we have Rosaceae (rose family), Liliaceae (lily family), Ranunculaceae (buttercup family).

floriferous. Full of flowers or producing many flowers.

follicle. A kind of seed pod with one chamber and opening by one lengthwise slit (e.g., columbine and milkweed pods).

frond. The leaf of a fern.

fruit. Botanically, the ripe container in which flowering plants produce their seeds. Some fruits are pods which split open; others become fleshy and are dispersed as a unit with the seeds inside.

genus (pl. genera). The next category under family. Most families consist of several genera. Example: larkspurs, columbines, buttercups, and meadowrues are genera belonging to the buttercup family Ranunculaceae. The technical genus name always begins with a capital and is italicized, and is the first of the two names given when the scientific name is requested. (See also *species*.)

gland. A sticky, often rounded structure which exudes a sticky substance on leaves or on hairs attached to various parts of the plant; or in flowers, the area which secretes nectar.

glaucous. A bluish or grayish green color.

granite. A rock type common in the Sierra and other mountains. It is recognized by its gray color and up close is mottled by several kinds of embedded crystals, such as mica and feldspar.

green-woody. Describes a plant whose oldest branches feel firm and woody but lack a brown, gray, or black bark, having instead a green skin.

habit. The overall form of a plant (low shrub, tree, vine). Don't confuse with *habitat*.

habitat. The kind of home in which a plant lives—its soil, slope, plant community, and other factors. Don't confuse with *habit*.

hardy. Usually applied in horticulture to plants which tolerate freezing temperatures. Often the degree of hardiness is stated as the minimum temperature at which a given species will survive.

head. Where many flowers are tightly clustered together at the end of a single stem. The head is the typical arrangement of flowers throughout the composite or sunflower family.

herb. Botanically, a plant with no wood or bark.

herbaceous. The condition of lacking woody tissue.

hummock. A raised area in a bog where conditions may be somewhat less soggy.

humus. Decayed or decaying leaves and twigs.

inflorescence. The general term for a clustering or arrangement of flowers. There are many kinds of inflorescences: heads, umbels, and racemes, for example.

introduced. Describes a plant which has been brought in, accidentally or intentionally, from another part of the world.

lanceolate. Lance shaped.

lateral. Pertaining to the side of something.

lobed. A leaf or petal which consists of several rounded sections separated by deep gashes.

naturalized. A plant which looks as though it belongs in an environment (as though it were native), but comes from another part of the world originally.

niche. The specific ecological conditions under which each species lives.

nutlet. A small, hard, one-seeded fruit which is shed as a unit (rather than the seed falling out). Nutlets are typical of members of the mint and borage families.

oblanceolate. A lance shape turned upside down.

offset. A small version of the original plant or part of plant (e.g., bulblets are offsets of bulbs; plantlets of many succulents are offsets of the main parent plant).

opposite. Where leaves are arranged two to a node or two at the same level on the stem (paired).

ovary. The swollen base of the pistil of a flower. The ovary contains the seeds and matures into the fruit when the seeds have ripened.

ovate. A leaf shape which is broad and rounded at the base, then tapers gradually to a point at the end.

pH. The measure of hydrogen and hydroxyl ions in the soil. When these are in balance, the pH is said to be neutral; more hydrogen ions makes an acid condition, and more hydroxyl ions creates an alkaline situation. The measure of pH is important in the kinds of plants which will grow in a soil; most plants do best near a pH of 7.

palmate. Divided, veined, or lobed in a pattern like the fingers on a hand (e.g., most maple leaves are palmately lobed).

panicle. A compound raceme of flowers. That is, a main long stem which carries many side branches, themselves rebranched.

pappus. The hairs or scaly structures (often nearly microscopic) attached to the fruits in members of the sunflower or composite family. A good example is the hairy parachutes attached to dandelion fruits which allow them to float on breezes.

peltate. A more or less circular leaf blade whose stalk is attached in the center like the handle of an umbrella.

perennial. A plant which lives three or more years. Horticulturally, "perennial" is often applied to plants which do not become woody, as do shrubs and trees.

petal. Usually, the showy, colored parts of a flower (although sometimes sepals or bracts take over this role). Typically, the petals are the second layer of a flower (the sepals being the outermost layer).

petiole. The stalk-like portion of a leaf; some leaves consist only of a thin blade without a stalk.

pinna (pl. pinnae). The segments or separate sections of a fern frond.

pinnate. Where lobes, leaflets, or veins are arranged like the whiskers of a feather.

pistil. The female and usually central part of a flower. The pistil typically consists of three parts: a top knob or section (the stigma), the slender tube below that (the style), and a swollen ovary at the base in which the seeds are produced.

pollen. The fine dust-like powder made by the stamens (most often colored yellow) which contains the male portion. (See *pollination*.)

pollination. The process of moving the pollen from its source (the stamen) to the top of the pistil (the stigma). From there, the individual pollen grains send out long tubes which eventually reach the preformed seeds inside the ovary (where fertilization then takes place).

prostrate. Growing flat along the ground.

pup. A miniature plantlet; typically several are produced in a circle around the parent plant.

race. A genetically different strain of a species, with a corresponding ecological or geographical distribution of its own.

raceme. A flower arrangement where a number of side branches are arranged along a long main stem. Generally, the flowers open from the bottom up.

ray flower. The outer flowers of a composite or sunflower or daisy. Each ray resembles a petal, although the ray itself consists of five petals fused together into a single strap- or tongue-shaped structure.

receptacle. The end of the stem to which all parts of the flower are attached.

In some cases, the shape of the receptacle is important in recognizing a particular flower (e.g., the cone- shaped receptacle in coneflower or *Rudbeckia*).

rhizome. A creeping, horizontal, thickened stem which grows at or below ground level (e.g., the rhizomes of irises). These are not the same as the roots.

rootcrown. The top of the root where it joins the stem. This is often the part most vulnerable to fungal attack and rot.

rootstock. A thickened, long stem which resembles a taproot or thick root. Many perennials spread by underground rootstocks.

rosette. A circular arrangement of leaves, usually at or near ground level.

ruderal. Describes a weedy plant which appears in or near cultivated areas, as along farms or pastures.

runner. A long, horizontal stem at ground level (the same as a stolon, described below).

scape. A naked, leafless flowering stalk.

scarification. Treating seeds by scratching, rubbing, or fraying the seed coat so that water can penetrate more easily for germination.

scree. Loose rocks, often on steep slopes.

scrub. A general term for shrubby vegetation.

shrub. A woody plant with multiple branches from the base, or at least lacking a prominent trunk.

simple. A leaf whose blade is in one piece, not compound (although such a leaf may be lobed).

sorus (pl. sori). The reproductive clusters of spore-bearing structures on ferns. To the naked eye, mature sori look like brown spots on the underside of fronds.

species. Often the smallest unit of classification, the specific kind of plant. For example, in the pine genus (*Pinus*) the many species include sugar pine (*Pinus lambertiana*), digger pine (*Pinus sabiniana*), and yellow pine (*Pinus ponderosa*). Notice that when the scientific name is cited both the genus name (the first word) and the species name (the second word) are given. Species names start with lower case letters and are italicized.

sphagnum. A special kind of moss which is very spongy and acid, and has the ability to absorb large amounts of water. Sphagnum bogs are wet areas dominated by these mosses, and because the conditions there are highly specialized, only a few plants are capable of living in these bogs.

spike. A clustering of flowers where the flowers are attached directly to a single long stalk (no side branches).

spur. Usually, a long, hollow tapered part of the petals or sepals which contains the nectar. Spurred flowers are most often pollinated only by special pollinators, such as butterflies, moths, and hummingbirds.

stamen. The male parts of a flower, generally occurring in a row between the petals and pistil. Each stamen consists of a stalk (the filament) and a sac-like part at the end (the anther) where the pollen is produced.

staminode. A sterile stamen, or stamen without the anther.

stigma. The top portion of the pistil, often enlarged, knob-like, or divided into lobes and sticky or fuzzy. This is where the pollen needs to be placed in order for pollination to be successful.

stipe. A stalk which carries the ovary above the rest of the parts of the flower (don't confuse with the stalk to which the other flower parts are attached).

stipule. Pairs of leaf-like structures at the side or base of an ordinary leaf. Stipules are sometimes modified into spines or glands, or in many cases, are absent.

stolon. The same as a runner. A slender stem which runs along the surface of the soil from the parent plant. At its end, a new plantlet is produced (e.g., in strawberries).

stratification. The process of wetting and chilling seeds before planting. Usually, seeds are wrapped in damp sphagnum moss or perlite and put in a refrigerator.

subalpine. The zone in the mountains just below timberline where there is still some tree growth. Typically, the subalpine in California mountains is characterized by western juniper, mountain hemlock, whitebark pine, and lodgepole pine.

subshrub. A bushy plant which is woody only toward the base. A half-shrub.

subspecies. Occurs where a species has two or more recognizable races which have their own separate geographic ranges. Subspecies are capable of forming hybrids where they overlap.

subtropical. Conditions close to those of the tropics, roughly on the edge of the zones marked by the Tropic of Cancer in the north and the Tropic of Capricorn in the south.

subwoody. A term sometimes used to describe the degree of woody tissues found in a subshrub. Also growth on shrubs or trees which is halfway between soft, green new growth and hard, woody mature growth.

succulent. Any plant in which part of the roots, stems, or leaves are modified to store water.

talus. Loose rocks on a steep slope. Much like scree.

taproot. A single thick, deeply penetrating root (such as a carrot).

tender. In horticulture, plants which are intolerant of frost or freezing conditions.

tendril. A coiled stalk-like extension of branches or leaves which helps support vines as they climb.

tepal. Used where the sepals and petals are colored and shaped similarly. Most members of the amaryllis and lily families have tepals.

terminal. At the end or top.

ternate. Divided into threes.

tomentum. A close, wool-like covering of hairs on leaves or stems.

tree. A woody plant with one or a few trunks (trunks are clearly more massive than side branches).

tribe. A category into which large plant families are subdivided. Thus, in the sunflower or composite family tribes are units containing closely related genera.

tropical. Plants coming from areas between the Tropic of Cancer and the Tropic of Capricorn and usually indicating conditions of nearly uniformly long and warm days all year.

tuber. An underground modified stem for storage of food and water not shaped like a corm (e.g., a potato).

tundra. Technically, the frozen lands of the Arctic and Antarctic where tree growth is not possible, but often used for the alpine zone of high mountains.

two-lipped. Flowers where the petals are arranged in two distinct lip-like portions with the entrance to the floral tube between. Typical of flowers in the snapdragon and mint families.

umbel. Formed by flowers arranged at the ends of spoke-like stalks which radiate from the end of a single larger stem (umbrella like).

umbellet. A small or secondary umbel. Applied mostly to the parsley family Apiaceae for the small flower clusters which themselves are arranged in larger clusters called umbels.

unisexual. Flowers which have either only stamens or only pistils.

variety. A loosely used subunit of the species. Often used for any variation within a species, such as different flower color, or greater or lesser size of the plant. Unfortunately, the term is so imprecise that it is often meaningless.

vegetative. Describes the leaves, stems, and roots of the plant as contrasted with the reproductive parts, such as flowers or cones. Vegetative reproduction involves making new plants directly from the stems, roots, or leaves.

vernal pool. A special depression in the grasslands of California's foothills, which holds water in winter and spring and gradually dries out by summer. Unusual plants are often associated with these pools.

viviparous. Literally, live bearing. Used where plantlets are produced directly on leaves or stems (e.g., the piggyback plant).

whorl. Where three or more leaves are attached at the same level of the stem.

index of species